R00090 14878

CHICAGO PUBLIC LIBRARY
HAROLD WASHINGTON LIBRARY CENTER

R0009014878

REF
TD   Mandel, S. (Samuel),
403   1918-
.M32
          Groundwater
          resources

DATE			

D0965873

© THE BAKER & TAYLOR CO.

Groundwater Resources

Investigation and Development

WATER POLLUTION

A Series of Monographs

EDITORS

K. S. SPIEGLER
Department of Mechanical
Engineering
University of California,
Berkeley
Berkeley, California

J. I. BREGMAN
WAPORA, Inc.
6900 Wisconsin Avenue, N.W.
Washington, D. C.

D. T. O'Laoghaire and D. M. Himmelblau. *Optimal Expansion of a Water Resources System.* 1974

C. W. Hart, Jr., and Samuel L. H. Fuller (eds.). *Pollution Ecology of Freshwater Invertebrates.* 1974

H. Shuval (ed.). *Water Renovation and Reuse.* 1977

C. W. Hart, Jr., and Samuel L. H. Fuller (eds.). *Pollution Ecology of Estuarine Invertebrates.* 1979

H. Shuval (ed.). *Water Quality Management under Conditions of Scarcity: Israel as a Case Study.* 1980

S. Mandel and Z. L. Shiftan. *Groundwater Resources: Investigation and Development.* 1981

Groundwater Resources

Investigation and Development

S. MANDEL
Groundwater Research Center
Hebrew University of Jerusalem
Israel

Z. L. SHIFTAN
TAHAL Consulting Engineers Ltd.
Tel Aviv, Israel

1981

ACADEMIC PRESS
A Subsidiary of Harcourt Brace Jovanovich, Publishers
New York   London   Toronto   Sydney   San Francisco

COPYRIGHT © 1981, BY ACADEMIC PRESS, INC.
ALL RIGHTS RESERVED.
NO PART OF THIS PUBLICATION MAY BE REPRODUCED OR
TRANSMITTED IN ANY FORM OR BY ANY MEANS, ELECTRONIC
OR MECHANICAL, INCLUDING PHOTOCOPY, RECORDING, OR ANY
INFORMATION STORAGE AND RETRIEVAL SYSTEM, WITHOUT
PERMISSION IN WRITING FROM THE PUBLISHER.

ACADEMIC PRESS, INC.
111 Fifth Avenue, New York, New York 10003

United Kingdom Edition published by
ACADEMIC PRESS, INC. (LONDON) LTD.
24/28 Oval Road, London NW1 7DX

Library of Congress Cataloging in Publication Data

Mandel, S. (Samuel), Date.
  Groundwater resources.

  (Water pollution series)
  Includes bibliographies and index.
  1. Water, Underground. I. Shiftan, Z. II. Title.
III. Series.
TD403.M32   553.7'9   80-990
ISBN 0-12-468040-2   AACR2

PRINTED IN THE UNITED STATES OF AMERICA

81 82 83 84   9 8 7 6 5 4 3 2 1

Contents

Chapter 4   Geophysical Methods

Chapter 5   Drilling for Exploration and Water Supply

Chapter 6   Pumping Tests

Chapter 7   Water Level Measurements, Hydrographs, and Water Level Maps

Contents   vii

Chapter 13   Criteria for the Regional Exploitation of Groundwater

Chapter 14   Groundwater Observation Networks   238

Chapter 15   The Methodology of Groundwater Investigations

Appendix   Units of Measurement and Conversion Factors   255

Preface

It is no longer necessary to preach the advantages of groundwater as a source of water supply. An extensive literature deals with theoretical aspects of groundwater movement, groundwater management and conservation, and other specialized aspects of the subject.

The application of advanced techniques relies on the availability of data, and it is in this field that a gap is often felt. In developed regions, the required data can usually be taken from files dating back to the precomputer era. Developing regions, however, have little data to start with. Therefore, it has become an accepted practice to carry out intensive investigations by teams of specialists when large-scale groundwater development is desired.

The purpose of this book is to show how groundwater investigations should be conducted, using a systematic, well-directed effort. In particular, the volume advises the person in charge what to do, what to avoid, and what kind of results one can reasonably expect from the application of different techniques under specific conditions.

We have attempted to explain succinctly various useful techniques, to evaluate their advantages and limitations, and to organize them into a logical structure.

The desire to cover a broad canvas in a short book has imposed restrictions: some detailed expositions were omitted, reference being made instead to specialized literature. Simple techniques are presented cheek by jowl with advanced ones, and together with organizational procedures. We ask the reader to understand the reason for this seemingly incongruous mixture; the presentation aims at utility rather than at sophistication.

We hope that this volume will provide in practical applicability what it perhaps lacks in universality.

Groundwater Resources

Investigation and Development

CHAPTER

1

Overview of Terms and Concepts

1.1 GROUNDWATER AS PART OF THE HYDROLOGIC CYCLE

Energy derived from the sun's radiation keeps the water on the earth's globe in a state of continual movement: from the oceans to the atmosphere by evaporation and vice versa by precipitation on oceanic surfaces; from the atmosphere to land and back by precipitation and evapotranspiration; and from land to the oceans by flowing surficial and underground waters. The term *hydrologic cycle* describes the sum of these global phenomena, although in reality only a small part of the global water traverses the full cycle from the ocean to atmosphere, to land, and back into the ocean. Figure 1.1a pictures the hydrologic cycle in the form of a *system* that is activated by an *input*, the sun's radiation, and produces an *output*, water flowing across the landmasses into the ocean. The global system thus defined can be applied only to the study of vast areas. In order to obtain detailed information of practical value, it is necessary to focus attention on a selected part of the hydrologic cycle.

The part of the hydrologic cycle that transforms precipitation into flowing surficial and underground waters is shown in Fig. 1.1b. One part of the precipitation generates the *surface runoff* component of streamflow; another part *percolates* to the saturated portion of an aquifer and reappears on the surface in the form of springs and seepages, or drains underground directly into the ocean. Streams and aquifers are often interconnected by the seepage of water from the riverbed into the aquifer or vice versa. A third,

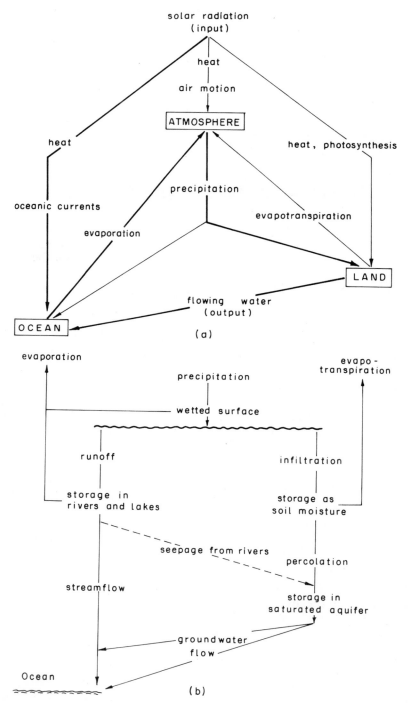

Fig. 1.1 (a) The hydrologic cycle, (b) terrestrial part of the hydrologic cycle.

and often the largest, part of precipitation is returned to the atmosphere by evaporation from the surface and by transpiration of soil moisture from the root zone of vegetation. These two processes are usually lumped together as *evapotranspiration*.

This scheme becomes useful only when it is applied to an appropriately defined region. Studies of surficial waters refer to a *watershed* (or *catchment*) characterized by the property that the addition or abstraction of water in any part of it influences streamflow and river stages further downstream. A watershed can easily be mapped, and all points in it are, in principle, accessible for observations and measurements. The region appropriate for *groundwater studies* should comprise one aquifer or several interconnected aquifers that are surrounded by impermeable rocks on all sides, except in areas through which natural replenishment and outflow are effected. If water is added to or abstracted from these aquifers at any point, water levels and the pattern of groundwater flow in the entire region are changed. The region thus defined will be denoted in this text by the term *groundwater system*. The term *groundwater basin*, which is widely used in the United States, denotes the part of a groundwater system that is easily exploited by wells. Since groundwater is accessible to observation only in isolated points, information about a groundwater system has to be pieced together from measurements at these points with the aid of geologic reasoning, the theory of flow in porous media, and other techniques.

Watersheds and groundwater systems perform identical functions in the hydrologic cycle. They convey water from higher elevations to lower ones and hold a certain volume of water in transient storage. The *depletion time* indicates how long it would take the watershed or the groundwater system to dry out if surface runoff or groundwater replenishment were stopped from the instant T onward and if outflow was maintained at the rate it had at this instant. The depletion time is defined as $V(T)/Q(T)$, where $V(T)$ equals volume of water stored and $Q(T)$ equals outflow at time T. Depletion times of surficial waters are usually of the order of hours to weeks. They may run into months or years if the river basin includes large lakes. Depletion times of aquifers are usually of the order of tens to hundreds, and often thousands of years. As a consequence, rivers react quickly to precipitation and to the abstraction of water, whereas groundwater systems react very sluggishly to these events.

The surface water hydrologist is concerned mainly with the study of the quick and often extreme responses of riverflow to short rainstorms or short dry spells, and with the statistical evaluation of *stochastic* series of unpredictable events. He has the advantage, however, of dealing with a visible physical system— the watershed. The groundwater hydrologist is concerned mainly with the delineation of the groundwater system and with the determination of the parameters that govern its behavior. His advantage is that he deals with a physical system in which changes take place so slowly that he is rarely forced to analyze the influence of short events such as single rainstorms. Therefore the two branches of hydrology need different approaches and have come to be regarded as two distinct specialized disciplines.

1.2   GEOLOGIC CLASSIFICATION OF ROCKS

Geologists classify rocks mainly according to genetic criteria. More detailed definitions of rock types refer to their mineral composition, texture (grain size), and degree of consolidation. Color, structure, and chemical composition may be taken as additional characteristics.

Igneous rocks (Nockolds, Knox, and Chinner, 1978) originate from the liquid magma that normally exists at depths exceeding 20 km below surface. *Intrusive rocks*, such as granite, are created when magma ascends to some distance below surface and solidifies there. *Extrusive rocks*, also known as volcanic rocks, are formed on the surface by the pouring out or ejection of fluid or solid magmatic materials. Extrusion of *lava*, that is magma from which gases and steam have escaped, forms broad, dome-shaped volcanoes or lava sheets and plateaus. Ejection of solid cinders and ash forms *pyroclastic rocks* that accumulate in cones around the centers of eruption or cover wider areas.

Sedimentary rocks (Carrozi, 1975) owe their origin to agents active on the surface of the globe. They are the result of erosion, transport, and deposition of rock materials by water, ice or wind, the accumulation of plant and animal remains, and the precipitation of salts from aqueous solutions. Layering and the presence of *fossils*—vestiges of plants and animals—are frequent characteristics. Classification of sedimentary rocks is based on a variety of criteria, such as mode and environment of formation (e.g., marine, fluviatile, organogenic), mineral composition (e.g., chert, limestone, gypsum), and size of constituent particles (e.g., gravel, sand, clay). Color, details of layering, sorting of particles, and the nature of included fossils are often used as additional attributes.

Clastic sediments are composed of particles of preexisting rocks, deposited after transport on the continents or in the oceans. Particle size is the criterion for the distinction of five major classes: *boulders and cobbles* (more than 5 cm), *gravels* (5–0.2 cm), *sand* (0.2–0.02 cm), *silt* (0.02–0.002 cm), and *clays* (less than 0.002 cm). Boulders, cobbles, and gravels have the composition of the mother rock. Sand grains are usually composed of a single mineral such as *quartz, calcite,* or, in very dry regions, *felspar (arcose sands).* Clays are derived from felspars by chemical weathering and consist of tiny crystals of *clay minerals. Conglomerates, sandstones, siltstones,* and *claystones* are the compacted and cemented equivalents of gravels, sand, silt, and clay, respectively. The most frequent cements are calcium carbonate, silicium dioxide, and iron oxides. *Shales* are fissile compacted clays. Gravels, sands and silt are deposited mainly by rivers (*fluviatile deposits*). Clays accumulate in lakes, swamps, and on the deep sea bottom. Heterogeneous masses of clastics deposited by glaciers are called *glacial drift* or *till.* Windblown sands form *dunes*; windblown silt and clay are often carried over large distances and eventually form *loess.* Ocean and lake beaches are covered by fine gravel and sand. In river deltas fine sands, silts, and clays are deposited and may eventually be redistributed in the shallow marine environment by sea currents.

   Carbonate rocks are another hydrologically important subclass of sedimentary rocks. *Limestones* are formed in the sea or in lakes by chemical precipitation, or by the accumulation of shells and skeletons of plants and animals (algal, corraline, shell limestones). *Dolomites* are generated from limestones by interaction with seawater. *Calcareous tufa* is often precipitated in the vicinity of springs.

   Siliceous sediments are precipitated, or coagulated, mainly in the shallow marine environment, or are composed of siliceous animal and plant remains (radiolarian chert, diatomite). *Siliceous sinter* is often found near thermal springs.

   Evaporites are rocks composed of relatively soluble salts (gypsum, rock salt, various potassium and magnesium salts) precipitated by evaporation of sea- or lakewater, or by evaporating groundwater.

   Soils are sedimentary materials resulting from the complex and combined effects of mechanical, chemical, and organic agents on rocks. Clay minerals are important components of most soils.

   Metamorphic rocks originate from igneous or sedimentary rocks that were subsequently subjected to intense heat or pressure, or both, so that their mineral composition and texture became greatly changed. To this group belong the various types of *gneisses, schists,* and *slates,* as well as *quartzites* and *marble.* Metamorphic and igneous rocks occur in close association over vast areas of the continents, and the term *crystalline rocks* is often used for these associations.

   Geologic formations (Dunbar and Rogers, 1966) or, in brief, *formations,* are rock units composed of one or several rock types that can be identified in the field by the naked eye. Their names derive from type localities, and their validity is restricted to a certain area. Large-scale geologic maps (1 : 20,000– 1 : 100,000) usually show the distribution of formations. The term *facies* is used to denote slight differences in the character of rocks within a formation. For example, a formation made up by a shaly sandstone may appear in a more shaly or a more sandy facies. The descriptive terms of rocks and formations have no relation to time. The absolute age of some rocks can be determined from the decay of their radioactive constituents, but it is more convenient to use a relative geologic time scale that is based on the fossil record of evolutionary changes in plants and animals. Geologic *time units* are denoted by a string of names, where each name serves to identify an interval on the geologic time sequence. Small-scale geologic maps (say, 1 : 250,000 and smaller) are based on these time units, which lump together different rock formations on the basis of their geologic age (Eicher, 1968).

In order to draw a three-dimensional picture of the geologic subsurface, it is necessary to know the sequence in which the rocks were originally deposited. Rock units by themselves are a poor guide in this respect since formations that look identical may represent different ages or, conversely, one and the same age may be represented by different formations in the investigated area. Hence the geologic age of rock units and the time interval they represent are not only of intrinsic scientific interest but also of great practical importance.

From a groundwater point of view, the most important property of rocks is the *pore space* they incorporate. The pore space may be contemporaneous with the rock *(primary porosity)*, or it may be due to subsequent processes, such as *fracturing, solution*, and *weathering* (*secondary porosity*). On the other hand, primary porosity may be partly or fully obliterated by subsequent processes such as mechanical compaction, secondary deposition of minerals, and filling with clay particles. There is no clear-cut correlation between the mode of rock generation, the subsequent geologic history of the strata, and the pore space the formations contain. Another descriptive classification distinguishes between *granular porosity* characterized by evenly distributed voids, *vugular porosity* characterized by large irregularly distributed voids, and *fissured porosity*, where more or less continuous voids are aligned in a certain direction.

The terms *aquifer, aquiclude, aquitard*, and *aquifuge* are used to describe the groundwater-bearing properties of different rock formations. Aquifers are formations from which useful groundwater supplies can be obtained. Aquicludes do not transmit water easily and do not yield water to wells, though they may retain much water in their fine pores. Aquitards occupy an intermediate position, yielding, under certain conditions, water in quantities that may be described as marginal. Aquifuges are rocks practically devoid of pores. It will be noted that the words *useful* and *marginal* take on a concrete meaning only with reference to local standards. Consequently, what would be termed an aquitard in one region may still be regarded as a useful aquifer elsewhere.

1.3 HYDROLOGIC CONCEPTS

The descriptive terms of groundwater hydrology are summarized in Fig. 1.2. A short recapitulation of the concepts on which quantitative work is based will be given below.

The flow of groundwater through the pore space of the aquifer is governed by Darcy's law, a linear function of the hydraulic gradient. The simplest formulation of this law, derived from the laboratory experiment shown in Fig. 1.3, is

$$Q/A = K(h_1 - h_2)/\Delta l \tag{1.1}$$

where Q is the discharge ($L^3 T^{-1}$), A the cross-sectional area (L^2), h_1, h_2 are the hydraulic heads measured at points 1 and 2, respectively (L), Δl is the distance between points 1 and 2 measured in the direction of flow (L), $(h_1 - h_2)/\Delta l$ the hydraulic gradient (dimensionless), and K the hydraulic conductivity, or permeability of the sample ($L T^{-1}$).

Darcy's law indicates that laminar conditions of flow prevail in the narrow interstices of the aquifer, in spite of their tortuosity and the innumerable interconnections among them. Deviations from Eq. (1.1) are

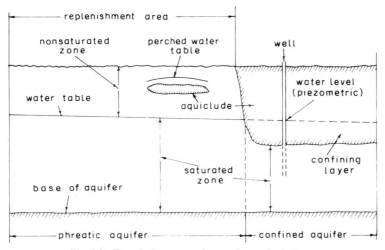

Fig. 1.2 Descriptive terms of groundwater hydrology.

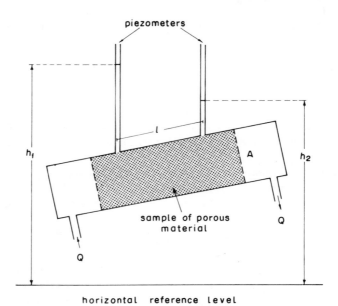

Fig. 1.3   Experimental verification of Darcy's law.

sometimes encountered in fissured aquifers, where the water flows through relatively wide channels.

Metric units of K are given in meters per day or centimeters per second. The USGS laboratory standard is defined as

$$K_s = \frac{1 \text{ gpd of water at } 60°\text{F}}{(1 \text{ ft}^2)(1 \text{ ft}/1 \text{ ft})} \qquad (1.2a)$$

The hydraulic conductivity K as defined by Eq. (1.1) depends on the properties of the pore space as well as on those of the liquid. The *intrinsic permeability*, which characterizes the pore space only, is defined by

$$K = k\frac{\gamma}{\mu} \qquad (1.2b)$$

where k is the *intrinsic permeability* (L^2), γ the specific weight of the liquid, and μ the dynamic viscosity of the liquid.

The unit of intrinsic permeability is the *darcy*. Petroleum engineers who work with liquids of widely varying properties prefer this unit, and it is also gaining acceptance in groundwater work. For groundwater the conversion formula is

$$1 \text{ darcy} = 0.835 \; m/d \text{ (at } 20°\text{C)} = 18.2 \; K_s \qquad (1.2c)$$

Hydraulic conductivity can be measured in the laboratory by *permeameters*, which work on the principle shown in Fig. 1.2.

A related parameter, *transmissivity*, is defined by

$$T = Kb \tag{1.3}$$

where T is the transmissivity ($L^2 T^{-1}$) and b the saturated aquifer thickness (L).

Transmissivity is measured in m²/d (metric units) or gpd/ft (American units) and can be determined by *pumping tests* in the field (Chapter 6).

The water content of a saturated aquifer equals its total *porosity*, which is defined by the ratio: volume of pores to volume of aquifer. However, only a part of the water can be made to flow through the interstices of the aquifer by the force of gravity. Another part is retained in very narrow channels by capillary forces or clings to the walls of the interstices as a thin film. This is expressed by the equations:

$$n = W/V \tag{1.4a}$$

$$n_e = W_e/V \tag{1.4b}$$

$$n > n_e \tag{1.4c}$$

where n is the total *porosity*, n_e the *effective porosity* (both dimensionless), V the total volume of the aquifer (L^3), W the volume of water in the saturated aquifer (L^3), and W_e the volume of water that can be drained from the saturated aquifer under the force of gravity (L^3).

The *storativity*, or *storage coefficient*, of an aquifer is defined by the following ideal experiment.

Imagine an aquifer with horizontal base, completely surrounded by impermeable vertical boundaries. Displace the water table, or—if the aquifer is confined—the piezometric surface, vertically downward or upward, measure the volume of water thus derived or taken up, and compute:

$$S = V_w/A\Delta h \tag{1.5a}$$

where S is the *storativity*, V_w the volume of water derived or taken up (L^3), A the base area of the aquifer (L^2), and Δh the vertical displacement of the water table or piezometric surface (L).

The ideal experiment assumes that depletion and replenishment are completely reversible processes. This is true only for relatively small, cyclic water level changes. If the water level is excessively lowered and kept low for a long period, irreversible *compaction* of rock formations accompanied by *soil subsidence* may occur. Unconsolidated formations are especially prone to this process. The volume of water squeezed out from interstices during compaction is not included in the definition of storativity (see Sections 2.4 and 13.1).

In a phreatic aquifer the experiment must be continued until the water has drained even from relatively narrow interstices. The constant value of S, which, by definition, equals n_e, will be approached only gradually (see also Section 6.2). In a confined aquifer, water is derived from elastic reactions of the whole system, the aquifer, the water, and the confining layers. Since elastic reactions are quick, the ideal experiment will yield an unequivocal value of S, provided that the rather narrow elastic limits of the system are not exceeded.

A representative value for the storativity of an aquifer, usually denoted by the term *specific yield*, can sometimes be obtained by the interpretation of long years' water level and pumping records. Pumping tests determine storativity from the velocity with which a local disturbance of the water level spreads through the aquifer. In phreatic aquifers the values of S thus determined appear to be a function of test duration (see Sections 6.1 and 6.2).

Table 1.1 cites several indicative values of K and S (phreatic) for several common rock types and correlates them with descriptive terms.

For the purpose of quantitative analysis the aquifer is regarded as *porous medium* (Bear, 1972), continuous—in the mathematical sense—and characterized by the parameters K and S. The water is assumed to be homogeneous, i.e., water samples taken from different parts of the aquifer have identical physical and chemical properties. Groundwater flow in the porous medium is governed by Darcy's law and by the *equation of continuity* (principle of the conservation of matter). The differential equation derived from this *conceptual model* is identical to the one that describes the flow of heat and of electricity. However, analytical solutions can be derived only for rather simple situations, such as those postulated in the theory of aquifer

TABLE 1.1

Indicative Values of K and S

Rock	Approximate hydraulic conductivity (m/day)	Approximate storativity	Descriptive term
Fine gravel	60	0.1	
Coarse sand	20	0.1–0.25[a]	Aquifers
Fine sand	10	0.25–0.35[a]	
Sand and silt	2	35[a]	Aquitards
Clay	0.001	—	Aquicludes
Confined aquifers	—	0.005–0.00005	

[a]Limiting values for considerations involving several months or longer periods.

tests. Solutions for the complex situations commonly encountered in real aquifers are derived by computerized *digital simulation techniques* (Remson, Hornberger, and Molz, 1971).

In practice, aquifers may be partially occupied by water of undesirable chemical quality. Examples are the wedge of seawater in the seaward portion of a coastal aquifer, the pockets of brackish groundwater commonly found in dry regions, and the many instances of man-made groundwater pollution. In such cases, changes of water quality are bound to occur when the aquifer is intensively exploited, and their prediction is even more important than the prediction of hydraulic states. Mixing processes in a porous medium are due mainly to the phenomenon of *hydrodynamic dispersion* (Bachmat and Bear, 1964), which depends on the average velocity of flow in the pore space and on the lateral and longitudinal *dispersion coefficients* of the porous medium. Additional factors are *molecular diffusion*, differences of gravity and viscosity, and in some instances *surface reactions* between chemical constituents of the water and clay minerals in the aquifer. Although a large amount of theoretical work has been done on *transport phenomena in porous media*, simulation models for the prediction of water quality are still in a less advanced state than those for the simulation of hydraulic states. The major difficulty seems to stem from the lack of reliable field methods for the determination of the relevant coefficients rather than from the mathematical complexity of the subject.

1.4 PHASES OF GROUNDWATER DEVELOPMENT

The ideal, orderly course of groundwater development runs from the drilling of the first successful well to sophisticated optimization schemes. It is convenient to distinguish four successive phases of groundwater development, each one being supported by an appropriate phase of investigations.

During the *phase of exploration* the principal purpose of the investigations is the drilling of successful water wells. The leading professions are geology, geophysics, and drilling. Usually not much attention is paid to the delineation of groundwater systems, which may, indeed, hardly be possible at this stage.

The *phase of increasing exploitation and quantification* is characterized by the fact that the location of successful wells has become, more or less, a matter of routine. Exploitation steadily increases as more and more wells go into production and, therefore, hydrologic considerations concerning the spacing of boreholes, the pumping lift, and the ultimate limitations of the supply capacity of the resource become important. It is now necessary to delineate the groundwater system(s), to determine aquifer constants, to estimate average annual replenishment, and eventually to formulate a rough theoretical model of the aquifer(s). Groundwater hydrology gradually becomes the leading profession.

The *phase of conservation* is concerned with the exploitation of the aquifer on a sustained basis. The *maximum sustained yield* (Section 13.2) depends on groundwater replenishment, on the *constraints* that are present, such as, for example, the danger of saline intrusions, and on the distribution of groundwater abstraction in the area. An additional factor to be evaluated is the danger of groundwater pollution by fertilizers and other chemicals and urban and industrial wastes.

The geology and hydrology of the aquifer should be known adequately long before actual groundwater abstraction approaches the level of the maximum sustained yield, so that there remains some leeway to direct the development of the resource according to hydrologic criteria and not only according to the preferences of water users. Groundwater hydrology, as well as legal and administrative means of control, dominates the scene at this stage.

The *phase of optimization* is concerned with operating the groundwater system in such a way that a certain cost benefit relation attains its maximum value, subject to the constraint that permanent damage to the resource must be avoided and to other constraints that may be imposed by criteria of water quality and water supply reliability, by environmental concerns (e.g., the drying up of groundwater fed streams), and by the social fabric of the region. The reservoir capacity of the groundwater system is now explicitly considered as a valuable asset. Operation of the groundwater reservoir may include temporary overexploitation or artificial replenishment and underground storage, or both. Optimization procedures are meaningful only if and when the wells are connected to a regional water supply system that may embody also other water resources. System analysis, aided by a calibrated model of the groundwater system, is the leading profession at this stage.

The above phases should be regarded as so many signposts on a road, telling the investigator not only where he is now but also which kind of problem will crop up next. A capable investigator will see a step ahead. The geologist should formulate semiquantitative ideas about the groundwater system already during the phase of exploration, and the groundwater hydrologist should try, as early as possible, to determine the optimal areal distribution of groundwater abstraction, knowing that this problem is sure to loom very large during the subsequent phases of the work.

Ideally, phased investigations presuppose the rather leisurely pace of development that prevailed in the past. Today it happens all too often that development overtakes research and that belated, so-called optimization studies have to be concerned more with staving off the worst consequences of uncontrolled development than with the optimal use of the resource. The best way to avoid ths serious situation is to carry out a relatively short campaign of intensive investigations that practically rolls all the first three phases into one and provides the basis for a rationally controlled use of groundwater supplies. Table 1.2 shows more specifically which hydrologic problems have to be solved at each phase as well as the appropriate techniques for solving them.

TABLE 1.2

Phases, Problems, and Techniques[a]

A. Phase of exploration
Practical aims: Find groundwater in the area and supply water for specific purposes.

Problems to be solved	Techniques of investigation
1. Identification of potentially aquiferous formations	
2. Nature and origin of porosity. Primary Fracturing Solution Weathering	Geology, geophysics (1), (2), (3), (4)
3. Position of water level. Elevation of natural outlet Perched horizons on impervious layers	Geohydrologic reasoning, drilling (2), (5)
4. Pumping lift. Depth of water level	Water level measurements; water level maps (7.1), (7.3); estimates of specific discharge of wells (6), (13)
5. Supply capacity of wells. Discharge–drawdown characteristics	Step drawdown tests (6.8)
6. Depth of drilling required	Inferences from geology and water levels (5)
7. Water quality	Chemical analyses, application of quality criteria, geochemical classification (9)

Continued

TABLE 1.2   (*Continued*)

B.   Phase of increasing exploitation and quantification
Practical aims: Locate more wells in area and increase groundwater supplies.

Problems to be solved	Techniques of investigation
1. Geometrical configuration of aquifer	Geophysics, drilling, subsurface mapping (4), (5), (3)
2. Minimum distance between wells. Aquifer confined, unconfined, hydrologic constants T, S	Geohydrologic reasoning, aquifer tests (6), (11), (13)
3. Constraints on location of wells. Depth of drilling Depth of water level Poor water quality Social (land ownership, etc.)	Geologic subsurface correlations, geophysics, water-level maps, chemical methods, drilling of research holes, information on requirements and social constraints (3), (4), (5), (7), (9), (15)
4. Boundaries of groundwater systems. Geologic boundaries Hydraulic groundwater divide	Geologic maps, geologic subsurface correlations, water level maps (3), (7)
5. Mechanism of replenishment. From rain From rivers Lateral inflow of groundwater Fossil water Man-made return flow	Geohydrologic inferences, water level hydrographs and maps, observations of river flow, geochemical methods, isotope methods (7), (9), (12), (10)
6. Mechanism of natural outflow. Through springs Seepage into rivers and lakes Evapotranspiration through phreatophytes, from salt marshes, and swamps Into ocean	Geohydrologic inferences, water level maps, salinity maps, geochemical methods, isotope methods, air photos (11), (7), (8), (2), (9), (10), (3)
7. Estimate of average annual replenishment	Simple water-balance methods (12)
8. Pattern of flow. Aquifer homogeneous isotropic Aquifer nonhomogeneous Aquifer anisotropic Aquifer with preferential flow channels	Geohydrologic inferences, geologic subsurface techniques, water level maps, pumping tests, geochemical methods (2), (11), (3), (6), (7), (9)

Continued

TABLE 1.2   (*Continued*)

9. Potential mechanisms of groundwater mineralization. Evaporites Seawater Brines of geologic origin Connate salts in fine-grained rocks Airborne salts	Geohydrologic inferences, geochemical methods, isotope methods, drilling of research boreholes (2), (11), (9), (10), (5)
10. Model of aquifer. Conceptual	Correlation and integration of all available data (3), (6), (7), (9), (8), (10), (11), (12), (14)
Digital or analog Stage 1	Beyond scope of this text

C.   Phase of conservation
Practical aims: Determine maximum sustained yield under given set of constraints

Problems to be solved	Techniques of investigation
1. Compute replenishment. Average annual replenishment Annual replenishment as a function of precipitation	Waterbalance methods (12)
2. Evaluate constraints. Pumping lift Decreased thickness of saturated section of aquifer Influence on spring flow and base flow of rivers Soil subsidence Economic, administrative, and social constraints	(13)
3. Calibrate model.	
4. Predict final equilibrium. Water levels for various alternatives of exploitation	Beyond the scope of this text
5. Rank constraints 6. Determine maximum sustained yield	(13)
7. Define observation network for monitoring and supervision	(14)

Continued

TABLE 1.2 (*Continued*)

D. Phase of optimization
Practical aims: optimization of exploitation (including storage operations)

Problems to be solved	Techniques of investigation
1. Model of water supply, including hydraulic, economic, and social variables	Beyond the scope of this text
2. Define target function to be optimized	
3. Define constraints. Hydrologic Hydraulic Economic Social and legal	Reevaluate criteria of preceding phase (13)
4. Determine groundwater storage. Dynamic Below level of outlet	Depletion curve analysis, residence time by radio isotopes, geohydrologic reasoning (8), (10), (13)
5. Generate series of replenishment events with varying probabilities	Beyond the scope of this text
6. Evaluate damages corresponding to various degrees of storage depletion	
7. Evaluate technical and economic feasibility of artificial replenishment	
8. Final calibration of hydrologic model	
9. Maximize target function	

[a] Figures in parentheses refer to the relevant sections in the text.

FURTHER READINGS

Bachmat, Y., and Bear, J., (1964). The general equations of hydrodynamic dispersion in homogeneous isotropic porous mediums. *J. Geoph. Res.* **69**, 2561–2567.

Bear, J. (1972). "Dynamics of Fluids in Porous Media." Elsevier, Amsterdam.

Bouwer, H. (1978). "Groundwater Hydrology." McGraw-Hill, New York.

Carozzi, A. V., ed. (1975). "Sedimentary Rocks: Concepts and History." Academic Press, New York.

Custodio, E., and Llamas, M. R. (1976). "Hidrologia subterranea." 2 vols. Ediciones Omega, Barcelona.

Dagan, G. (1979). Models of groundwater flow in statistically homogeneous porous formations. *Water Resour. Res.* **15**, 47–63.

Davis, S. N., and DeWiest, R. J. M. (1966). "Hydrogeology." Wiley, New York.

De Josselin De Jong, G. (1958). Longitudinal and transverse diffusion in granular deposits. *Trans. Amer. Geophys. Un.* **39**, 67–74.

Domenico, P. A. (1972). "Concepts and Models in Groundwater Hydrology." McGraw-Hill, New York.

Donovan, D.Th. (1966). "Stratigraphy, an Introduction to Principles." Murby, London.

Dunbar, C. O., and Rogers, J. (1966). "Principles of Stratigraphy." Wiley, New York.

Eicher, D. L. (1968). "Geologic Time." Prentice Hall, Englewood Cliffs, New Jersey.

Gignoux, M. (1955). "Stratigraphic Geology." Freeman, San Francisco.

Goldthwait, R. P. (1975). "Glacial Deposits." Academic Press, New York.

Halek, V., and Seč J. (1979). "Groundwater Hydraulics." Elsevier, Amsterdam.

Holmes, A. (1965). "Principles of Physical Geology." 2nd ed. Nelson, London.

Irmay, S., Bear, J., and Zazlavsky, D. (1968). "Physical Principles of Water Percolation and Seepage". UNESCO, Paris.

Mandel, S., and Weinberger, Z. (1972). Analysis of a network model for dispersive flow. *J. Hydrology* **16**, 147–157.

Nemec, J. (1972). "Engineering Hydrology." McGraw-Hill, New York.

Nockolds, S. R., Knox, R. W. O'B, and Chinner, G. A. (1978). "Petrology for Students." Cambridge Univ. Press., London and New York.

Neuman, S. P. (1972). Theory of flow in unconfined aquifers considering delayed response of the water table. *Water Resour. Res.* **8**, 1013–1045.

Pinder, G. F., and Gray, W. G. (1977). "Finite Element Simulation in Surface and Subsurface Hydrology." Academic Press, New York.

Remson, I., Hornberger, G. M., and Molz, F. J. (1971). "Numerical Methods in Subsurface Hydrology." Wiley, New York.

Selley, R. C. (1976). "An Introduction to Sedimentology." Academic Press, London.

Todd, D. K. (1959). "Groundwater Hydrology." Wiley, New York.

Thomas, R. G. (1973). "Groundwater Models." Irrigation and Drainage pap. No. 21, FAO, Rome.

Verrujt, A. (1970). "Theory of Groundwater Flow." Civil Engineering Hydraulic Series. Macmillan, New York.

2

Aquifer Types and Groundwater Environments

Similar climatic and geologic conditions engender similarities of groundwater occurrence in widely distant regions, but a consistent world-wide typology of groundwater occurrence is still outstanding.

The investigator has to appraise the conditions and difficulties he is going to encounter in a given area so as to forestall, as much as possible, disagreeable surprises. Adopting this point of view and eschewing any pretense at systematic thoroughness, several common types of aquifers and of groundwater environments are described in this chapter. Voluminous information on groundwater occurrence and conditions is available in reports and publications, but it is futile to expect an exact duplication of conditions in two different areas, despite great apparent similarities.

2.1 ALLUVIAL AQUIFERS

The term *alluvium* is widely used to describe terrestrial sediments of recent geologic age deposited by flowing water. The sediments are composed of clastic material of greatly varying grain size. If the particles are of a fairly uniform size, the material is said to be *well sorted*; if particle sizes are distributed over a wide range, the material is said to be *poorly sorted*. Aquifers in alluvial deposits are very common and constitute in many regions the only exploitable source of groundwater. They can be classified according to the environment of deposition into (1) alluvial fans and piedmont deposits, (2) alluvial plains, and (3) deltaic terrains.

Piedmont Deposits

Alluvial fans form where a stream leaves its inclined mountain tract and enters the plain, dumping most of its sediment load, because of the sudden decrease in flow velocity. The accumulation of great masses of material forces the river from its point of emergence from the mountains into frequent changes of course, into various directions. Thus its sediment load is spread over a fan-shaped area. Alluvial fans, distinct near the points of emergence of the valleys from the mountain belt, tend to merge farther downstream. The resulting complex of coalescent alluvial fans is often called *piedmont*. The sediments of alluvial fans are composed of particles of all sizes, from large boulders and blocks to clay with greatly differing degrees of sorting. The coarsest materials are found near the mountain border, generally mixed with finer fractions, and particle size diminishes toward the lowlands. Stratification is very imperfect in the upper ranges of the piedmont belt. Units of similar lithologic composition and sorting are lens-shaped in a section across the fan and stringlike in the direction of the river channels. It is difficult, therefore, to extend stratigraphic correlations over any appreciable distance. In addition, each period of high river flow truncates part of the previous sediments and redeposits them further downstream. In the lower part of alluvial fans, more continuous and better-sorted layers are present and the part of the finer-grained materials increases. Thus the thickness of aquiferous beds in a given section is reduced, and simultaneously confined aquifers are formed (Fig. 2.1).

Groundwater in alluvial fans is replenished mainly by percolation of river water, which may reach a remarkable rate over relatively short stretches, especially near the mountain border. The water may reappear in the form of springs and seepages around the toe of the fan, or it may continue its subsurface flow toward more distant downstream areas (see following discussion of alluvial plains). Relatively deep drilling in the downstream part of the fan often taps confined aquifers, because of the interstratification of aquiferous and confining beds.

Where recent uplift of the mountain border zone or lowering of the base level of erosion has caused the dissection of the alluvial fan by deeply incised river channels, it turns into a thin aquifer and loses much of its capacity to absorb and store river flow.

The hydrologic properties of alluvial fans depend on the physical and chemical nature of the constituent rocks. Fine and plastic components may

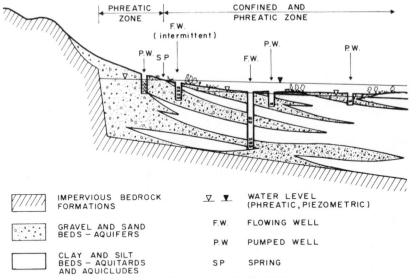

IMPERVIOUS BEDROCK FORMATIONS	▽ ▼	WATER LEVEL (PHREATIC, PIEZOMETRIC)
GRAVEL AND SAND BEDS – AQUIFERS	F.W.	FLOWING WELL
	P.W.	PUMPED WELL
CLAY AND SILT BEDS – AQUITARDS AND AQUICLUDES	S P	SPRING

Fig. 2.1   Section through alluvial fan.

lose their primary porosity by compaction. Calcareous rock debris can be transformed into a compact breccia or conglomerate by alternating solution and precipitation of carbonates. Where the rock material and the climate are conducive to mudflows, fans may be so rich in clay-sized particles as to be practically impervious.

The importance of alluvial fans as sources of groundwater is amply demonstrated in many areas. Examples are the Los Angeles Basin (Thornbury, 1958) and the foothill belt bordering the Himalaya ranges on the south in India and Nepal (Tahal,1979).

Another type of clastic deposits of recent age, though not deposited by flowing water, but by gravitational sliding of rock debris from cliffs and steep slopes, is *talus* or *scree* deposits. They form steeply inclined half-cones or wedges at the foot of the slopes or cliffs. The material is poorly sorted, consisting of huge blocks and angular fragments mixed with washed-down clay and soil. The outcrop area of this kind of deposits is restricted to a narrow, often discontinuous belt along the mountain border, so that not much replenishment from rainfall can be expected. Springs arising at the foot of scree slopes often represent groundwater emerging through them from aquifers pertaining to the adjoining mountain region.

Alluvial Plains

Alluvial plains are built up by clastic material deposited by meandering or braided rivers. The sediments formed within or close to river channels are much more coarse-grained and permeable than those deposited on the floodplains. The coarsest-grained gravels and sands make up the traction load of present and ancient buried stream channels. On the inside of meander bends, coarse-grained *point-bar* deposits are formed. Natural *levees* often flanking the channels are generally built up by fine sand and silt. During high-water stages a slowly moving sheet of water covers the floodplain and deposits silt and clay. Coarser material may reach the floodplain when the levees are pierced during floods. Ancient river channels can frequently be identified on aerial photographs, but for the detection of deeper-buried channels subsurface exploration methods must be applied. Many alluvial plains conceal, in their subsurface, deposits of former lakes and bogs, which are composed mostly of fine-grained and hence little permeable material. The deposits often contain noxious components, such as compounds containing nitrogen, iron, manganese, and others, which may cause a deterioration of water quality when the water table is lowered (see Sections 13.1 and 9.4).

According to a schematic concept of depositional history, coarser-grained materials should prevail in the upstream part of the plain and in older, deeper layers that were deposited during early more vigorously erosive phases. Although this is borne out by many examples, there are also many exceptions. Often the scarcity or absence of aquiferous gravel and sand deposits that were expected in depth is deduced only by the wisdom of hindsight from unsuccessful wells (Fig. 2.2). A large alluvial plain should be visualized as a complex of more or less lens-shaped, elongated bodies—or discontinuous layers—of gravel, sand, silt, and clay, including various mixtures of these components. Geophysical methods can generally be applied to distinguish between more gravelly–sandy and more clayey–silty parts of the plain's subsurface. Where data from boreholes and from geophysical surveys are well spread over the area, it is possible to work out a reasonably correct stratigraphic correlation or at least a regional distribution pattern of coarser- and finer-grained sediments. Such a regional image, however, is not sufficient to eliminate completely the element of chance from the siting of wells. An area in which gravels and sands are known to

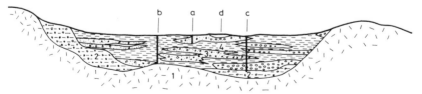

Fig. 2.2 Section through alluvial plain. 1, bedrock; 2, old consolidated terrace deposits; 3, gravel, sands, silt; 4, clay. a, Shallow well; b, unsuccessful deep well; c, successful deep well; d, present river channel.

predominate may, nevertheless, contain unexpected lenses of clay. Resistivity depth probes on sites selected or considered for drilling are always indicated in such terrains. Pumping tests are useful to detect local inhomogeneities in the aquifer and to evaluate the extent and continuity of confining layers (Chapter 6). Simulation models may require a very strong simplification of the complex subsurface conditions. Hence, locally, rather large deviations from hydrologic predictions are to be expected. Because of the nature of the deposits and the presence of semipermeable layers, the aquifer is markedly anisotropic, vertical permeabilities being smaller at least by one order of magnitude than horizontal ones. Local cones of depression tend, therefore, to be much deeper than the values predicted on the basis of horizontal transmissivities only. If the aquifer complex incorporates a continuous semipermeable layer of silty sand or silt, leaky aquifer concepts have to be applied (Section 6.7).

Deltaic Terrains

Deltaic deposits are formed where a river dumps much more material than the sea currents are able to sweep away. Not all rivers are capable of building deltas. Sediments consist predominantly of fine sand and silt. Gravels reach delta areas only in rare cases. Coarser sand and sandstones originate from beach sands, dunes, sand bars and banks, and river channel deposits. Clay and silt are deposited in tidal flats and shore lagoons. As a consequence of the variety of depositional environment over short distances and in time, sedimentary units are lens-shaped and discontinuous. Therefore the appraisal of subsurface conditions presents the same difficulties as on alluvial plains. Information on the subsurface distribution of beds of various aquiferous properties must be obtained mainly from boreholes, since geophysical methods—especially electrical resistivity methods—yield ambiguous results because of the frequent presence of brackish or saline groundwater.

Brackish water may be encountered even in shallow boreholes and in locations far removed from the sea. These occurrences can be ascribed to vestiges of trapped seawater, ancient lagoons, spring tides, or salt spray, but this does not make them, unfortunately, more predictable. In rapidly growing deltas such as the Mississippi Delta (Fig. 2.3) saline water may also be forced upstream in confined beds because of increasing sediment load on the delta deposits and rapid compaction.

On the other hand, the occurrence of freshwater under some artesian pressure, even below shallower patches of saline water, is not uncommon. It is due to infiltration into truncated delta deposits that become confined in a downstream direction.

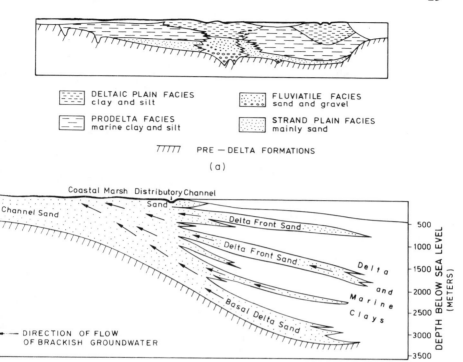

Fig. 2.3 The subsurface of deltas. (a) Section through the Quaternary Mississippi delta, (b) hypothetical section through a delta showing flow of groundwater due to load compaction of sediments. (After Jones, 1971.)

2.2 GLACIAL TERRAINS

Glacial terrains cover large areas in the cool-temperate zone of the Northern Hemisphere and smaller areas in the corresponding zone of the Southern Hemisphere. An extensive literature deals with the glacial and interglacial stages of the Pleistocene, which gave final shape to the morphology of these vast areas and witnessed the ascent of man to his present position. Remnants of much older periods of glaciation are of little hydrologic interest. Pleistocene glacial deposits present, in many cases, the only prospect for locating groundwater in vast areas of the continental platforms in the cold and temperate zones.

The streams of ice that issued during the successive glacial stages from polar regions and from high mountains churned up huge volumes of rock. Since the carrying capacity of moving ice is practically independent of its

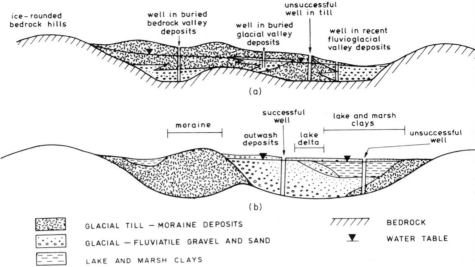

Fig. 2.4 Groundwater in glacial terrains. (a) Buried valley aquifers, (b) glacial outwash aquifers.

flow velocity, clay, silt, gravel, boulders, and sometimes huge rocks were carried indiscriminately over large distances. Where—and when—the ice melted, the entire unsorted load of material was dumped, thus creating *glacial till*, characterized by very small hydraulic conductivity. The thickness of glacial deposits varies between several meters and several tens of meters, but rarely exceeds 100 m. They often form elongated ridges called *moraines*. Sometimes they form plains smothering the remnants of the preexisting topography (Fig. 2.4).

Streams that issued from the edge of melting ice masses picked up big loads of the unconsolidated glacial sediments, dumping the coarser constituents at some distance downstream. These *outwash gravels* occur in the form of *outwash fans* and *outwash terraces* and constitute shallow but useful aquifers. Their thickness rarely exceeds several tens of meters. Frequently, the outwash gravels are intimately connected with recent river gravels. In some places the meltwater was dammed up by moraines, thus forming lakes in which delicately layered (*warved*), fine-grained sediments were deposited. These are aquitards or poor aquifers. The finer-grained materials, deposited further downstream, were often eroded by wind and redeposited as *loess* layers (*circum-glacial loess*).

Groundwater prospection in glacial terrains is concerned mainly with the location of outwash gravels and buried stream channels. This is accomplished by morphologic considerations and by the application of geophysical methods.

Drawdowns in these thin outwash gravel aquifers increase nonlinearly when the water table is lowered, thus restricting well discharges in spite of the sometimes very large conductivity of the gravel beds. Discharges of several m^3/hr must be considered as acceptable results, several tens of m^3/hr as good, and 100 m^3/hr or more as rare exceptions.

The hydrology of these terrains is characterized by the close connection between surface and groundwater. In central Canada, in areas where groundwater is recharged from rainfall (400–600 mm/year), each small stream forms the basis of drainage for the groundwater in the adjoining part of the plain, so that water level contours follow rather closely the subdued topography of the region (Tóth, 1966). In the Lowell area of New England, crossed by the Merrimack River, best groundwater conditions obtain in buried preglacial valleys (Baker, 1964). The aquifers are outwash deposits adjoining the river, which constitutes a practically unlimited source of recharge. Quantities of groundwater that can be extracted are limited mainly by the permeability of the sediments and the small saturated thickness of the aquifer. In the Canterbury region of New Zealand, groundwater seems to be replenished mainly from the large rivers descending from the eastern slopes of the Southern Alps, which loose large volumes of water into outwash fans. Geochemical evidence and water-level observations in boreholes indicate that the major part of groundwater flow follows well-defined gravel-filled channels (Mandel, 1974).

2.3 SANDSTONE–SHALE AQUIFERS

Sequences of alternating sand, or sandstone and shale, or clay are characteristic of many sedimentary successions. Deposition of such sequences takes place in the marine, deltaic, littoral, and arid-continental environment. The main difference between such sequences and similar rock associations shown on geologic maps under the definition *alluvium* or *recent deposits* is the greater age and hence the more advanced stage of consolidation. In contrast to alluvial sediments, sandstone–shale sequences usually exhibit a rather persistent stratigraphy. The primary porosity of a layer of sandstone is often strongly reduced by compaction and cementation. Zones with secondary porosity are usually aligned along bedding planes, fractures, and joints. Near the surface sandstones are often indurated by almost impermeable crusts.

Alternating sandstone–shale formations occur under a great variety of geologic conditions. On some of the continental platforms they fill vast bowl-shaped depressions or basins and constitute large regional, often confined aquifers. Famous examples are the Karroo sandstone of South Africa, the Botucatu sandstone of southern Brazil, the Dakota sandstone of

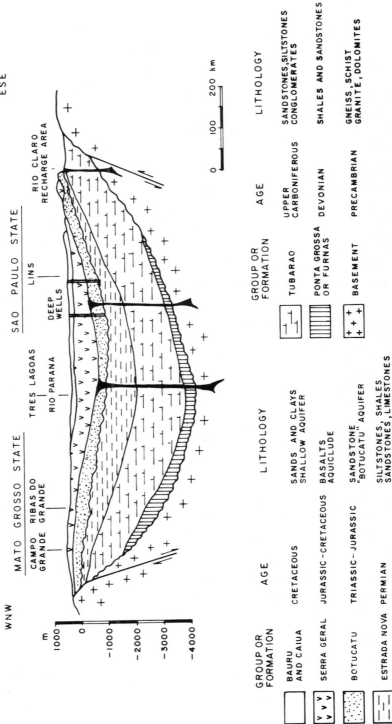

Fig. 2.5a Regional sandstone aquifers on continental platforms. Schematic section through the Parana Basin, Brazil. (After Gilboa *et al.*, 1976.)

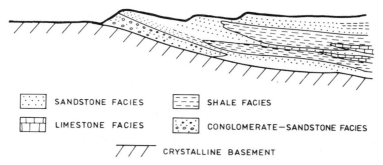

SANDSTONE FACIES   SHALE FACIES

LIMESTONE FACIES   CONGLOMERATE–SANDSTONE FACIES

CRYSTALLINE BASEMENT

Fig. 2.5b Facies changes in a sandstone–shale sequence on a continental platform.

North America, and the so-called Nubian sandstones of Northern Africa and the Arabian Peninsula (Fig. 2.5). In regions dominated by a normal fold pattern, conditions are also conducive to the formation of regional confined aquifers, such as in the Paris Basin and the folded northern Negev of Israel. In strongly deformed regions, however, intense tectonic forces often compact the rocks, or even transform them through metamorphic processes into quartzite–slate formations, so that the original water-bearing properties are lost. In addition, tectonic movements disrupt the continuity of aquiferous strata.

In gently folded and dissected regions, a fairly complete image of the aquiferous properties of the sandstone–shale formations can be obtained from surface observations. In plane regions, however, with more or less horizontal strata, where outcrops are rare, interpolation or extrapolation based on distant information points may be misleading.

2.4 CARBONATE ROCKS

Carbonate rocks are composed of the carbonates of calcium and magnesium in varying proportions, often admixed with clay and siliceous components. *Limestones* consist mainly of the mineral calcite ($CaCO_3$). *Chalks* are soft, friable limestones. *Dolomites* consist mainly of the mineral dolomite [$CaMg(CO_3)_2$]. Rocks composed of calcite and dolomite, in varying proportions, are *dolomitic limestones*. Rocks built of the mineral magnesite ($MgCO_3$) are rare.

Dolomites can be distinguished from limestones by the rougher surface they display when freshly broken and by the fact that they do not effervesce with hydrochloric acid. In the field, dolomite formations are often of a dull gray color and form characteristic landscape features.

Only carbonate rock formations with a thickness of at least several tens of meters make potential aquifers. Formations composed sandwich fashion of thin layers of carbonate rock alternating with shales offer poor prospects for groundwater. Soft chalks generally make poorer aquifers than hard limestones and dolomites.

Carbonate rocks are eroded by dissolution in water containing carbon dioxide. The peculiar landscape thus formed is called *karst* after a type locality in Yugoslavia. A mature karst morphology develops on hard, fissured carbonate rocks under humid–subhumid climatic conditions. It is characterized by the disruption of surficial drainage patterns. River valleys are replaced by arrays of closed depressions (*dolines*), surface runoff disappears into *sinkholes*, and in extreme cases, entire rivers flow for some distance in *caverns* underground. In dry climates morphologic karst features remain relatively undeveloped because of the scarcity of water. In the saturated zone, however, solution proceeds continually and eventually creates a system of solution channels.

Solution by groundwater proceeds according to the following principles:

(1)   Imagine a limestone aquifer having some initial—primary or secondary—porosity. The water picks up carbon dioxide in the nonsaturated zone above the water table, dissolves calcite during its flow through the aquifer, and emerges from the natural outlets saturated with calcium bicarbonate.

(2)   Consider a flow channel leading from the water table to an outlet and assume, for simplicity, that it is not connected to any other channels. Under these conditions the rate of erosion by dissolution is proportional to the discharge of the channel.

$$\Delta M = Q \Delta t \, \alpha (C_s - C_0) \qquad (2.1a)$$

$$\frac{\Delta M}{\Delta t} = Q \alpha (C_s - C_0) \qquad (2.1b)$$

where ΔM is the mass of rock matrix dissolved (M), Δt the time interval (T), $\Delta M / \Delta t$ the rate of erosion (MT^{-1}), Q the discharge of the channel ($L^3 T^{-1}$), C_0, C_s are the concentration of $CaCO_3$ near water table and the saturated concentration at outlet respectively (ppm), and α is the proportionality factor depending on channel geometry and on the chemical and mineralogic characteristics of the aquifer.

(3)   The largest rate of erosion will occur along flow paths that offer the least resistance to the passage of water through the aquifer. These preferred flow paths may be formed by interstices along bedding planes, by faults, or by fissures. The point is that openings that carry a relatively large discharge are preferably widened by karstic erosion.

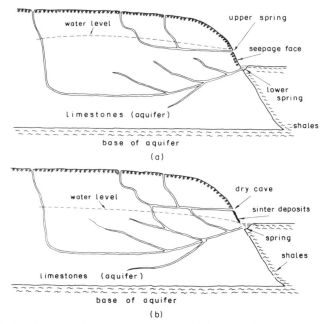

Fig. 2.6 Development of solution channels by flowing groundwater. (a) Initial stage, (b) advanced stage.

(4)   An array of solution channels, even though each one is only one or several millimeters wide, strongly increases the hydraulic conductivity of the aquifer and, consequently, the discharge in a particular direction. Thus an ever-increasing part of the water flowing through the aquifer is concentrated into a system of solution channels.

(5)   The water table is lowered and outlets fed from the upper part of the aquifer gradually cease to function. The pore space between solution channels, where the water becomes semistagnant, may be plugged by calcite deposits. In the vicinity of a natural outlet, where flow paths converge, veritable caverns are created. Eventually one spring—usually the one at the lowest outcrop—grows into giant proportions, leaving older spring outlets "high and dry" (Fig. 2.6).

(6)   When karstic erosion runs its full course, the pore space of the aquifer is replaced by a few wide caverns, and eventually the whole limestone massif collapses and is washed away. These spectacular developments are of interest to geomorphologists. The hydrogeologist is concerned mainly with the invisible initial and intermediate stages of the process, which enhance aquiferous properties rather than destroy them.

This conceptual model of karstic erosion by groundwater is amply supported by observational evidence.

Giant springs are a characteristic feature of carbonate massifs. The spring is usually located near the lowest outcrop and drains an area not necessarily congruent with surface watersheds. Ancient, higher spring outlets are often marked by dry caverns above the present spring level. Cores from boreholes frequently exhibit solution channels as well as calcite veins, thus demonstrating the delicate balance between solution and precipitation.

Several authors concluded that dissolution can occur only near the water table, since the limited supply of carbon dioxide swept in from the root zone of vegetation should be quickly exhausted. This idea may be supported by evidence from some areas, but it should not be generalized. Under natural conditions chemical equilibria may take a long time to be established (Mercado and Billings, 1975). Karstic solution channels are sometimes noticed in boreholes at depths exceeding 1000 m. The supply of carbon dioxide may be augmented by the oxidation of fossil organic matter or by volcanic exhalations. Finally, it should be remembered that the hydrologic effects sketched above are brought about by very slow solution processes. They do not depend on the existence of very aggressive waters and on quick reaction rates.

The influence of chemical and mineralogical rock characteristics on the dynamics of the solution process is imperfectly known. In one area solution channels may be concentrated in a certain limestone facies, whereas dolomitic rocks remain relatively tight. In another area the situation may be reversed. The only valid criterion is that systems of solution channels are more likely to develop in hard rocks than in soft ones.

The aquifer feeding the Yarkon and Tanninim springs, located in the eastern part of the coastal plain of Israel, serves as an example for a carbonate rock aquifer. It consists of limestones and dolomites that crop out on the western flanks of the Judea–Samaria mountain range and plunge toward west below the coastal plain (Fig. 2.7). The hydrostratigraphy of the aquifer and adjoining formations is shown in Table 2.1 (see also Fig. 3.1).

The structure is characterized by a series of normal folds with axes running roughly in a SW–NE direction. Faults provide connections between the upper and lower aquifer. The replenishment area extends over approximately 1,400 km^2. Its boundaries are, in the west, the limits of outcrops of the upper aquifer; in the east, the groundwater divide between the Mediterranean and the Jordan depression, which generally coincides with the crests of the anticlinal axes; in the south and north, structural depressions. Rainfall on the replenishment area ranges between 650 and 350 mm/av year; 550 mm/yr may be taken as representative areal average.

The Yarkon spring about 12 km east of Tel Aviv rises at an elevation of 16.5 m above Mediterranean Sea level (M.S.L.) from a small pool fed by several vertically ascending channels. In the natural state the average annual discharge was 200 million cubic meters per year (MCM/yr). The Tanninim

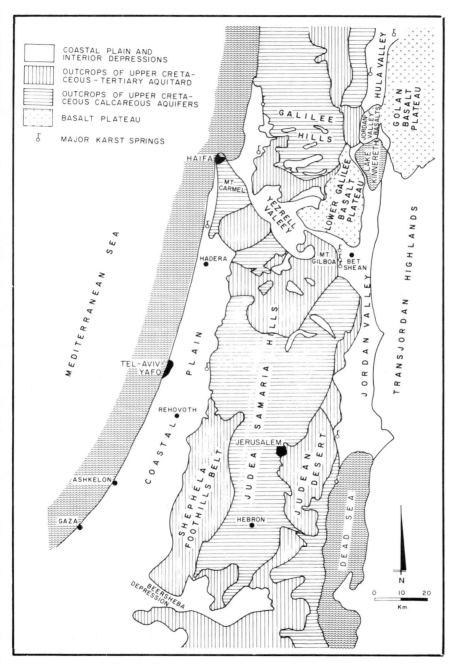

Fig. 2.7 Key map of northern Israel and adjoining territories.

TABLE 2.1

Hydrostratigraphy of the Aquifer Feeding the Yarkon and Tanninim Springs and Adjoining Formations

Age	Lithology	Approximate thickness (m)	Hydrologic properties
Neogene Eocene Senonian	Chalks, partly siliceous, marls	250	Aquiclude
Turonian and Cenomanian (upper part)	Mainly limestones and dolomitic limestones	300	Upper aquifer
Cenomanian (middle part)	Soft, marly dolomites and limestones with chalk and marl beds	150	Aquitard
Cenomanian (lower part) Albian (upper part)	Mainly dolomites	300	Lower aquifer
Albian (lower part)	Marls	100	Base of aquiferous sequence

springs rise at elevations of 2–4 m above Mediterranean Sea level near the southern tip of Mt. Carmel. They discharged in the natural state approximately 100 MCM/yr of brackish water with about 1800 parts per million total dissolved solids (ppm TDS). A few very small springs and seepages appear in some locations near outcrops of the Cenomanian (middle part) aquitard. Their combined discharge is estimated at 5 MCM/yr.

The upper aquifer is exploited by about 150 wells drilled mainly into the confined part of the aquifer, all along the foothills. Water levels were in the natural state 25 m above Mediterranean Sea level in the south and 19 m above M.S.L. in the north. Salinities vary generally between 250–575 ppm TDS, except for synclinal, heavily confined parts of the aquifer, where much higher salinities are frequently encountered. Salination of the Tanninim springs occurs near a fault, just south of the spring.

The lower aquifer is exploited mainly in the vicinity of Jerusalem, where its water level rises to 500 m above M.S.L. because of perching above Albian marls. The wells have small specific discharges of 2–10 cubic meters per hour per meter drawdown ($m^3/hr/m$).

Water quality is excellent, 75–150 ppm TDS. A few deep wells in the foothill region showed that here water levels in both aquifers are almost equal and that the lower aquifer is much less saline than the upper one.

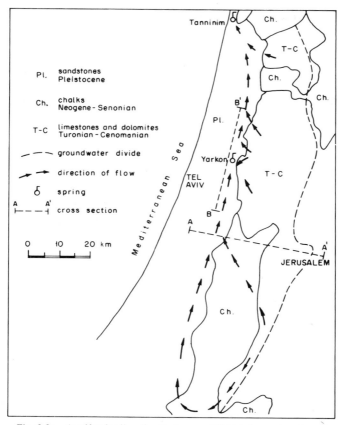

Fig. 2.8a Aquifer feeding the Yarkon and Tanninim springs (map).

The flow pattern is shown in Fig. 2.8a,b. Along the mountain border groundwater flow is directed from south to north. The uncertain groundwater divide between the Yarkon and Tanninim springs is probably a movable boundary, reflecting hydrologic conditions.

The surficial drainage pattern of the area is characterized by deeply incised, dry river valleys. Morphological karst features are the curiously dissected rock surface known as *lapies*, a few caves, a few closed depressions, and small sinkholes.

The very rudimentary state of morphological karst development strongly contrasts with the far-reaching effects of erosion by dissolution in the saturated aquifer. During drilling, losses of circulation are frequent, and cores usually show solution channels side by side with calcitic veins. Groundwater abstraction through boreholes lowered the water level almost

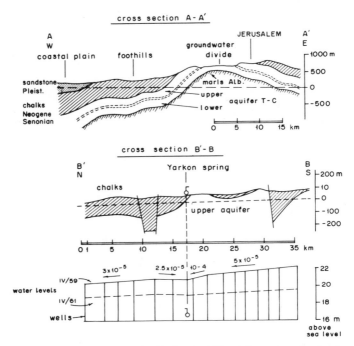

Fig. 2.8b   Aquifer feeding the Yarkon and Tanninim springs (sections).

parallel to itself, thus indicating an enormously enlarged transmissivity. The two springs that are situated at the lowest outcrops discharge approximately 37% of the rain falling on an area of 1400 km². Flow directions toward the springs cut across surface watersheds, fold structures, and fault lines and thus demonstrate that a process of capturing due to the development of solution channels has taken place.

The above description refers to the natural state of the aquifer. The effects of intensive groundwater abstraction from this aquifer are discussed in Section 8.2.

2.5   VOLCANIC TERRAINS

Volcanic terrains are built up by lava rocks, or pyroclastic deposits, or both, in varying proportions. Many predominantly volcanic formations include also sedimentary rocks, such as river alluvium, ancient soils, and lake and marine deposits.

Volcanic rocks have widely varying hydrologic properties, making predictions about groundwater possibilities uncertain. Some lavas contain excellent aquifers; others are practically impermeable. Many lava rocks exhibit *vesicular porosity* caused by the gas bubbles contained in the lava during eruption. But the pores thus formed are not interconnected. It appears that mainly lavas of fairly recent age (Quaternary, Late Tertiary) are aquiferous, whereas in most older lavas the formation of secondary minerals and the partial disintegration into clay have clogged voids and fissures. Acid lava rocks containing a high proportion of silica (66% or more) are generally poorer aquifers than the more frequent basic lavas, such as *olivine basalt*, named after the conspicuous olive-colored mineral it contains. Lavas formed by submarine eruptions—so-called *pillow lavas*—are poor aquifers, or aquifuges, since no voids or fissures are formed because of the rapid chilling and the presence of large amounts of minerals precipitated by steam. Loose pyroclastic rocks (scoria, cinders, pumice, ash) are quite permeable when fresh, but the finer-grained varieties lose much of their permeability through compaction and weathering. *Mud flows* that owe their origin to torrential rains on steeply inclined, soft pyroclastic strata are practically impermeable. They can be discerned by morphologic characteristics and by the lack of stratification.

In volcanic terrains, highly mineralized, more or less thermal waters are of frequent occurrence. Noxious ions such as boron, arsenic, and fluoride may be present in harmful concentrations even in normal-tasting waters.

From the viewpoint of groundwater occurrence, three principal types of volcanic terrains can be distinguished: basalt plateaus, central volcanic edifices, and mixed pyroclastic–lava terrains.

Basalt plateaus are the result of repeated effusions of low-viscosity lavas over extensive areas. The flows of these low-viscosity lavas have issued from numerous fissures and sometimes contain the conspicuous mineral olivine. Preexisting relief tends to be leveled-out and transformed into a flat morphology, or into a steplike one, if successive flows terminate at different distances from the erupting fissures. Clay-rich soils that form by weathering between eruptions, or sands, are sometimes found between successive sheets. The original continuity of basalt plateaus aquifers is often disrupted by deeply incised valleys cutting into underlying formations or by tectonic disruption, into fault blocks (Fig. 2.9a,b). Some volcanic plateaus are built up by *ignimbrites*—ashes erupted in an incandescent state and welded together by heat.

The hydrologically important porosity of basalt terrains is due to more or less vertical shrinkage cracks—often also observed in ignimbrites—and to the essentially horizontal voids and rubble zones left between successive flows. Streams flowing over basalt plateaus frequently lose much water by infiltration. Large springs are formed where the contact between the basalts and an impervious substratum is exposed in incised valleys or along escarpments of the plateau. Smaller springs may issue at various elevations

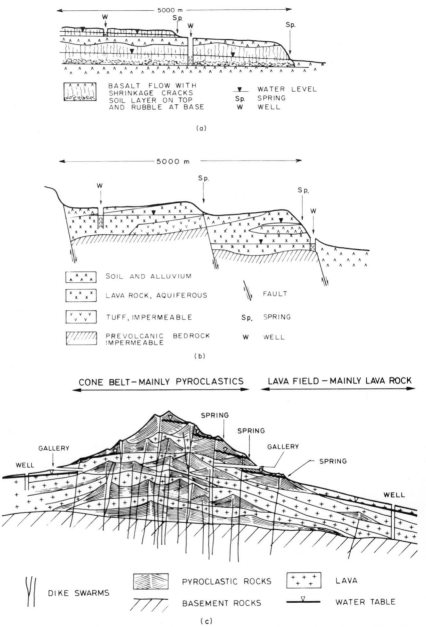

Fig. 2.9   Groundwater in volcanic terrains. (a) Lava plateau, (b) volcanic tilted-block region, (c) central volcano.

from perched horizons, such as ancient soils and tuffs. The presence of major fissures or faults largely determines the occurrence of the larger springs. In some basalt plateaus, permeability of the formation may be as high as in karstic limestone aquifers, and fairly evenly distributed, so that wells stand a fair chance of success where the saturated section is thick enough. Under less favorable conditions, well siting must be guided by the distribution and alignment of major fissure systems that are visible on the surface or indicated by hydrologic phenomena.

The use of geophysical methods for groundwater prospecting in lava terrains is beset with peculiar difficulties. High electrical resistivities are sometimes, though not always, associated with impervious, compact flows, and low to medium resistivities are associated with more porous, water-saturated ones. The application of the *magnetotelluric* method has recently been advocated, but no practical experience is yet available. *Seismic refraction* is more successful in defining lateral changes in rock velocity than in determining the vertical thickness. *Magnetometry* may help to locate impervious dikes forming hydrologic boundaries.

A well frequently must penetrate several vertically superimposed perched horizons in order to attain satisfactory results. With increasing depth, the water level in the well may descend while shallower perched horizons are successively connected through the borehole to deeper ones—a situation reverse to the one encountered when drilling into progressively more confined aquifers. Care has to be taken not to block thin perched horizons by "blind" (unperforated) sections of the well casing. The capacity of wells varies greatly. Discharges of up to 500 m^3/hr have been reported from the Snake River Basin (Idaho, U.S.A.) and 200 m^3/hr from some wells in Lower Galilee (Israel), but a relatively large number of failures or modest successes have probably to be accepted in most basalt-plateau regions. Obviously, the hydrogeologic realities of basalt plateaus are far removed from the concept of a homogeneous, isotropic porous medium.

Central volcanic edifices are cone-, dome-, or shield-shaped volcanoes composed of lava flows and layers of volcanic ash and coarser materials ejected in the solid state. The surrounding lowlands are often covered with thick accumulations of volcanic ash and fine-grained pumice. Only the most copious lava flows reach large distances from the center of eruption (Fig. 2.9c).

The recent surficial products of eruption, almost bare of vegetation and not much affected by weathering and compaction, have a large infiltration capacity. Compacted impermeable tuff or soil layers between lava flows and subvertical impermeable dikes divide the subsurface into a number of groundwater compartments, each with its own water level and its own outlet, either into an adjacent lower compartment or into a spring. Thus the groundwater passes through a number of "steps" down the mountainside into the plain (Fig. 2.9c). At higher elevations, on the mountain slopes, groundwater can be exploited by galleries, and this has been the traditional method in many volcanic mountains and volcanic islands. Groundwater flow is encountered when a dike is pierced. The initial flow tends to decrease with time, and galleries are therefore extended into additional groundwater compartments to maintain the supply. This practice exploits the groundwater steadily infiltrating into the galleries from above but also entails the exploitation of reserves.

On the lower parts of volcanoes, at a greater distance from the center of eruptive activity, dikes are less frequent, and the aquifers pass from the "compartment" type to the layered type common in sedimentary layered rocks. The accumulations of volcanic ash, consisting of alternating layers of larger and smaller permeability—together with lava sheets or flows—create confined subartesian and artesian conditions. In these parts groundwater is better exploited by vertical wells. During drilling a steady rise of the water table is often noted attesting to progressive confinement of the layers, though visual inspection of samples may not permit to discern more or less permeable layers among the fine-grained pyroclastics. In the coastal volcanic regions, the freshwater–seawater interface problem has to be faced. In some cases, impermeable layers may isolate sections of the aquifer from contact with seawater and thus facilitate exploitation. Where no separation exists and highly pervious lava rocks border on the sea, the freshwater lens can be extremely thin, and exploitation by horizontal galleries is then the only way to skim off the freshwater effectively.

The Hawaii Islands are a typical example for groundwater occurrence and utilization on volcanic islands (Peterson, 1972). Although rainfall is abundant, surface flow is scarce because of the great infiltration capacity of the volcanic rocks. Rainwater percolating through the rocks accumulates in three principal types of groundwater bodies: (1) on the highest levels, in local aquifers perched on ash beds or other impermeable materials; (2) at high and medium levels, in groundwater compartments formed by dikes; and (3) in basal aquifers, where freshwater floats on saltwater.

Much groundwater is obtained from the dike aquifers. Copious, initial flows from tunnels result from the depletion of groundwater stored in the dike compartments. The establishment of a more steady, equilibrium flow takes several years and equals more or less the flow originally available from natural springs. Bulkheads have been installed in tunnels to regulate the outflow and conserve stored groundwater. The basal aquifers are the principal source of fresh groundwater. Wells penetrate both artesian and unconfined aquifers, and groundwater is also extracted from skimming tunnels. Confined conditions are created by relatively little permeable coastal sediments overlapping the highly permeable basalts.

On islands with less abundant rainfall than Hawaii, such as the Canary Islands (off the west coast of desert Africa), discharges obtained from tunnels quickly decline to meagre equilibrium discharges, and the freshwater lens of the basal aquifer is thin and technically more difficult to exploit.

Mixed lava–pyroclastic terrains of regional extent stem from prolonged periods of intensive volcanic activity. If older than Pleistocene, the morphology is often one of maturely dissected hills that bear little resemblance to the original volcanic landscape forms. Where volcanic activity has persisted into the Pleistocene, better-preserved volcanic features are superimposed on the ancient landscape. The best aquifers in such terrains are the more recent lavas, coarse pyroclastics (scoria, cinders), and some alluvial deposits. Fine-grained pyroclastics tend to become little permeable or impermeable through compaction.

The alluvial fill of plains and valleys, consisting of gravel, sand, and clay of volcanic origin, may present important groundwater possibilities, but the alluvial deposits are as diversified and variable as those in any region. Ancient volcanic craters and subsidence calderas (large depressions marking the area of former eruption centers) are often filled by lakes that represent an outcrop of the groundwater table, and could be described as giant natural wells. They can be a convenient source of water supply, provided the water quality is satisfactory and not impaired by noxious constituents.

Some coarse- to medium-grained pyroclastic deposits have a very large porosity. When confined aquifers composed of pyroclastics are dewatered by intensive exploitation, soil subsidence may result. The best-known instance is that of the center of Mexico City, which subsided to the extent of 7 m between the years 1910 and 1970. During this period a total of an estimated 5000 million m^3 was withdrawn through wells, most of it after World War II.

The contrast in productivity between lava rocks and pyroclastics is well demonstrated in Central America. The water supply of San Salvador City is derived mainly from wells drilled into basalts of the Boqueron Volcano and from natural springs emerging from these basalts. Well capacities are of the order of 200 m^3/hr. Wells drilled into fine-grained and compacted pumice deposits in the same area yield only up to 20 m^3/hr and are used for local consumption. Central America also provides numerous examples for the hydrogeologic difference between young volcanic rocks and older ones. Older, Tertiary lavas and pyroclastics in El Salvador (Balsam Range), Costa Rica, and Nicaragua are much less permeable than the more recent Quaternary lavas, pyroclastics, and alluvial materials and often are aquicludes.

2.6   CRYSTALLINE ROCKS

A great variety of rocks of igneous, mainly intrusive, and metamorphic origin form vast terrains on the continental platforms. The term *Precambrian Basement* is also used for this rock association, describing its age. Intrusive igneous and metamorphic rocks, of younger age, are found within many of the major mountain belts of the world. When of regional extent, they are called *batholites*. The most common igneous rocks of the Precambrian Basements are granites and other acid and intermediate rocks related to them (*diorites*, *syenites*). The metamorphic rocks are mostly gneiss, mica schists, quartzites, marble, and others. Less extremely metamorphic rocks such as *phyllites* and *slates* also are of widespread occurrence. The Basement Complex is traversed generally by numerous dikes and has been invaded locally by bodies of fine-textured intrusive rocks (Mehnert, 1969).

All rocks composing the Basement Complex are poor aquifers. In the fresh state, the rocks are aquifuges. Groundwater in modest quantities can be obtained from them only where they are fractured or jointed or where weathering has disintegrated the mineral fabric and produced a surficial layer of sandy clay. Its thickness generally does not surpass a few meters (Fig. 2.10). In the tropical humid environment, this weathered layer is generally covered by *laterite*, an almost impermeable, red soil. Open fractures and joints rarely extend to depths exceeding 100 m, and in many cases water-bearing fissures close at shallower depths. Some notable exceptions to this rule have been observed in mines. Gneisses differ from granites by having a foliated structure, but are similar in their mineral composition. Permeability down to a few meters depth is often due to foliation.

Mica schists consist of mica and quartz. Weathering products are micaceous sands that in some cases constitute valuable shallow aquifers. Well-cleaved and well-jointed schists can have relatively favorable aquiferous properties in comparison with other crystalline rocks. These rocks, however, are softer than granites and gneisses, and therefore water-bearing joints are closed already at shallow depth. *Quartzites* may be extensively fissured and fractured near the surface, thus creating the impression of a high secondary permeability, resembling that of fractured hard carbonate rocks. Fissures, however, are closed already at shallow depth, and the truly metamorphic quartzites are bad aquifers, even in comparison with granites, gneisses, and schists, because of their resistance to chemical disintegration. Metamorphic carbonate rocks (*metamorphic marbles*) are poor aquifers. Their secondary fissures are often filled with calcite, and they have a rather irregular and limited distribution. All *fine-grained* metamorphic rocks, such as slates and phyllites, are aquicludes. The sometimes impressive fissile

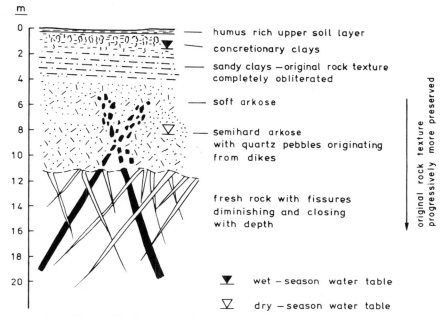

Fig. 2.10 Profile of subsurface in crystalline terrains of the intertropical belt.

disintegration of *slates* near the surface should not deceive the investigator. In the subsurface, at shallow depth, these rocks are completely tight and nonaquiferous. Dikes and other intrusive bodies composed of fine-textured rocks act as impervious barriers to groundwater flow. Coarsely crystalline, so-called pegmatitic dikes associated with large intrusive granite masses are, on the other hand, among the most permeable crystalline rocks.

Practical conclusions from experience gained in many different areas and climatic zones are as follows:

(1) Little is gained by drilling to depths exceeding 100 m.

(2) Well discharges to be expected are a few m³/hr. Discharges exceeding 10 m³/hr are exceptional.

(3) A considerable number of unsuccessful wells must be expected. Therefore, drilling campaigns are best organized with a view to rapid testing of a great number of prospective sites.

(4) The degree and depth of weathering are greatly influenced by moisture. Water-bearing properties due to rock decomposition are better in humid than in arid regions.

(5) Valleys are to be preferred for well sites where they coincide with zones of intense fracturing. In rolling terrain greatest depth of weathering

prevails, according to some investigators, on hilltops, whereas on sloping ground erosion has generally removed part of the weathered material. Flat uplands are recommended for drilling for this reason.

(6)   Geophysical methods can be of great assistance in the location of fracture zones and in the definition of the thickness of the weathered, decomposed rock zone. A combination of shallow refraction seismic and surface resistivity methods gives the best results.

(7)   Chemical quality of the water is generally good, with a tendency to alkalinity. Higher than acceptable salinities are frequent in semiarid regions with strongly seasonal rainfall. Fluoride content should be checked in all such terrains. Groundwater in zones rich in highly mineralized veins may contain other noxious ions.

(8)   In tropical–humid basement areas, there is often no alternative but to search for fracture zones, for greatest depth of weathering, and for comparatively most favorable rock types. The transition from bedrock into the lateritic soil is gradual and consists of a zone of slightly decomposed rock, a sandy horizon rich in mineral grains of the original rock with some clay ("soft arenas," Lelong, 1964), sandy clay, and finally concretionary clays and a humus layer. In order to be of practical interest for even modest but perennial water supplies, the thickness of the weathered section must exceed 10 m, in view of the annual variations of the water table. The surficial layer of laterite impedes infiltration of rainfall.

(9)   In high-latitude Basement terrains (e.g., northern U.S., Canada), glacial outwash deposits often present alternatives, and buried river channels should be searched for.

2.7   COASTAL AQUIFERS

Coastal plains generally consist of a wedge of sediments resting on the seaward inclined surface of a substratum (Fig. 2.11). Within this wedge, frequent alternations between sediments of marine and terrestric origins attest to ingressions and regressions (retreats) of the sea. Some coastal plains, however, are of different character, being rised marine abrasion plains carved out of preexisting geologic formations. The predominant young sedimentary character of coastal plains is sometimes modified by volcanic features or uplifted fault blocks consisting of older formations. Subsurface sections show an intricate interfingering of marine sands, sandstones, silts and clays, littoral sands and conglomerates—in places reef limestones—lagoonal or tidal-marsh silts and clays, sand bars and sand dunes, ancient soils, river alluvium, and deltaic silts and sands. Geophysical

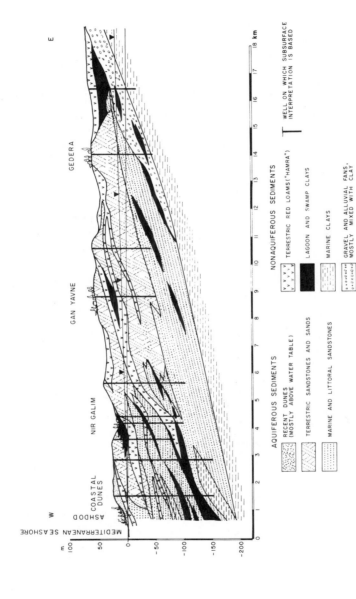

Fig. 2.11 Cross section through a coastal plain (southern coastal plain, Israel). (Courtesy of TAHAL Consulting Engineers Ltd.)

AQUIFEROUS SEDIMENTS

RECENT DUNES (MOSTLY ABOVE WATER TABLE)

TERRESTRIC SANDSTONES AND SANDS

MARINE AND LITTORAL SANDSTONES

NONAQUIFEROUS SEDIMENTS

TERRESTRIC RED LOAMS ("HAMRA")

LAGOON AND SWAMP CLAYS

MARINE CLAYS

GRAVEL AND ALLUVIAL FANS, MOSTLY MIXED WITH CLAY

WELL ON WHICH SUBSURFACE INTERPRETATION IS BASED

ASHDOD   COASTAL DUNES   NIR GALIM   GAN YAVNE   GEDERA

MEDITERRANEAN SEASHORE

W   E

0 1 2 3 4 5 6 7 8 9 10 11 12 13 14 15 16 17 18 km

100 50 0 -50 -100 -150 -200 m

measurements may indicate the most salient subsurface features, but a detailed picture can be derived only from a network of closely spaced boreholes. Subsurface correlations call for the recognition of regressive and ingressive phases in drilling samples.

In the seaward portion of a coastal aquifer freshwater floats on seawater, the two kinds of water being separated by a *zone of transition* in which salinity changes gradually (Fig. 2.12). In an undisturbed, well flushed aquifer the zone of transition is relatively thin, of the order of 10 m, and may be simulated by a sharply defined *freshwater–seawater interface*. The depth of the interface below sea level is computed by assuming that two immiscible liquids are in hydrostatic equilibrium. This procedure yields a relation known as *Ghyben–Hertzberg rule*:

$$z = h\frac{\gamma_f}{\gamma_s - \gamma_f} = h\alpha \qquad (2.2)$$

where h is the elevation of the water level above sea level, γ_f and γ_s are the specific weights of freshwater and seawater, respectively, and z is the depth of the interface below sea level. The density contrast α between fresh groundwater and oceanwater equals approximately 38.

The *toe of the interface* is situated at the point where z equals the depth D of the impermeable aquifer base. At the landward side of the toe the aquifer contains only freshwater. The following relations can be deduced for a strip of unit width, say, 1 km, represented by Fig. 2.12 (Bear, 1979).

$$L = D\sqrt{\frac{K}{\alpha R}} \qquad (2.3)$$

$$Q_L = \frac{KD^2}{2\alpha L} - \frac{RL}{2} \qquad (2.4)$$

$$Q_o = \frac{KD^2}{2\alpha L} + \frac{RL}{2} \qquad (2.5)$$

$$L_{opt} = \sqrt{\frac{KD^2}{\alpha R}} \qquad (2.6)$$

where K is the permeability, D the depth of the aquifer base below sea level, L the distance of the toe from the seashore, R replenishment on unit length of the strip, Q_L and Q_o are inflow of groundwater from the landward side and outflow into the ocean, respectively, and L_{opt} is the distance that minimizes Q_o.

A change of the water level has two effects. (a) The interface moves to another position, and (b) the zone of transition widens because of hydrodynamic dispersion. The velocity of the movement and the widening of the zone of transition are difficult to predict. Two principal situations that occur during groundwater exploitation are discussed below.

Groundwater Abstraction from a Freshwater Lens

The cone of depression around the pumped well causes a corresponding upconing of the interface (Fig. 2.12). Seawater will be drawn into the well if upconing exceeds a certain *critical rise*. In this context it should be remembered that freshwater containing only 4% oceanwater is already unusable for most purposes (Section 9.6). Theoretical considerations and field evidence indicate that the critical rise equals, approximately, one half of the original distance interface–well bottom (Schmorak and Mercado, 1969). This criterion places two restrictions on wells exploiting the freshwater lens: (a) screens have to be set high above the interface, and (b) drawdowns and, consequently, discharges have to be kept relatively small. If the freshwater lens is thick, say, more than 70 m, reduced but still acceptable discharges may be obtained. In an intensively exploited aquifer, however, the thickness of the lens is bound to decrease. The exploitation of a thin lens requires very shallow boreholes and drawdowns of the order of 10 cm. Under these conditions it is very difficult to obtain economically feasible discharges. Various technical solutions have been proposed, such as the construction of horizontal wells or the simultaneous pumping of seawater from below the interface, but a safe and inexpensive method for *skimming off freshwater* from a thin lens is still outstanding.

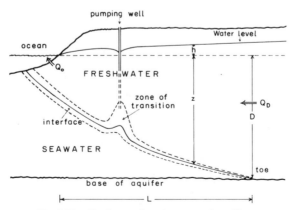

Fig. 2.12   Freshwater lens in a coastal aquifer.

Groundwater Abstraction from the Landward Part
of a Coastal Aquifer

Intensive groundwater abstraction at the landward side of the toe lowers the water level in the entire aquifer. As a consequence, the interface moves inland and upwards. If exploitation is kept within reasonable bounds, a new equilibrium position will eventually be established (Section 13, Fig. 13.2). The velocity of this transversal movement is small. It may take several years until a shift of the interface can be observed in observation holes near the shore (Section 5.3) and several decades until the interface approaches a position commensurate with hydrostatic equilibrium. During this time seawater does not intrude into the exploited wells, even if the water level is lowered below sea level. Considerations relevant to the intensive exploitation of a coastal aquifer are discussed in Sections 13.2 and 13.3.

2.8   ARID REGIONS

A region is arid if potential evapotranspiration (see Section 12.3) considerably exceeds precipitation. A more intuitive definition of aridity as well as a rough classification of degrees of aridity is easily achieved by reference to the natural vegetative cover. The brush of stunted trees (*Garriga, Maquis*) that covers large areas around the Mediterranean indicates dependable, relatively abundant winter rains and hot dry summers. Grasslands (*steppe, savannah, pampa*) indicate seasonal but less abundant rainfall. The scant vegetation of deserts is adapted for surviving very long dry periods that are only occasionally interrupted by short rainstorms.

Systematic classifications of aridity are based on climatic parameters. Koeppen (1936) assumed that temperature is the principle factor controlling evapotranspiration and derived the following rules. (1) A region with winter rains is arid if annual precipitation in millimeters is less than twice mean annual temperature in centigrades. (2) A region with summer rains is arid if annual precipitation is less than twice mean annual temperature, augmented by 14. Thornthwaite (1948) related water availability to the water requirements of plants by computing a monthly moisture index. Into the formula for the calculation of this index there enter monthly precipitation, mean monthly temperature, correction factors for the length of the month and for the duration of daylight in relation to geographic latitude, and a factor expressing the water-holding capacity of an average soil. If precipitation is just adequate to supply all the water that would be need for maximum evapotranspiration in the course of a year, the moisture index is zero.

Climates with a moisture index between 0 and -20 are called subhumid, between -20 and -40 semiarid, and below -40 arid. This section refers mainly to regions that are arid according to the preceding definition.

The most important hydrological characteristics of groundwater in arid regions are as follows: (1) Replenishment is effected mainly by seepage of water from rare river flows. Infiltration of rainfall plays a minor role. (2) Poor water quality is the almost universal constraint to groundwater exploitation. Basically all quality problems stem from the fact that in an arid region accumulated salts are recycled in the environment; they are not washed away at a significant rate. (3) Because of the irregular occurrence of replenishment, the storage capacity of the aquifer assumes special importance. Only aquifers that hold a very large volume of water in storage yield a dependable water supply. (4) Large-scale groundwater development almost always entails overexploitation. In an arid region groundwater cannot be considered as a wholly renewable resource, but rather as a one-time resource that will be "mined out" sooner or later (see Section 13.3).

In many arid regions conditions of aridity have persisted or recurred during geologic periods and left their traces in the stratigraphic column. The geology of groundwater occurrence is therefore strongly influenced by the processes of erosion and sedimentation that are peculiar to arid regions. This is true, in particular, of clastic formations of Quaternary age that frequently form important aquifers. Processes of mechanical rock disintegration are more active in arid than in humid regions. Deeply weathered soils are therefore rare, but disintegration of granular rocks into a loose grit is common. The absence of soil cover and of weathering products facilitates the attack of atmospheric agents. Scarcity of rainfall prevents the activation of large river systems. As a consequence, the products of rock weathering accumulate in basins and depressions that act as local base levels of erosion and drainage. The basins are gradually filled up with sediments while the surrounding mountains are being worn away. Thus slopes become more gentle and the carrying capacity of flowing water decreases. The gradual lowering of the mountains brings about a decrease in orographic rainfall over them and further aggravates aridity.

Some deserts are traversed by large perennial streams originating in distant, more humid regions. Such "exotic" streams are important sources of water, but their influence on geomorphological processes remains generally limited to narrow strips in their immediate vicinity. On the other hand, even ephemeral streams descending from mountains into nearby desert lowlands play an important part in the formation and shaping of a sediment cover, as well as in the dissection of the hill country. Rare and short, but often violent, rainstorms produce flash floods, which are the principal agent of sediment transport. Products of rock disintegration available over the catchment are easily picked up by the streams. Mudflows can carry materials of every grain size, even large boulders. These conditions lead to the accumulation of huge alluvial fans on the mountain borders. The finest-grained materials are deposited in the lowest parts of the basin, where flood waters often form a temporary lake called *playa*. On evaporation, the precipitated salts impregnate the sediments or form a salt crust. Salts thus accumulated can be redistributed over the region by wind action. The lowest parts of desert basins receive not only occasional floods, but are often permanently moist because of the proximity of the groundwater table to the surface. Saline mud flats from which groundwater evaporates are a feature so characteristic for deserts that local names exist in many regions (*chott* in North Africa, *sebkha* in the Middle East, *kevir* in Iran, *salina* or *salar* in the Americas). Where permanent terminal lakes exist, solid sediments and the dissolved salts carried by the streams accumulate in them. Because of the scarcity of flowing water, the erosive action of the wind assumes relatively great importance. Wind removes loose particles up to sand size, leaving behind a surface covered by *lag gravels*. The finest particles are often carried as dust to great distances. Sand grains can be carried by traction along the surface or at small elevations above it, to accumulate in inland dune areas. It is believed that the deflating action of the wind is responsible in places for the lowering of the desert floor down to the groundwater table, exposing it to evaporation and creating in this manner saline mud flats.

In the following pages some typical groundwater environments of arid regions are discussed.

Mountain Ranges

Desert mountains are characterized by a sharply dissected morphology. The mountains produce orographic rainfall with marked differences between windward and leeward slopes. Freezing temperatures and snowfall are not uncommon on the mountain tops. The valley floors are covered with heterogeneous alluvial material. Exploitable aquifers may exist where the alluvial fill attains a thickness of at least a few meters. The best conditions for groundwater exploitation can be expected where coarse deposits of relatively large thickness have accumulated on the upstream side of swells of an impermeable bedrock, thus forming a natural subsurface dam and reservoir. Natural outflow from such a reservoir may take the form of springs or of subsurface spills.

Fig. 2.13 Key map of Sinai and the Negev. (Courtesy of TAHAL Consulting Engineers Ltd.)

In the high, granitic mountains of the Sinai desert (Fig. 2.13) small perennial springs are fed from snowfall. They emerge generally near dikes and are used for drinking water supplies and for small-scale irrigation. An alluvial aquifer was located in the El-Quaa depression that extends from the mountains toward west and is separated from the Gulf of Suez by a coastal range. The aquifer is replenished by floods and is exploited for drinking water supplies in the small town of At-Tur.

A subsurface reservoir formed behind a natural barrier is exploited in Nahal (stream) Paran in the Negev (Figs. 2.13 and 2.14). The watershed of Nahal Paran extends over approximately 3800 km in the mountains of Sinai and of the Negev and drains toward the Arava valley in the east. Mean

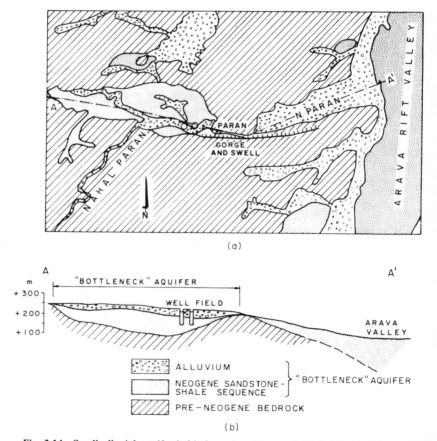

(a)

(b)

Fig. 2.14 Small alluvial aquifer behind a subsurface swell (Nahal Paran, Negev desert, Israel). (a) Map, (b) section. (Courtesy of TAHAL Consulting Engineers Ltd.)

annual rainfall ranges from 25 to 100 mm. The bedrock consists of more or less impermeable chalks and shales with patches of hard limestones. Over most of the catchment, groundwater prospects are unfavorable. Test drilling revealed small amounts of strongly mineralized water in the bedrock, as well as in the shallow alluvial deposits. About 20 km upstream from the Arava, the river passes through a narrow gorge cut into practically impermeable hard chalks. Upstream of this gorge there is a basin extending over about 100 km^2 filled with alluvial deposits that overlie sandstones and shales of Neogene age. These clastic sediments reach a maximum thickness of 100 m, 50% of which are aquiferous sands and gravels.

The stream is ephemeral, its average annual discharge is estimated at 2.6 million m^3 (MCM). The upstream entrance to the gorge was considered as a prospective dam site, and the aquifer was discovered in the course of test drilling in connection with site investigations. The first water well passed 138 m of sand, gravel, and shale and discharged 150 m^3/hr with a drawdown of 30 m. At present 1 MCM/yr is exploited and delivered to a small town. In view of this solution, the construction of the dam was deferred. Subsequent test drilling and geophysical investigations revealed that exploitable conditions occur over at least 27 km^2 and that the aquifer contains about 120 MCM of water in storage. The average annual throughflow of groundwater is estimated at 2 MCM. A long-term exploitation of 2–3 MCM/yr is contemplated, involving a slight draft on groundwater reserves, in order to make storage space available for the infiltration of large floods.

Piedmont-Bajada Belts

Many deserts comprise mountain ranges and plains, separated by a sharp borderline of structural origin. Geomorphologists distinguish between two zones: an upper one subjected to erosion, where bedrock is exposed or covered only by a thin layer of rock waste, called *pediment*, and a lower zone over which great amounts of clastic materials accumulate in the form of alluvial fans, or of a continuous belt of fans called *bajada*. The term *piedmont* is used for the belt of alluvial fans, but some authors include under this term also the pediment zone. At their lower end, alluvial fans often border on playas or mud flats. In arid regions, alluvial fans attain larger dimensions and are more conspicuous as landscape forms than in humid regions, and also play a more important role as potential aquifers. Most of the infiltration of floodwater takes place along the braided channels of the major streams in the upper and middle reaches of the bajada belt. In the lower parts, percolation is impeded by the presence of greater amounts of clay and silt in the near-surface sediments. Groundwater is phreatic below the higher parts of the piedment belt, where the water table is often at depths that make exploitation unattractive. In a down-slope direction, the water table gradually approaches the surface and finally intersects it as evidenced by the appearance of springs or seepages. In the middle and lower parts of the piedmont belt, groundwater becomes progressively confined because of the increasing number and thickness of semipermeable and impermeable layers and the simultaneous wedging out of aquiferous sand and gravel beds. Some of the fine-grained beds may stem from ancient playas and can be the source of excessive groundwater salinity.

At the lower end of the piedmont belt, or below the adjoining playa or mud flat, groundwater moves upward through semiconfining layers and appears on the surface as dispersed seepages, or occasionally, as more centralized springs. Most of the emerging groundwater is used up by vegetation or evaporates on the surface.

Best results from well drilling are to be expected in the middle part of the Piedmont belt where the water table is not too deep, a fair amount of aquiferous beds can be expected, and salinity may still be relatively low. The surface features of alluvial fans do not indicate the subsurface extent of possible aquifers. Electrical resistivity methods may give ambiguous results because of the presence of groundwater of greatly varying salinity. Refraction seismic techniques may provide clearer results.

Bolsons

Bolsons, the lowest parts of closed desert basins, are characterized by mud flats and playas. Shallow groundwater in this environment is generally too saline for use. Water of better quality can often be obtained at greater depths from confined gravel and sand aquifers that are hydrologically connected with the piedmont belt. Test drilling is the only way to ascertain water quality. Exploration wells should be logged by techniques that permit the differentiation of layers of different permeability and of water of different salinity ranges.

The sedimentary cover is sometimes very thick. A borehole in the playa of Qom in Iran penetrated 350 m of clastic strata. The uppermost part of the section consists of five salt beds interbedded with brown clay and silt, and two sand horizons. The middle part consists of brown clay and silt with salt crystals, and the lowest part is composed mainly of coarse-grained sand (Krinsley, 1970). The Chott Chergui in Algeria is a very large bolson framed by the Atlas mountains. The surface catchment extends over about 100,000 km^2, and the basin itself covers 40,000 km^2. Its center is occupied by an immense (2000 km²) flat saline plain. Though inundations are rare, the surface is always moist, in spite of the dry air and the frequent winds. Rainfall over the catchment reaches a maximum value of 280 mm/yr. Several thermal springs arise along the mountain border, but most of the groundwater leaks upward from aquifers underlying the center of the depression, through semiconfining layers, and evaporates on the surface. The hydrological regime was elucidated by a large number of exploration wells. Surface resistivity measurements gave misleading results because of the high salinity of the upper layers. Seismic techniques produced more satisfactory results (Drouhin, 1953). The exploitation of a bolson type aquifer in the Arava valley is described under the relevant heading.

Basin and Range Provinces

Basin and range provinces are landscape forms composed of a series of more or less parallel valleys separated by elongated ridges. The term stems from the Great Basin region of western North America, where this type of landscape is due to block-faulting. Folding has created similar landscape forms elsewhere. Basin and range provinces differ from erosional landscapes by the relatively large width of the structurally conditioned basins. The ranges separating the valleys are usually of moderate height and cannot produce much orographic rainfall. Therefore runoff is scarce. Under more strongly arid conditions, valleys may not be connected by surface drainage, and correspond to the definition of bolsons. Where sufficient runoff is supplied from nearby mountains, the basins may be traversed by streams that often take a circuitous course, following the length of one valley or basin until a breach or gap in the range permits passage into the next, lower basin. In other cases, a major stream may follow a course more or less perpendicular to the principal trend of the valleys and ranges, with tributaries from each basin joining it along its course.

Where permeable formations are present in the ranges and rainfall is sufficient to produce some infiltration, springs may appear along the foot of the ranges, or groundwater may pass from the ranges through alluvial formations of the basin into streams, contributing to their base flow. In basins, alluvial fan deposits, alluvial materials brought by the major streams from higher mountains, and clay and silt deposited in ancient lakes should be anticipated. Subsurface passage of groundwater from one basin into another can take place where the ranges are built wholly or in part of permeable formations (e.g., carbonate rocks, sandstones). Where the ranges are essentially impermeable, the gaps in them may make it possible to quantify subsurface flow in the alluvium, by a few observation holes. A reliable subsurface section based on well logs and possibly supported by geophysical investigations must be available. Conclusions from such appraisals are representative of long-years average groundwater flow, provided that there is no significant abstraction upstream of the observed section.

Where small rivers are coupled to small groundwater basins, problems stemming from intensive groundwater exploitation may become acute within a short time. At first, groundwater is usually exploited by private owners without regard to the hydrologic implications. Within a few years, the dry-weather flow of the river is seriously diminished, users dependent on river water suffer and start using groundwater, thus aggravating the effect. On a regional scale, the replacement of surface water supplies by groundwater only redistributes available total water resources according to the demand curve.

The catchment of the Rio Magdalena (Sonora, Mexico) covers about 26,000 km^2 from the water divide of the Sierra Madre Occidental to the shores of the Gulf of California (Fig. 2.15). The basin-and-range zone adjoins the higher parts of the Sierra to the west. In this zone, the Rio Magdalena crosses a number of approximately north–south-aligned valleys following a generally east–west-directed course. The intermountain valleys cover an area of about 2500 km^2. Mean annual rainfall ranges from 500 mm over the high mountains to about 200 mm in the basin-and-range zone and 100 mm at the coast. Over the last decades the region experienced a vigorous development of irrigated agriculture. In 1970 about 45,000 ha out of a total irrigated area of 50,000 ha were irrigated with groundwater. Annual groundwater withdrawal amounted to 550 MCM. This rate of exploitation led to a rapid decline of the water table in parts of the valleys. A hydrologic study was carried out during 1969–1970 (Planimex, 1970).

The aquifers are contained in the upper part of the alluvial fill of the basins. Their thickness varies from 50 to 200 m. The material is badly sorted and has good aquiferous properties only along the major stream channels. Water levels range from a few meters to 40 m below surface. The saturated thickness of the aquifers varies from 35 to 80 m. Groundwater salinity is 330 to 550 ppm TDS, with some isolated higher values. Salinity increases in the direction of the coast. Groundwater balance calculations showed that at the present rate of exploitation, an average reduction of the saturated section of the aquifer by 1.5 m yr must be expected. Within 20 years the exploitation by pumping would become difficult. A more even distribution of wells over the aquiferous terrains can mitigate the effects of overexploitation. This case, like many others, demonstrates that where groundwater of good quality is found in arid regions the temptation to overexploit the resource is hard to resist.

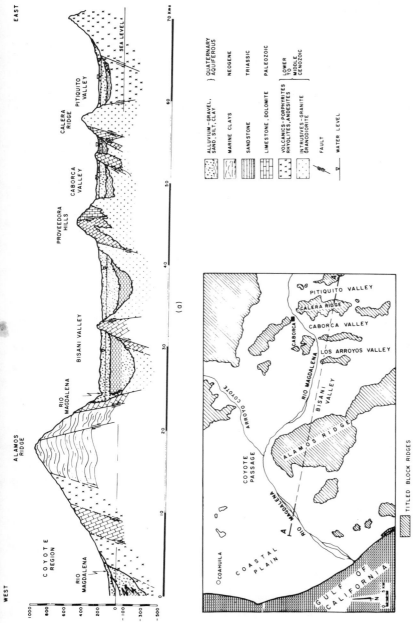

Fig. 2.15 Basin-range region in an arid zone—Rio Magdalena catchment, Sonora, northwestern Mexico. (a) Section, (b) map. (After Planimex, Ingenieros Consultores S.A., 1970.)

Coastal Deserts

In true coastal deserts groundwater occurs only in alluvial fans and in the alluvial fill of river valleys. In semiarid coastal areas exploitable quantities of groundwater may also be located in sand dunes, sandstones, and coral rock that are replenished by the direct percolation of rainfall. Scarcity of replenishment and the proximity of the ocean are reflected in the following salination effects: (1) Vestiges of oceanwater from Pleistocene ingressions may remain in fine-grained aquitards and even in aquifers because of poor flushing by freshwater. (2) Pockets of brines may stem from ancient lagoons that were cut off from the sea and covered by clastic sediments. (3) The thin wedge of freshwater mixes with the underlying seawater to such an extent that it changes into a wedge of brackish water. (4) Quick evaporation of salt spray creates a relatively large amount of windblown salt crystals that are rarely washed down by rain and are therefore carried farther inland than in temperate regions. (5) Deflation by wind, possibly in combination with structural accidents, may create depressions that reach below sea level and attract seawater (Jones, 1971).

The eastern coast of the Sinai peninsula is formed by rugged mountains reaching down to the sea. Where major wadis emerge, small deltas have been formed. The detritic material forms small aquifers that are replenished by sporadic floods, and exploited to satisfy the modest domestic and agricultural needs of two villages, Di-Zahav and Nevioth. In the vicinity of El Arish on the Mediterranean shore of the Sinai peninsula there is a narrow belt of dunes breached at one place by the El Arish wadi. Rains that amount on the average to 100 mm/yr replenish a shallow, brackish groundwater horizon in the dune area. Fresh groundwater is found only in and near the alluvial fill of wadi El Arish. In the area of Gaza further to the north rainfall is on the average 300 mm/yr and replenishes groundwater in the coastal belt of sandstone and dunes. Exploitation amounts to approximately 110 million m^3/yr; replenishment is estimated at 60 million m^3/yr. Seawater intrusion has already caused some damage.

The city of Aden in southern Arabia obtains most of its water supply from wells drilled into the alluvium of ephemeral streams. Recharge originates from floods created by rainfall (300 mm/year) in nearby highlands. Attempts to obtain groundwater from wells drilled into older formations have mostly resulted in small capacities and saline water (Cederstrom, 1971).

In Peru, near the small town of Pisco, the Pampa de Lanchas (Fig. 2.16) represents an extremely dry coastal desert (Gilboa, 1973). Here about 10 million m^3/yr are drawn from wells. Groundwater quality ranges from good to brackish. Recharge is due mostly to infiltration losses in the valley of the

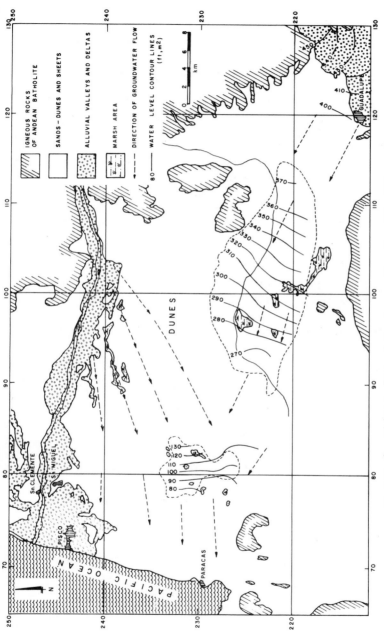

Fig. 2.16 Coastal desert—Pampa de Lanchas, near Pisco, Peru. (After Gilboa, 1973.)

Pisco River, which create a groundwater flow toward the Pampa de Lanchas. In addition, there is some inflow from an adjoining aquifer, also recharged by a stream originating in the Andes mountains (Rio Ica).

Regional Confined Aquifers

Regional confined aquifers are exploited in several desert regions. The confined sandstone aquifer termed *continental intercalair* of the Sahara is probably the best known. Other examples are the aquifers of the Australian Great Basin and, on a smaller scale, of the Sinai peninsula and the Negev. Natural replenishment of these aquifers is probably effected only through small outcrop areas around mountains. Natural drainage takes place through mud flats and through brackish to saline, sometimes thermal springs.

In the Sahara, increased withdrawal of groundwater has resulted in local declines of piezometric water levels, and in many cases in the cessation of artesian flow. In the Sinai peninsula and in the Negev of Israel the regional aquifer is formed, as in the Sahara desert, by sandstones of Lower Cretaceous and older age. The water is brackish containing around 1500 mg/1 of total solids (TDS). In the Negev hill country wells are deep, around 1000 m, and piezometric water levels are low, 200 m and more below surface. Better conditions for exploration exist in the Arava valley.

Investigations in the Sahara and in the Negev have revealed the old age of the water (*fossil water*). Stable isotope studies in the Sinai–Negev aquifer (Gat and Issar, 1974) showed that the water stems from a cooler period that probably prevailed during the Pleistocene and that the age of the water exceeds 10,000 years. These findings correspond to the very long residence times to be expected in a large aquifer with a small through flow (Eq. (1), Section 1.1). With regard to the hydrologic regime, one may entertain either of the two assumptions: (1) The aquifers "filled up" during a colder and presumably also wetter period and are now emptying down to their base levels and (2) present-day replenishment balances present-day outflow. Neither of these assumptions can be proven on the basis of available data, but both are compatible with a Pleistocene age of the water.

Groundwater in the Arava Valley

The Arava is an elongated valley stretching over 165 km from the Dead Sea in the North to the Gulf of Elath in the South (Figs. 2.13 and 2.17). Its width measures 10–20 km. The international boundary between Israel and the Hashemite Kingdom of Jordan runs in the center of the valley. Average annual rainfall ranges from 100 mm/yr at the Dead Sea to 25 mm/yr near Elath.

In the east the mountains of Edom descend into the valley from elevations of 1000 m in steep fault escarpments. The western border is formed by a more gradual descent of the Negev mountains, which attain near the valley border elevations of about 300 m. The valley itself rises from approximately 400 m below Mediterranean Sea level at the Dead Sea to about 230 m above Mediterranean Sea level in its central part, gradually descending again to sea level at Eilat. The northern part is drained toward the Dead Sea by an ephemeral water course—Nahal Arava. In the southern part, surface drainage is not integrated and "sebkhas" form local bases of drainage.

The stratigraphic succession consists of four major units:

(1)   The Precambrian Basement Complex, built up by metamorphic and igneous rocks. This formation outcrops on the western side of the Arava Valley only in the Elath region but forms great parts of the fault escarpment along the eastern border.

(2)   A sandstone–shale sequence of Paleozoic to Lower Cretaceous age, generally known as "Nubian Sandstone." It unconformably overlies the Basement Complex. Along the western side of the Arava Valley, outcrops are confined to the southernmost section, near Elath, but in the high Negev and Sinai mountains, this sequence is exposed in some of the major anticlines. Along the eastern border of the Arava the sandstone–shale sequence is extensively exposed on the fault escarpments. Its thickness is around 300 m.

(3)   A predominantly shallow-marine sequence of carbonate rocks and shales, grading upward into chalk and shales containing some conspicuous chert layers. This sequence constitutes the major part of the Sinai and Negev mountains, which form the western catchment of the Arava Valley. Thickness ranges from about 200 m in the south to about 700 m in the Dead Sea region. The age is Upper Cretaceous to Lower Tertiary.

(4)   A clastic sequence deposited in depressions of Tertiary to Recent age. This sequence includes a number of formations: The *Hatzeva* formation consists of semiconsolidated sandstones, shales, and conglomerates. It is of Neogene Age and reaches a thickness of 300 m in the northern part of the valley. The *Lashon marls* consist of warved clays with thin, intercalated gypsum beds. They were deposited by a Pleistocene lake that extended as far as 30 km south of the present Dead Sea (Figs. 2.17 and 2.18). Recent alluvium in the Arava merges with alluvial fans along the mountain borders. In the center of the southern Arava there are mud flats, sebkhas, and sand dunes.

Hydrological conditions near the Dead Sea are shown in Fig. 2.17. There are two confined aquifers, interconnected by faults. Groundwater in the

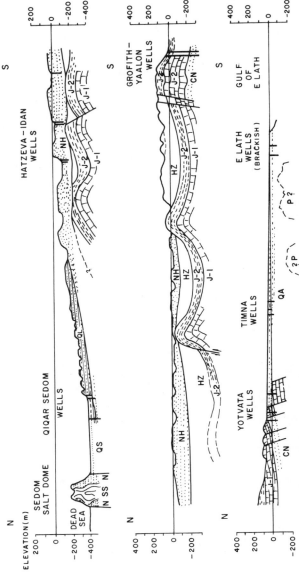

Fig. 2.17 Section along the Arava depression from the Dead Sea to the Gulf of Elath. QA, alluvium of Sedom salt marsh; QL, Lissan Formation—sediments of ancient Dead Sea; N, Neogene of Sedom salt dome; NH, Neogene Hatzeva Formation—sandstones, silts, shales, conglomerates; HZ, Har—Hazofim Group—chalk, shales, chert, Cretaceous to Eocene; J–2, Judea Group, upper part—chalk, shales, limestone, Upper Cretaceous; J–1, Judea Group, lower part—dolomite, limestone, shales, Upper Cretaceous; CN, "Nubian" sandstones, Lower Cretaceous; P, crystalline basement, Precambrian.

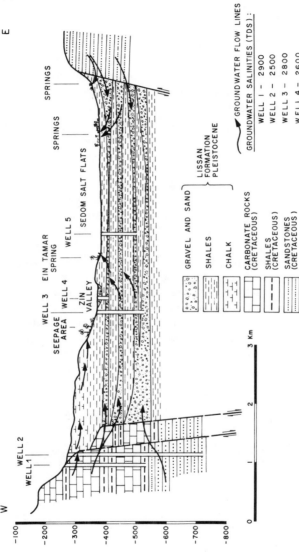

Fig. 2.18 Section across the southern Dead Sea depression. (Courtesy of TAHAL Consulting Engineers Ltd.)

lower sandstone aquifer is fossil. The upper carbonate aquifer is replenished at a small rate through short river courses that traverse outcrops in the Negev mountains. Exploitation wells are situated in the fault zone limiting the Dead Sea depression. Salinity ranges around 2000 mg/l total dissolved solids. The bulk of the water is derived from the lower aquifer and is used for the processing of minerals that are extracted from the Dead Sea.

The Hatzeva formation is exploited in the northern part of the Arava. The aquifer is replenished by seepage of surface flows in the piedmont zone. Salinity ranges between 800–1500 mg/l total dissolved solids. The sustained yield of the aquifer is estimated at six million m^3/yr, and this quantity is at present abstracted for irrigation. Impounding of floods is contemplated in order to increase groundwater replenishment. Additional groundwater is obtained in the northern Arava from carbonate rocks and from fissured flint layers of the Upper Cretaceous sequence.

Near Yotvata in the southern Arava groundwater is exploited from the Upper Cretaceous carbonate aquifer, from the Lower Cretaceous sandstone aquifer, and from a bolson type of environment in the vicinity of the sebkha (Fig. 2.19). The largest discharges, up to 350 m^3/hr, are obtained from wells in the carbonate aquifer. The water contains 600–800 mg/l chloride and up to 800 mg/l sulfate. Water from the sandstone aquifer is of better quality—about 500 mg/l chloride and similar concentrations of sulfate. Stable isotope studies showed that the water in the steplike carbonate blocks derives in part from infiltrated storm runoff and in part from the reservoir of fossil water in the sandstone aquifer. Exploration wells in the clastic strata near the sebkha showed that groundwater ascends vertically upward and that salination occurs near the surface. Down to a depth of 10 m chloride concentrations range from more than 100,000 mg/l to 27,400 mg/l, between 10 and 20 m depth they decrease to about 1000 mg/l, and between 50–100 m depth the water contains only 500–600 mg/l chloride. Stable isotopes indicate that the water is a mixture of recent and fossil waters (Naor, 1978). Groundwater abstraction from all three aquifers combined amounts to approximately eight million m^3/yr. The water is used for irrigation. Evapotranspiration from the sebkha, prior to the development of groundwater resource intensification of groundwater abstraction, amounted to about six million m^3/yr (Galed, 1968). At present the sebkha is rapidly shrinking.

At Timna, about 20 km north from Elath, groundwater is exploited from large alluvial fans that reach down into the valley. Salinity ranges from 2200 to 2700 mg/l total dissolved solids. Parts of the aquifer contain even more saline water, and a steady increase of salinity is expected if exploitation exceeds two million m^3/yr. The water is used for processing copper ores of

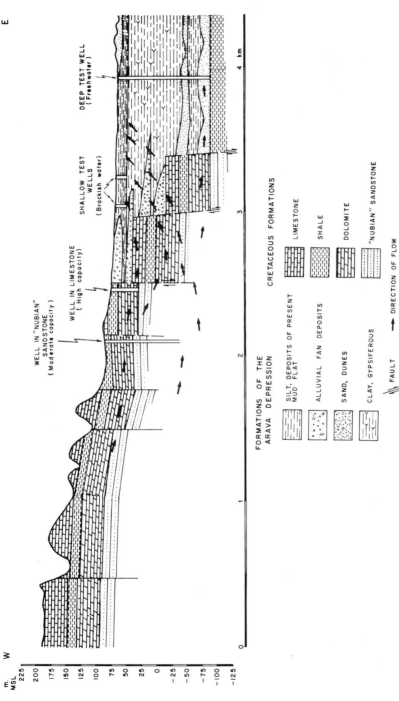

Fig. 2.19 Section from the southeastern Negev hills to the Yotvata salt flat (southern Arava Valley).

FORMATIONS OF THE
ARAVA DEPRESSION

SILT, DEPOSITS OF PRESENT
MUD FLAT

ALLUVIAL FAN DEPOSITS

SAND, DUNES

CLAY, GYPSIFEROUS

CRETACEOUS FORMATIONS

LIMESTONE

SHALE

DOLOMITE

"NUBIAN" SANDSTONE

FAULT

DIRECTION OF FLOW

WELL IN "NUBIAN"
SANDSTONE
(Moderate capacity)

WELL IN LIMESTONE
(High capacity)

SHALLOW TEST
WELLS
(Brackish water)

DEEP TEST WELL
(Freshwater)

W

E

m.
MSL
225
200
175
150
125
100
75
50
25
0
-25
-50
-75
-100
-125

0   1   2   3   4 km

the Timna mines. Brackish water in the mud flats adjoining the Gulf of Elath will be used for desalination.

Groundwater development in the Arava started in the 1950s. Today groundwater abstraction amounts to about 30 million m^3/yr. Most of the water is used for irrigation and a part for domestic and industrial supplies. The following conclusions from groundwater development in this extremely arid area can be drawn: (1) Initial estimates of groundwater availability were greatly exceeded. The most important discoveries were the great thickness of the Hatzeva aquifer in the northern Arava, the excellent water-bearing properties of limestone blocks near Yotvata, and the reserves of fossil freshwater in Nubian sandstone. (2) The quality limit for irrigation supplies was initially set at about 1000 mg/l TDS, and much effort was spent in a fruitless search for water conforming to this standard. A breakthrough was achieved through agrotechnical innovations, such as drip irrigation, that made it possible to use water in the range 1000–2000 mg/l TDS for the irrigation of highly valued crops for export.

FURTHER READINGS

Anonymous (1967). La nappe du Continentale Intercalaire. *Chron. Hydrogeol.* No. 11, 97–102.

Bear, J. (1979). "Hydraulics of Groundwater." McGraw-Hill, New York.

Baker, J. A. (1964). Ground-water resources of the Lowell area. Massachusetts. *U.S. Geol. Serv., Water-Supply Pap.* No. 1669-Y.

Bannerman, R. R. (1973). Problems associated with development of ground water in igneous and metamorphic rocks—a case study in Ghana. *Groundwater* **11**(5), 31–34.

Beaumont, P. (1971). Qanat systems in Iran. *Bull. IASH* **16**(3), 39–40.

Bedinger, M. S., and Jeffrey H. G., (1964). Ground water in the Lower Arkansas River Valley, Arkansas. *U.S. Geol. Serv., Water-Supply Pap.* No. 1669-L.

Biscaldi, R. (1971). Cartographie hydrogéologique des régions a socle cristallin et cristallophyllien affleurant. *Int. Assoc. Hydrogéol., Mem. Congr., Tokyo* **9**, 30–35.

Bolelli, E. (1957). Proprietés aquifères des schistes primaires en pays subarides en particulier. *Mém. Int. Geol. Congr., 20th., Mexico City 1956*, 3–16.

Born, S. M., Smith, S. A., and Stephenson, D. A. (1979). Hydrogeology of glacial terrain lakes, with management and planning applications. *J. Hydrol.* **43**, 7–39.

Bredehoeft, D. J., and Safdi, M. (1963). Disposition of aquifers in intermontane basins of northern Nevada. *IASH Gen. Assem., Berkeley, Calif.* pp. 197–212.

Burdon D. J., and Papakis, N. (1963). "Handbook of Karst Hydrogeology." U.N. Special Fund—Inst. for Geol. and Subsurface Res., Athens.

Burdon, D. J. (1977). Flow of fossil ground water. *Q. J. Eng. Geol.* **10**, 97–124.

Burdon, D. J., and Alsharhan, A. (1968). The problem of the paleokarstic Dammam Limestone aquifer in Kuwait. *J. Hydrol.* **6**, 385–504.

Burger, A., and Dubertret, L. (1975). Hydrogeology of Karstic Terrains. *IAH, Ser. B* No. 3.

Callahan, J. T. (1964). The yield of sedimentary aquifers of the Coastal Plain, Southeast River Basin. *U.S. Geol. Surv., Water-Supply Pap.* No. 1669-W.

Carozzi, A. V. ed. (1975). "Sedimentary Rocks, Concepts and History." Academic Press, New York.

Cederstrom, D. J. (1971). Groundwater in the Aden Sector of Southern Arabia. *Groundwater*, 9(2), 29–34.

Chenevart, C. (1971). Géologie structurale du Sahara septentrional appliquée a l'éxploration petrolière et l'hydrogéologie. *Eclogae. Geol. Helv.* 64(3), 529–566.

Coates, D. R. (1973) "Coastal Geomorphology," Publications in Geomorphology. State Univ. of New York, Binghamton.

Cohen, P. (1963). Specific yield and particle size relations of Quaternary alluvium, Humboldt River Valley, Nevada. *U.S. Geol. Surv., Water-Supply Pap.* No. 1669-M.

Cooke, U., and Warren, A. (1973). "Geomorphology in Deserts." B. T. Batsford, Ltd., London.

Cordova, R. M. (1963). Reconnaissance of the ground water resources of the Arkansas Valley Region, Arkansas. *U.S. Geol. Surv., Water-Supply Pap.* No. 1669-BB.

Dagan, G., and Bear, Y. (1966). "The Transition Zone at the Rising Interface Below the Collector," Joint Experimental Coastal Groundwater Collector Project, Tech. Rep. No. 7. Technion Res. Dev. Found., Ltd., Technion, Isr. Inst. of Technol., Haifa.

Dagan, G., and Shamir, U. (1971). Motion of the seawater interface in coastal aquifers, a numerical solution. *Water Resour. Res.* 7, 644–659.

Davis, J. N., and Turk, L. J. (1964). Optimum depth of wells in crystalline rocks. *Groundwater* 2(2), 6–11.

Domenico, P., and Stephenson, D. (1964). Application of quantitative mapping techniques to arid hydrologic systems—analysis of alluvial aquifers. *J. Hydrol.* 2, 164–181.

Drouhin, G. (1953a). The problem of water resources in north-west Africa. *Ankara Symp. Arid Zone Hydrol., UNESCO, Paris* pp. 9–41.

Drouhin, G. (1953b). Reactions on the hydrological balance of the exploitation of underground water resources. *Ankara Symp. Arid Zone Hydrol., UNESCO, Paris* pp. 125–133.

Durozoy, G. (1972). Hydrogéologie des basaltes du Harrat Rahat (Saudia). *Bull. B.R.G.M., Sect. III* No. 2, 37–50.

Eckstein, Y. (1969). Hydrogeology of a volcanic island Che Ju Do, Korea. *Bull. IASH* 14(12), 45–60.

Fairbridge, R. W., and Bourgeois, J. (1978). "'The Encyclopedia of Sedimentology." Dowden, Hutchinson and Ross, Inc. (distributed by Academic Press).

Fink, M., Columbus, N., and Naor, H. (1976). "Estudio del Potencial de las Fuentes de Agua Subterranea de Monterrey," Rep. submitted to Comision de Agua Potable, Monterrey, Vols. 1 and 2. Planimex Ing. Consult., Mexico, D. F.

Florquist, B. A. (1973). Techniques for locating water wells in fractured rocks. *Groundwater* 11(3), 26–28.

Ford, T. D., and Cullingford, C. H. D. (eds.) (1976). "The Science of Speleology." Academic Press, New York.

Forth, J. (1971). "The Great Australian Basin as a Regional Aquifer," Students Project. Groundwater Cent., Hebrew Univ., Jerusalem.

Galed, D. (1968). Lysimeter investigation of evaporation from the Yotvata mudflat. The Hydrological Service of Israel, Jerusalem (in Hebrew).

Gallaher, J. T., and Price, W. E., Jr. (1966). Hydrology of the alluvial deposits of the Ohio River Valley in Kentucky. *U.S. Geol. Surv., Water-Supply Pap.* No. 1818.

Gat, J. R., and Issar, A. (1974). Desert isotope hydrology, water sources of the Sinai desert. *Geochim. Cosmochim. Acta* 38, 1117–1138.

Gautier, E. F. (1935). "Sahara—The Great Desert" Columbia Univ. Press, New York.

Gautier, M. (1952). La résource aquifère du bassin du Chott Chergui (Oranie). *Congr. Geol. Int., 19th Sess., Algiers* 2, 00–00

Gilboa, Y. (1967). The groundwater resources of Uruguay. *Hydrol. Sci. Bull.* **22**, 115–126.

Gilboa, Y. (1973). La recarga de los acuiferos en las pampas de Villacuri y de Lanchas, Departamento de Ica. *Bol. Soc. Geol. Peru* **43**, 19–24.

Gilboa, Y., Mero, F., and Mariano, I. B. (1976). The Botucatu aquifer of South America, model of an untapped continental aquifer. *J. Hydrol.* **29**, 165–179.

Goldschmidt, M. J. (1961). On the mechanism of the replenishment of aquifers in the Negev (the arid region of Israel)—A Progress Report. *Groundwater Arid Zones; IASH Publ.* No. 57, 547–550.

Hall, D. W., and Turk, C. J. (1975). Aquifer evaluation using depositional systems—an example in North Central Texas. *Groundwater* **13**(6), 472–483.

Hanshaw, B. B., and Back, W. (1979) Major geochemical processes in the evolution of carbonate aquifer systems. *J. Hydrol.* **43**, 287–311.

Hanson, H. J. (1971). Common stratigraphic boundaries associated with coastal plain aquifers. *Groundwater* **9**(1), 5–12.

Harshberger, J. W. (1968). Ground-water development in desert areas. *Groundwater* **6**(5), 2–4.

Havens, J. S. (1966). Recharge studies on the High Plains in northern Lea County, New Mexico. *U.S. Geol. Surv., Water-Supply Pap.* No. 1819-F.

Herak, M., and Stringfield, V. T. (1972). "Karst—Important Karst Regions of the Northern Hemisphere." Elsevier, Amsterdam.

Issar, A. (1969). The groundwater provinces of Iran. *Bull. IASH* **14**(1), 87–99.

Issar, A. (1972). On the ancient water of the Upper Nubian sandstone aquifer in central Sinai and southern Israel. *J. Hydrol.* **17**, 353–374.

Jacobs, M., and Schmorak, S. (1960). Salt water encroachment in the Coastal Plain of Israel. *IASH Publ.* No. 52, 408–423.

Johnson, A. J., and Bredinger, M. S. (1967). Hydrogeological mapping of quantitative properties of an alluvial valley by use of laboratory data. *Bull. IASH* **8**, 138–146.

Jones, J. R. (1971). Ground-water provinces in Libya. *Symp. Geol. Libya, Fac. Sci., Univ. Libya*, pp. 449–479.

Jones, P. H. (1970). Hydrology of Quaternary delta deposits of the Mississippi River. *IASH-UNESCO Symp. Hydrol. Deltas*, **1**, 49–63.

Kahana, Y., Naor, I., and Lindenbergh, P. C. (1965). Joint experimental coastal groundwater collectors project, final report. TAHAL, Tel Aviv. Publ. No. 445.

Knetsch, G., Shata, A., Degens, E., Muennich, K. O., Vogel, J. C., and Shazly, M. M. (1962). Untersuchungen an Grundwaessern der Ost Sahara. *Geol. Rundschau* **52**, 587–668.

Koeppen, W. (1930). "Handbuch der Klimatologie," Gebrüder Bornträger, Berlin.

Kohout, F. K. (1962). The pattern of fresh and salt water in the Biscayne aquifer of the Miami area, Florida. *IASH Gen. Assem., Helsinki.* Publ. No. 52, 440–448.

Krinsley, D. B. (1970). "A Geomorphological and Paleoclimatic Study of the Playas of Iran," *Geol. Surv., U.S. Dep. Inter.*, Parts 1 and 2. U.S. Gov. Print. Off., Washington, D.C.

Landers, R. A., and Turk, L. J. (1973). Occurrence and quality of ground water in crystalline rocks of the Llano area, Texas. *Groundwater* **11**(1), 5–10.

Larsson, I. (1963). Tectonic and morphologic studies in precambrian rocks and groundwater prospecting in south Sweden, *Geol. Foeren. Stockholm Foerh.* **85**, 320–340.

LeGrand, H. E. (1967). Groundwater of the Piedmont and Blue Ridge provinces in the southeastern states. *U.S. Geol. Surv., Circ.* No. 538.

LeGrand H. E. (1970). Comparative hydrology—an example of its use. *Bull. Geol. Soc. Am.* **81**(4), 1243–1248.

LeGrand, H., and Stringfield, V. T. (1966). Development of permeability and storage in the Tertiary limestones of the southeastern states U.S.A. *Bull. IASH* **11**, 61–73.

LeGrand, H. E., and Stringfield, V. T. (1971). Water levels in carbonate rock terrains. *Groundwater* **9**(3), 4–10.

LeGrand, H. E. (1979). Evaluation techniques of fractured rock hydrology. *J. Hydrol.* **43**, 333–345.

Lelong, F. (1964). "Recent Data on the Arena Aquifers Following a Hydrogeological Reconnaissance in North-Central Dahomey (Parakou and Nikki Regions)." Bur. Cent. Etud. Equip. Outre-Mer, Paris.

Lesser-Jones, H. (1967). Confined fresh water aquifers in limestone in the north of Mexico with deep wells below sea level. *Hydrol. Fractured Rocks, Proc. Symp. Dubrovnik; IASH Publ.* No. 74, **2**, 526–539.

Lloyd, J. W., and Farag, M. H. (1978). Fossil groundwater gradients in arid regional sedimentary basins. *Groundwater* **16**(6), 388–393.

Lobeck, A. K. (1939). "Geomorphology." McGraw-Hill, New York.

Lombard, A. (1972). "Séries Sédimentaires, Genèse, Evaluation". Masson, Paris.

Lukovic, M. T. (1961). Distribution and circulation of groundwaters in carbonate rocks. *Assoc. Int. Hydrogeol. (A.I.H.), Mem. Reunion Rome* **4**, 73–75.

Mandel S. (1966). A conceptual model of karstic erosion by groundwater. *Bull. IASH* **11**(1), 5–7.

Mandel, S. (1974). The groundwater resources of the Canterbury Plains. *N. Z. Agric. Eng. Inst., Lincoln Pap. Water Resour.* No. 12.

Mandel, S., Gilboa, Y., and Mercado, A. (1972). Groundwater flow in calcareous aquifers in the vicinity of Barcelona, Spain. *Bull. IASH* **12**(14), 74–83.

Maxey, G. B. (1968). Hydrogeology of desert basins. *Groundwater* **6**, 10–21.

Mehnert, K. R. (1969). Precambrian basement complex. *Geophys. Monogr., Am. Geophys. Union* **13**, 513–518.

Meigs, P. (1966). "Geography of Coastal Deserts." Arid Zone Res., UNESCO, Paris.

Mercado, A., and Billings, G. K. (1975). The kinetics of mineral dissolution in carbonate aquifers as a tool for hydrological investigations. *J. Hydrol.* **24**, 303–331.

Mijatovic, B. and Bakie, M. (1967). Le Karst du Liban, étude de son évolution d'après les récherches hydrogéologiques. *Chronique d'Hydrogéologie* **10**, 95–107.

Motts, W. S. (1965). Hydrologic types of playas and closed valleys and some relations of hydrology to playa geology. *U.S. Air Force Cambridge Res. Lab., Environ. Res. Pap.* No. 96.

Mundorff, M. J., Crosthwaite, E. G., and Kilburn, E. (1964). Ground water for irrigation in the Snake River basin, in Idaho. *U.S. Geol. Surv., Water-Supply Pap.* No. 1654.

Naor, H. (1979). Hydrogeology of Aquifers in the Grufit Yotvata Area. M.Sc. Thesis, Groundwater Research Center, Hebrew Univ. Jerusalem (in Hebrew).

Neal, J. T., ed. (1975). "Playas and Dried Lakes—Occurrence and Development," Benchmark Papers in Geology. Hutchinson & Ross, London.

Peterson, F. L. (1972). Water development on tropical volcanic islands—type example: Hawaii. *Groundwater* **10**(5), 18–23.

Picard, L. (1953). Outline of ground-water geology in arid regions. *Ankara Symp. Arid Zone Hydrol., UNESCO, Paris* pp. 165–176.

Picard, L., and Wakshal, E. (1975). Evolution of fossil karst aquifers in Israel. *Proc. 12th, Int. Congr. IAH on karst hydrology, Huntsville, Alabama. Abstr. Ala. Geol. Surv.*, 78–79.

Planimex (1970). "Estudios Hidrogeologicos en la Cuenca del Rio Magdalena (Concepcion)," Vol. 1. Mexico D.F.

Plote, H. (1968). La récherche d'eau souterraine dans les régions arides à substratum cristallin et métamorphique de l'Afrique occidental. *Bull. B.R.G.M., Sect. III* No. 2, 97–111.

Poland, J. F., Piper, A. M., et al. (1956). Ground-water geology of the coastal zone, Long Beach–Santa Ana area, California. *U.S. Geol. Surv., Water-Supply Pap.* No. 1109.

Saines, M. (1969). Map interpretation and classification of buried valleys. *Groundwater* **6**(4), 32–37.

Samuel, E. A., Baker, J. A., and Brackley, R. A. (1966). Water resources of the Ipswich river basin, Ma. *U.S. Geol. Surv.*, *Water-Supply Pap.* No. 1826.

Sarocchi, C., and Levy-Lambert, H. (1967). La nappe aquifere de l'Albien dans le bassin de Paris. *Chron. Hydrogeol.* No. 11, 33–56.

Schmorak, S. and Mercado, A. (1969). Upconing of the freshwater-seawater interface below pumping wells, field study. *Water Resour. Res.* **5**(4), 1290–1311.

Schneider, R. (1963). Groundwater provinces of Brazil. *U.S. Geol. Surv.*, *Water-Supply Pap.* No. 1663-A.

Schneider, R. (1967). Geological and hydrological factors related to artificial recharge of the carbonate rock aquifer system of Central Israel. *IASH Publ.* No. 72, 37–45.

Shata, A. (1971). A new light on the ground-water potential of the Nubian sandstone aquifer in northeast Africa. *Symp. Geol. Libya, Fac. Sci., Univ. Libya* pp. 483–486.

Shiftan, Z. L. (1961). New data on the artesian aquifers of the southern Dead Sea Basin and their geological evolution. *Bull. Res. Counc. Isr., Sect. G* **10**(1/2), 267–291.

Shiftan, Z. L., Issar, A., and Rosenthal, E. (1961). Fault zones and ground-water in arid parts of Israel. *Assoc. Int. Hydrogeol. (A.I.H.), Mem. Reunion Rome* **4**, 245–253.

Shuster, E. T., and White, W. B. (1971). Seasonal fluctuations in the chemistry of limestone springs: a possible means for characterizing carbonate aquifers. *J. Hydrol.* **14**, 93–128.

Speelman, H., and Ryckborst, H. (1976). Hydrogeology of the quaternary and tertiary formations along the south coast of the Algarve, Portugal. *Hydrol. Sci. Bull.* **21**, 345–356.

Springfield, V. T., Rapp, J. R., and Anders, R. B. (1979). Effects of karst and geological structure on the circulation of water and permeability in carbonate aquifers. *J. Hydrol.* **43**, 313–330.

Stearns, H. T., and MacDonald, G. A. (1946). Geology and ground-water resources of the island of Hawaii. *Hawaii Div. Hydrogr., Bull.* **9**.

Summers, W. K. (1972). Specific capacities of wells in crystalline rocks. *Groundwater* **10**(6), 37–47.

TAHAL (1979). "Bhairawa–Lumbini Groundwater Irrigation Project, Feasibility Study II—Hydrology," 2 vols. Tel Aviv.

Tanaka, H., and Holowell, J. R. (1966). Hydrology of the alluvium of the Arkansas River, Muskogee, Oklahoma to Fort Smith, Arkansas. *U.S. Geol. Surv.*, *Water-Supply Pap.* No. 1809-T.

Thornbury, W. D. (1958). "Principles of Geomorphology." Wiley, New York.

Thornthwaite, C. W. (1948). An approach toward a rational classification of climate. *Geophys. Rev.* **38**, 55–94.

Tilahun, A. (1975). Goundwater in crystalline rocks and a hypothetical tectonic model. M. Sc. Thesis, Univ. of Helsinki, Dpt. Geol. and Paleontol.

Tolson, J. S., and Doyle, F. L. (eds.) (1977). Karst Hydrology. *Proc. 12th Int. Congr. I.A.H. on karst hydrology, Huntsville Alabama 1976. Ala. Geol. Surv.*

Toth, T. (1963). A theoretical analysis of groundwater flow in small drainage basins. *J. Geol.* **68**, 4795–4811.

Toth, J. (1966). Mapping and interpretation of field phenomena for ground-water reconnaissance in a prairie environment, Alberta, Canada. *Bull. IASH* **11** (2), 20–67.

U.N. Department of Economic and Social Affairs (1973). "Groundwater in Africa." U.N., New York.

Verdeil, P. (1961). Principes généraux de l'hydrologie des karsts. *Assoc. Int. Hydrogéol. (A.I.H.), Mem. Reunion Rome* **4**, 94–98.

White, W. B., and Schmidt, V. A. (1966). Hydrology of a karst area in east-central West Virginia. *Water Resour. Res.* **2**, 549–560.

Williams, P. W. (1977). Hydrology of the Waikoropupu springs, New Zealand, a major tidal karst resurgence. *J. Hydrol.* **35**, 73–92.

CHAPTER

3

Maps and Sections

3.1 MAPS AND AERIAL PHOTOGRAPHS

Geographic and geologic maps of some sort exist today for almost any region on the globe. Small-scale maps and satellite photographs depicting vast areas are appropriate for researches on regional geologic structures, but for the practical investigation of groundwater resources maps on a larger scale are required. Useful map scales range from 1 : 500,000 to 1 : 20,000. The most useful scale for groundwater investigations is probably 1 : 100,000 which shows an area of 10,000 km² on sheets of convenient size (1 × 1 m), but still enables the accurate location of important features. Maps on a larger scale are needed for the selection of well sites in complex areas. Maps on a smaller scale permit a synoptic view of regional hydrologic features at the price of suppressing local details. The scale of a map should do justice to the detail it shows. For working purposes it is sometimes useful to enlarge ("blow up") a finely printed map.

Good topographic maps may reveal important information on groundwater, such as springs, swamps, and dune areas. The density and pattern of surface drainage may furnish clues to the infiltration capacity of the terrain and hint at hidden geologic features. Aerial photographs can often be obtained for regions without topographic maps. They may reveal features that are almost invisible at ground level, such as ancient river courses or the alignment of fault lines (Voûte 1967, Seker 1966). The disadvantages of aerial photographs are distortions of scale, the lack of measured vertical elevations, and in many cases, obscurement of part of the terrain by cloud

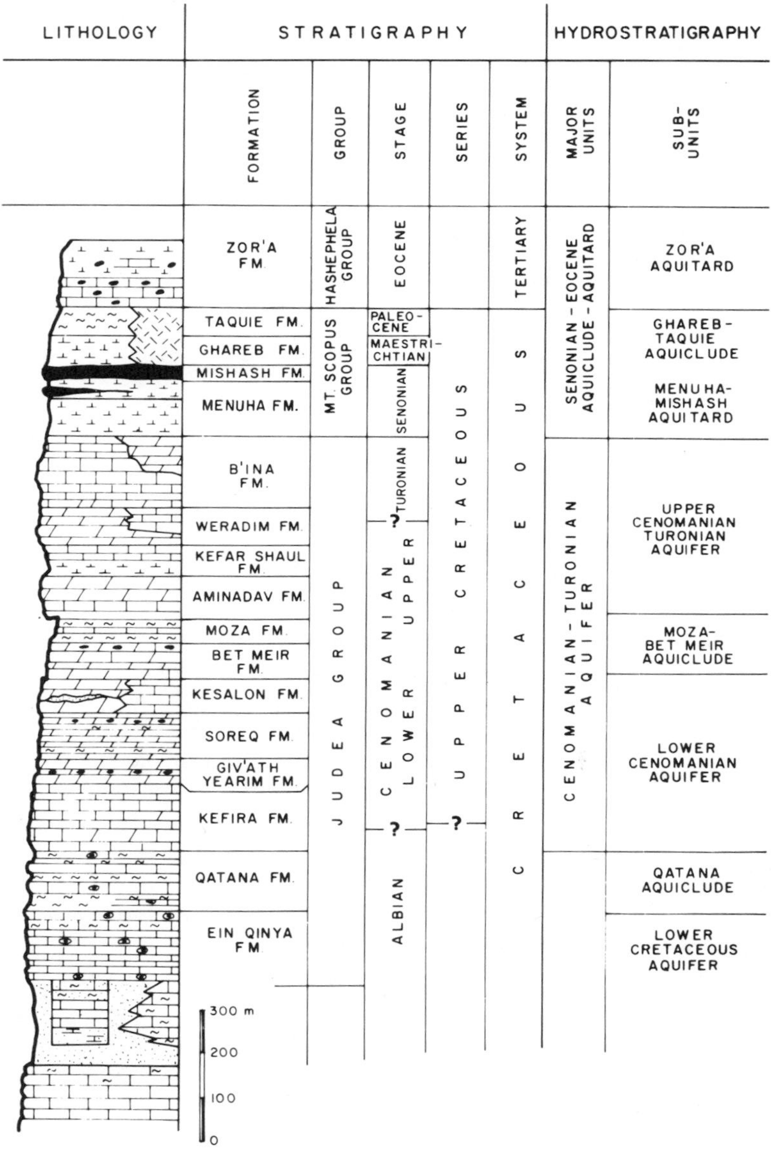

Fig. 3.1 Lithologic, stratigraphic, and hydrostratigraphic columnar section, Judean Hills region, Israel.

cover or by vegetation. Infrared photography yields relatively clear pictures even under difficult atmospheric conditions but accentuates vegetation, which appears as black or red mass.

Geologic maps depict not only visible reality but also the interpretation given to it by the geologists who drew them. Different geologists working in the same area may adopt different stratigraphic divisions or structural concepts. This feature becomes rather disconcerting when the uncoordinated efforts of two different geologists result in discrepancies between adjoining map sheets.

Geologic maps on the scale 1 : 100,000 and larger should emphasize formations (see Section 1.2) rather than time units, and they should be accompanied by detailed columnar sections that describe the various formations, their stratigraphic sequence, and their thickness (Lahee 1950). The columnar section should also point out type localities where the newcomer to the area can get acquainted with each one of the rock units. Formation maps on the scale 1 : 100,000 are often based on photogeologic surveys combined with field work and their reliability depends strongly on the actual ground control that was exercised over photogeologic interpretations.

In a new area it is one of the first tasks of the investigator to transform the lithostratigraphic sequence of rock units on which large-scale maps are based into a *hydrostratigraphic sequence* of aquifers (potential or proven), aquitards, and aquicludes (Maxey 1964). This can be done by lumping together several formations or picking out parts of them. The hydrostratigraphic sequence is usually simpler than the lithostratigraphic one (Fig. 3.1).

Geologic maps on a still larger scale and detailed geologic maps of alluvial strata are rarely available but have to be made to order. The amount of work depends on the geologic complexity of the region, on its accessibility, and on the availability of good topographic base maps.

When starting the study of a region the investigator should consult and compare all the available geologic maps and the best available topographic maps and air photos. The identification of similarities and discrepancies will give him a much better grasp of the characteristics and problems of his research area than the uncritical acceptance of any set of maps. In addition, the investigator should familiarize himself with his terrain through reconnaissance field trips. Even the best maps and aerial photographs are no substitute for field reconnaissance.

3.2   GEOLOGIC CROSS SECTIONS AND SUBSURFACE MAPS

Geologic cross sections are the easiest means of representing subsurface conditions (Moore 1963). Some sections, especially those that accompany small-scale maps, are intended to convey general ideas about the structure of the area rather than any particular subsurface configuration. A section that is to be used for practical purposes must represent a vertical cut through the geologic strata along an identifiable straight line, or on a line composed of several straight segments. For the drawing of such sections the following working procedures are suggested (Fig. 3.2).

The best representation of geologic structures is obtained by sections drawn perpendicular to strikes and major faults. The stratigraphic complexities of alluvial strata are best represented on several sections criss-crossing the area. When the section is intended mainly to illustrate hydrologic data and concepts it is usually drawn along a flow line. The information on which the section is based, outcrop areas, boreholes, and geophysical measurements, must be clearly shown on a map. The points for which subsurface information is available do not always lie on a straight line; frequently it is necessary to project them onto the line from a small distance, say 300–1000 m, depending on local conditions, but projection over larger distances can lead to serious errors.

The information from each point is graphically represented on a strip of millimetric paper about 1–0.5 cm wide. The vertical scale depends on the stratigraphic detail that has to be shown. Useful scales are 1 : 1000 to 1 : 10,000. A common reference level, usually mean sea level, must be marked on all the strips. Accuracy is important, especially in areas with an intricate stratigraphy, such as alluvial terrains. Obviously, strata of 10–20 m thickness cannot be correlated if their elevation is known only to the same order of magnitude. Reading of these tiny strips is facilitated by using colors, as well as graphical symbols.

In order to obtain the required stratigraphic detail, vertical scales must always be larger than horizontal ones. Distortions are, therefore, unavoidable. Very large distortions make mountains out of hills and steep cliffs out of gentle slopes; they also play havoc with the apparent thickness of strata, so that in an inclined position they appear to be much thinner. The largest distortion a trained eye can still compensate for is about 1 : 20. Therefore, if the strips are drawn on the scale 1 : 1000, the horizontal scale of the cross section should be at least 1 : 20,000, but an even larger scale, say 1 : 10,000, will facilitate correlations and yield a more readable picture.

When the horizontal scale has been chosen in accordance with the preceding criteria, a topographic cross section is drawn. The information points are marked at the appropriate distances on a datum line and the strips are attached with their common reference level on this line. At this point the actual geologic interpretation can begin. The most important geologic criterion is the stratigraphic sequence of the formations. Figure 3.3 demonstrates how strongly spatial correlations depend on the time correlation of the strata. In alluvial and volcanic terrains where time correlations

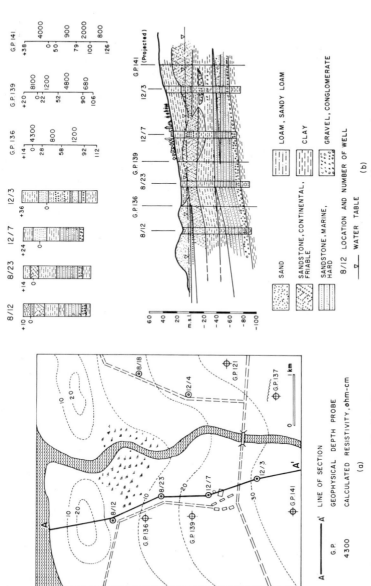

Fig. 3.2 Preparation of section from subsurface information.

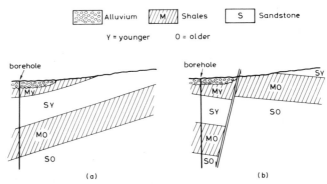

Fig. 3.3 Spatial correlation and time correlation in subsurface interpretation. (a) Correlation results if shales on outcrop are of the same age as upper shales in borehole. (b) Correlation results if shales on outcrop and lower shales in borehole are of the same age.

are often difficult to establish, it is necessary to keep in mind the probable geologic history of the area and to resist the temptation of drawing lines just on the basis of a superficial resemblance of strata.

Geologic sections are still more influenced by subjective personal views than geologic maps. A sequence of strata that appears at different elevations in two points may be connected by an unbroken line by one author, whereas another may assume a fault between the two points, each one citing tenuous field evidence or other arguments in favor of his interpretation. In alluvial layers it may happen that a clay encountered at approximately the same elevation in several boreholes is interpreted as a continuous layer by one author, while another favors the concept of several unconnected lenses.

Water levels should be indicated on the cross section, so that the saturated, nonsaturated, and confined parts of the aquifer can be seen at a glance, but hydraulic gradients will appear to be almost horizontal. The best way to visualize hydraulic gradients conjunctively with a geologic cross section, is to draw a separate section of water levels at the same horizontal scale and a much more exaggerated vertical one (Fig. 2.8b). Salient surface features, such as river valleys, swamps, forests, and towns should be shown on the section because they help the eye to compensate for the vertical distortion and make it easier for the reader, who is familiar only with the surface, to orient himself. Three-dimensional block diagrams can convey a still more vivid picture if they are executed by a competent artist. They are drawn mainly for the purpose of illustrating publications.

Geologic subsurface maps show the elevation of the top or the base of a certain formation, or the varying thickness of the formation (*isopach maps*). They are used mainly for studies concerning the geologic structure and history of the region. *Base and top-aquifer contour maps* are often useful for the purposes of well siting and aquifer delineation. *Aquifer thickness maps* enable the extrapolation of transmissivity values that were obtained in isolated boreholes over a wider area. When the aquifer consists of alternating layers of aquiferous and practically impermeable strata, such as sandstone alternating with shales, it is useful to draw a map showing the true combined thickness of the aquiferous layers by subtracting the thickness of the impermeable layers from the total thickness of the aquiferous formation (see also Section 6.14).

Any reasonably reliable subsurface map requires a far larger number of information points, boreholes, and geophysical measurements than geologic cross sections. When the data are available, the office work for drawing the maps is worthwile. Obviously the execution of expensive drilling or geophysical work for the sole purpose of completing the geologic subsurface picture is rarely justifiable in the context of groundwater investigations.

FURTHER READINGS

Arkin, Y., Braun, M., and Itzhaki, Y. (1967). "Cenomanian Mapping Units and their Correlation in the Negev." *Bull.* **43**, *Geol. Surv. Israel*, Jerusalem.

Bishop, M. S. (1960). "Subsurface Mapping." Wiley, New York.

Eardley, A. J. (1942). "Aerial Photographs: Their Use and Interpretation." Harper, New York.

Howe, H. L. (1958). Procedures for applying airphoto interpretation in the location of ground-water. *Photogramm. Eng.* **24**, 35–47.

Kottlowski, F. E. (1965). "Measuring Stratigraphic Sections." Holt, New York.

Lahee, F. H. (1959). "Field Geology." McGraw-Hill, New York.

Lattman, L. H., and Ray, R. G. (1965). "Aerial Photographs in Field Geology." Holt, New York.

LeRoy, L. W., ed. (1950). "Subsurface Geological Methods (A Symposium)." Colorado Sch. of Mines, Golden.

Maxey, G. B. (1964). Hydrostratigraphic units. *J. Hydrol.* **2**, 124–129.

Mekel, J. F. M. (1970). "The Use of Aerial Photographs for Geological Mapping." Int. Inst. for Aerial Survey and Earth Science. Its textbook manual VIII, Delft, Netherlands.

Moore, C. A. (1963). "Handbook of Subsurface Geology." Harper, New York.

Ray, R. G. (1960). Aerial photographs in geologic interpretation and mapping. *U.S. Geol. Surv., Prof. Pap.* No. 373.

Seker, J. (1966). Hydrologic significance of tectonic fractures detectable on airphotos. *Groundwater* **4** (4), 23–27.

Van Everdingen, R. O. (1964). Distortion of groundwater flow patterns in sections with exaggerated vertical scale. *J. Hydrol.* **2**, 11–14.

Voûte, C. (1967). The use of airphoto interpretation techniques in water resources surveys. *IASH Gen. Assem., Bern*, pp. 75–80.

Voûte, C. (1968). "The Changing Art of Geological Surveying." Int. Inst. for Aerial Survey and Earth Science, Delft.

CHAPTER

4

Geophysical Methods

4.1 GEOPHYSICAL METHODS IN GROUNDWATER INVESTIGATIONS

Geophysical methods measure natural or induced physical phenomena in the earth's crust and interpret the results to obtain information on the subsurface. The widest use of geophysical methods is made in prospecting for economically valuable resources of minerals and petroleum. Application in groundwater investigations takes third place.

The subsurface data of interest in groundwater investigations that can be produced by various geophysical methods are

(1) depth of contact between layers of different aquiferous properties (base, top aquifer);

(2) horizontal changes in the aquiferous properties (facies changes in aquifer, buried hills of impervious formations);

(3) vertical geologic boundaries (faults, dikes, buried escarpments);

(4) thickness of aquiferous and nonaquiferous formations (depending on the power of resolution of method and depth of layer);

(5) a rough estimate of permeability;

(6) groundwater salinity, within the general definition of fresh or saline water (only under favorable conditions).

Geophysical methods used in groundwater investigations are broadly classified as *surface methods*, applied from the ground surface; *borehole geophysics*, applied in drilled boreholes; and *remote sensing techniques*,

76

applied from some distance above the surface of the ground, mainly from airplanes and satellites.

Surface geophysical methods (Dobrin 1976) are indirect; there is no technique capable of directly indicating the presence of exploitable groundwater in the subsurface. Some methods can aid in the approximate determination of the depth of the water table, but their application for this purpose is hardly ever indicated. Successful application of surface geophysical methods depends largely on the correct choice of the method, or combination of methods; the quality of the instruments; competent field work; and correct processing and interpretation of field results, and their correlation with geologic data.

All possibilities to clarify the geologic structure of a given region by direct surface and subsurface geologic observations should be thoroughly pursued prior to the application of surface geophysical methods. Without some basis for correlation with observed geologic and borehole data, conclusions from surface geophysical investigations are likely to remain ambiguous.

The geologic or hydrogeologic problem at hand must be clearly defined to enable the selection of the most appropriate techniques. No single method should be regarded as a panacea for the solution of all possible problems. The geophysicist should not be expected to take on himself a task defined simply as "finding water-bearing layers," or worse, "discovering water," without some concept, idea, or briefing on the geologic structure of the terrain and the expected hydrostratigraphic and structural conditions.

Surface geophysical techniques are of greatest value where an overburden conceals deeper-seated hydrogeologic features. Alluvium-covered plains and other regions with flat-lying sediments are the most frequent examples. In hill regions, where surface geology permits a good insight into the structure of the subsurface, the contribution of surface geophysical methods is more limited. Applicability is also limited sometimes by lack of geophysical contrast between aquiferous and nonaquiferous formations or by the depth range of available equipment.

Geophysical investigations are often one of the more costly items on the budget of groundwater projects. Substantial savings, however, can result through the reduction of the expenditure required for exploration drilling. Other benefits are greater confidence in the selection of well sites and the provision of information within a relatively short time. Test drilling is comparable in cost to surface geophysical methods only if the investigation is concerned with depths and formations that can be penetrated by very light drilling equipment.

Downhole geophysical or logging techniques (Keys and MacCary, 1971) are an important aid in obtaining the full range of information from

78   4 Geophysical Methods

boreholes concerning subsurface geology and groundwater quality and movement. Logging techniques are mainly used in the uncased holes produced by rotary drilling equipment. Techniques based on nuclear radiation can be applied also in cased holes and can provide hydrogeologic data from older wells with incomplete records.

Remote sensing techniques (Sabins 1978) used for a multitude of surveying purposes in different fields, are to be regarded in groundwater investigations mainly as another tool for the clarification of geologic conditions and some hydrogeologically important details, such as faults, fissure zones, abandoned stream courses, and offshore springs. Their main advantage of providing information on regions of difficult access does not play a decisive part in groundwater investigations, because in such regions demand for water supplies is generally small.

Geophysical methods are useful in all four phases of groundwater resources development but are needed mostly in the course of the first two phases (see Section 1.4).

4.2   ELECTRICAL RESISTIVITY METHODS

Electrical resistivity methods (Keller and Frischknecht, 1969) are the most widely used geophysical methods in groundwater investigations. The reasons are mainly relative simplicity of instruments and their operation, relatively low operational costs, a depth range commensurate with the depths required in most groundwater problems, suitability to a wide spectrum of subsurface problems, and easy, though not always reliable, methods of interpretation.

The resistivity of earth materials is defined by the ohm-meter, the electrical resistance of a cube of material with dimensions of 1m on a side. the ohm-centimeter, equaling 0.01 ohm-meter, is also often used. Some investigators find it more convenient to present *conductivity* of a rock rather than resistivity. Conductivity is the reciprocal of resistivity, and the dimensions of the unit for expressing it are either the mho per meter or mho per centimeter. Some characteristic ranges and values of resistivities of rock materials are shown in Fig. 4.1.

Because of the high resistivity of most rocks, electrical currents pass almost entirely though the water contained in their pores. The resistivity of a rock layer depends on the following factors: (1) total porosity expressed as fraction of rock volume, (2) degree of saturation with water expressed as fraction of total porosity, (3) salinity of the water, (4) geometrical configuration of the pore space. In strata saturated with water, resistivity is a good

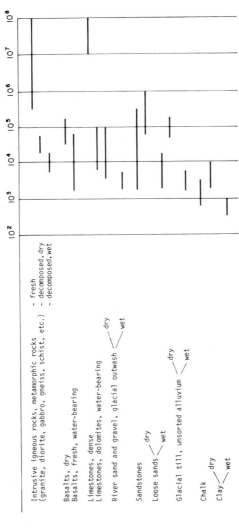

Fig. 4.1 Resistivity ranges of some common groups of rocks (in ohm-cm). (Based in part on data by Atlas Copco ABEM AB, AHB 33-15.)

indicator of hydrologic characteristics. Generally, the fine-grained rocks that compose aquicludes and aquitards are characterized by a larger porosity and a smaller resistivity than the coarse-grained rocks that compose aquifers. The most notable exceptions to this simple correlation are: (1) Strata containing waters with widely different salinities: for example, sands saturated with saline water may exhibit the low resistivity generally associated with clays. (2) Rock sequences containing aquifuges: for example, layers of hard basalt are often characterized by high resistivities, whereas intercalated, weathered, aquiferous zones are characterized by relatively low resistivities. (3) Metallic ores sometimes have low resistivities irrespective of their water content.

In the unsaturated zone the percentage of water contained in the interstices changes with time and seasons, and in a different manner with different rock types. Shales, for example, may retain water for much longer periods than sandstones.

From experimental work in oil fields an empirical relationship between resistivity and primary porosity of water-saturated rocks has been derived. It is known as Archie's law and states that resistivity varies approximately with a negative power of porosity:

$$\rho = a\rho_w n^{-m} \tag{4.1}$$

where ρ is the bulk resistivity of the rock, ρ_w is the resistivity of the water contained in the pores, n is the total porosity expressed as a fraction per unit volume of rock, and a and m are empirical parameters. The parameter m is sometimes called the "cementation factor" because its value appears to vary with the degree of cementation of a granular rock.

The parameter a varies from slightly less than 1 in clastic detrital rocks to 3.5 in rocks with very large voids. The parameter m varies from 1.3 in packed sand to 2.3 in tightly cemented clastic rocks.

The principle of the electric resistivity methods is shown in Fig. 4.2. An electric current is passed into the ground through a pair of *current electrodes*, and the resulting electrical field is measured between a pair of potential electrodes. The *apparent bulk resistivity* of the subsurface is computed from the measured values of current strength, potential difference, and electrode spacing. In principle, direct current should be used, but in practice the direction of the current has to be reversed at short time intervals in order to cancel polarization effects.

The four electrodes are arranged in fixed patterns, or *arrays*. *Wenner* and *Schlumberger* arrays are most commonly used (Fig. 4.3). The *Polar Dipole* array has found relatively little application. The apparent resistivity in ohm-m, for the Wenner array, is calculated by

$$\rho = 2\pi a V / I \tag{4.2}$$

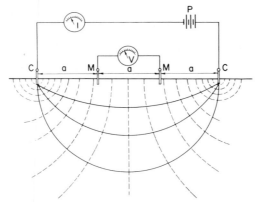

Fig. 4.2 Electrical resistivity method—potential field around electrodes in a homogeneous subsurface. C, current electrodes; M, measuring electrodes; P, current source; I, amperemeter; V, voltmeter; a, electrode distance;—, lines of current flow;---, equipotential lines.

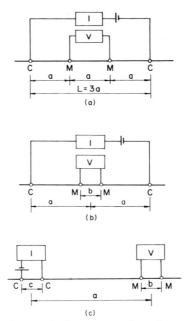

Fig. 4.3 Electrical resistivity method—common electrode arrays. (a) Wenner array, (b) Schlumberger array, (c) dipole–dipole array. I, amperemeter; V, voltmeter; C, current electrodes; M, measuring electrodes. (After Keller and Frischknecht, 1969. From Geological Survey of Canada, *Econ. Geol. Rep.* **26**, *Figure* 4.)

where a is the distance between adjacent electrodes, V the potential difference measured between the potential electrodes (volts), and I the applied current strength (amperes).

In the Schlumberger array the potential electrodes are kept at a closer distance. The apparent resistivity is determined by

$$\rho = \pi (L/2)^2 - (b/2)^2 V/I \qquad (4.3)$$

where L is the distance between the current electrodes (m) and b the distance between the measuring electrodes (m).

When the distance between the current electrodes is increased, the depth of penetration of the current also increases, and the apparent resistivity computed by the preceding equations reflects the influence of deeper layers (*depth probing* or *sounding*). In an ideal homogeneous subsurface, ρ should remain constant for all electrode spacings. If the subsurface is built up by different layers ρ changes more or less sharply when increased electrode spacing brings a deeper layer into play (Fig. 4.4). For interpretation, the apparent resistivity is plotted versus electrode spacing. The simplest and most reliable method of interpretation relies on a measurement carried out near a well with known section. The curve thus obtained is then compared with measurements at some distance from the well (Fig. 4.5).

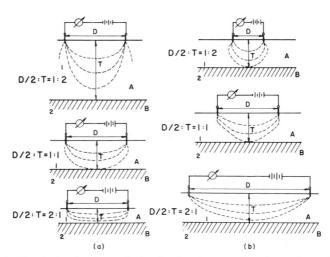

Fig. 4.4 Electrical resistivity method—density of current lines in two-layered subsurface. (a) Constant electrode distance—changing depth of nonconductive substratum, (b) changing electrode distance—constant depth of substratum. A, conductive near-surface layer; B, nonconductive substratum; T, thickness of conductive layer A; D, distance between current electrodes.

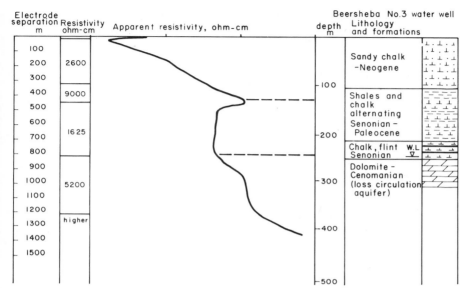

Fig. 4.5 Graph of resistivity depth probe. (Courtesy of TAHAL Consulting Engineers Ltd.)

A more sophisticated method derives specific resistivities of layers by matching the empirical curve against a selection of theoretically computed type curves. Results thus obtained are, however, not uniquely determined and should be accepted with caution unless they can be correlated with geologic data. Visual curve matching may resolve two- to three-layer problems. Computerized methods may theoretically solve even six-layer problems.

A variant of this method consists of moving the electrode array over the terrain with constant electrode spacings. The observed apparent resistivities reflect conditions within a more or less constant depth. The distinction of individual resistivity layers of a given thickness becomes more difficult with increasing depth. There is, however, no unique depth limit. Depth effectiveness depends on the complexity of the subsurface in terms of layers of distinct resistivities, the resistivity contrast between different hydrostratigraphic units and the nature of the instrument applied. Marked resistivity discontinuities have been successfully discerned in two-layer situations to depths of about 1000m. On the other hand, the identification of thin but hydrologically important strata of high resistivity, alternating with low-resistivity layers is often impossible within much smaller depth ranges.

The simultaneous interpretation of a series of measurements from a given region is, in general, easier than the interpretation of a single measurement, because it permits pattern recognition and may help to overcome difficulties arising from equally plausible alternative interpretations. For this reason it is desirable to carry out a number of measurements even if information concerning only one single possible drilling location is sought.

The instrumentation hardware needed for the application of geoelectric resistivity measurements consists of three basic elements:

(1)   a current source with instruments for the control of current strength;
(2)   a set of current and potential electrodes, with the necessary connecting wires;
(3)   a voltmeter or potentiometer for reading potential differences.

The current source can be a battery or a generator. In order to minimize polarization effects, low-frequency square-wave currents are used with periods of a tenth of a second to several tens of seconds. A commutator or relay reverses the polarity of the voltage from the measuring electrodes each time the direction of the current flow in the ground is reversed. Current electrodes are generally steel or copper-clad steel stakes driven a few inches into the ground. In dry areas the soil around the electrodes may have to be moistened.

Sometimes nonpolarizing electrodes have to be used in order to overcome strong polarization effects. They consist of a copper bar immersed in a copper sulfate solution that is contained in a porous ceramic pot.

Resistivity equipment varies greatly in dimensions and depth penetration potential. Lightweight equipment for simple shallow depth application —down to about 100 m—ranges from about 12 to 16 kg in weight, including batteries. Field operations with small instruments can be carried out on a "do-it-yourself" basis, by the project geologist, geophysicist, or hydrogeologist, and the light instruments available on the market are generally offered with detailed operation manuals. With lightweight equipment it is possible to perform 5–10 soundings per work day, depending on the skill of the operating personnel and on terrain conditions.

Greater depths, up to more than 1000 m, can be attained by truck-mounted equipment that incorporates a strong source of current, very sensitive instrumentation, and long cables for the required long base lines. The current strength that can be used is obviously limited by the risk involved and by the weight and bulk of power sources and cables. Therefore efforts have concentrated on more refined receiving equipment. Constraints in this direction are increasing noise–signal ratios, stemming from natural earth currents and also industrial currents. These heavier types of equipment require a specialized operator and workmen to move the electrodes over relatively long distances.

Such a crew can accomplish three to five deep depth probes per day, depending on terrain conditions.

The three principal electrode arrays described have their specific advantages and disadvantages. The Wenner array has the advantage of not requiring very sensitive measuring instruments. It was often preferred in the past because of the reputed closer correlation between electrode spacing and depth penetration, but this assumption has proved erroneous. A disadvantage in comparison with the Schlumberger array is the need to employ four workmen for moving each of the four electrodes from place to place.

The Schlumberger array requires only two workmen because during most of the time only the current electrodes have to be moved. This also minimizes problems brought about by inhomogeneities in the surface. On the other hand, a sensitive measuring instrument is needed because the potential difference between closely spaced electrodes is relatively small.

The polar dipole array dispenses with the need for long cables and uses higher operating voltages. This provides a great logistic advantage, but depth penetration is considerably smaller for a given separation than with the previously mentioned arrays. The polar dipole array in which the dipoles are placed along a common line is considered more sensitive to lateral changes in resistivity than the Wenner or Schlumberger arrays, and therefore more applicable to the detection of faults and other vertical discontinuities in the subsurface. Dipole arrays with one current electrode submersed below the water table in a well are recommended for tracing groundwater-conducting fissures and cavities.

The greatest success in the application of the electrical resistivity method is attained with two-layer problems not involving too great a depth. Examples of problems that can be solved by the surface resistivity method are the depth of alluvium–bedrock contact, identification of aquiferous and non-aquiferous zones and layers in alluvial deposits, determination of contacts between shales and aquiferous limestones, sandstones or basalts, depth and thickness of decomposed or fissured zones in bedrock, and position of the freshwater–saltwater interface in a lithologicallly homogeneous aquifer.

4.3 ELECTROMAGNETIC METHODS

Electromagnetic methods (Collet, 1969) are based on phenomena that occur when natural or artificially created electromagnetic waves impinge on the earth. They developed as an outgrowth of mine detecting techniques and were initially used for the detection of highly conductive ore bodies. A great variety of ground and airborne electromagnetic methods has come into existence, most of them applied for mineral prospection. Since the 1950s electromagnetic methods have been used also for more general mapping purposes, such as the detection of faults and shear zones, differentiation between various soil and rock types, and mapping of sand and gravel deposits. Up to the present time, the application of electromagnetic methods in groundwater investigations has been limited. In the following, a few methods that appear promising in connection with groundwater investigations are reviewed.

Radio broadcast frequency waves passing along the surface, are in part refracted into the earth, giving rise to currents. These, in turn, are influenced by the electrical properties of the upper layers of the earth's crust, including resistivity. Using radio broadcast waves as an energy source, resistivity maps can be prepared for areas surrounding broadcast antennas up to distances of 30–40 km. This method was found useful in the USSR for mapping contacts of dissimilar rocks, such as limestones, clay, shales, sandstones, and porphyrites, and also for detecting karst cavities. Radiofrequency methods appear to be best suited for the study of the electric properties of the soil cover and overburden, because of their relatively shallow penetration. Successful experiments have been conducted in Canada using VLF (very-low-frequency) transmitters to locate fault zones.

The AFMAG (audio-frequency magnetometric) method is an inductive electromagnetic method using as energy source the frequent thunderstorms of the tropical belt of the earth. It is used both as a ground and as an airborne method and has proved its value mainly as an instrument for the detection of faults, shear zones, and dikes. There are limitations to the use of the AFMAG method, such as seasons and hours of the day, and surveys have to be repeated several times to obtain reliable results. The use of this method in groundwater investigations has been recommended.

The *Turam* method uses a fixed energy source in the form of large rectangular wire loops, from 200 by 200 m to 3000 by 5000 m, (Fig. 4.6). Field strength ratios and phase differences are measured between successive observation points by two receiving coils connected to a compensator

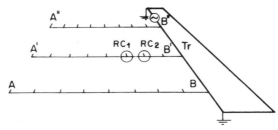

Fig. 4.6 Turam method. Tr, transmitter loop; RC_1, RC_2, mobile receiving coils; A-B, traverse lines and stations; Θ, alternating current source. (After Collet, 1969. From Geological Survey of Canada, *Econ. Geol. Rep.* **26**, *Figure* 5.)

bridge. By changing the coil distances or by moving the set of coils along profiles it is possible to obtain results corresponding to electrical sounding or profiling, respectively. The Turam method has been reported to be useful in the search for groundwater in lava terrains (Von Seggern, 1967). It is assumed that fissure zones will show as anomalies, either more or less conductive than the surrounding terrain. It can possibly be useful also in carbonate rock terrains.

A variation of this method is the *galvanic inductive Turam* method, which uses a grounded energy source. It is especially useful in the detection of elongated cylindrical conductive bodies and might be applicable in the search for flow channels in karstic terrains.

The disadvantage of the Turam method lies in the need to set up large wire loops in the field; its advantage is great depth penetration where this cannot be attained by the galvanic resistivity and other methods.

Lately, groundwater investigators have shown interest in the *magneto-telluric resistivity* method that relies on electrical currents induced in rocks by fluctuations in the earth's magnetic field.

The magneto-telluric method has several advantages over the older galvanic methods. Since measurements are made with currents induced in the earth, no problem is encountered in determining resistivity beneath a highly resistant bed. Resistivity may also be probed to great depths, which with galvanic methods would require the use of tremendous power. The main disadvantage of the magneto-telluric method is the instrumental difficulty in measuring the amplitude of very small, rapid changes in the magnetic field.

4.4 MAGNETOMETRIC METHODS

Magnetometric methods are based on the observation of anomalies in the magnetic field of the earth that are caused mainly by the different magnetic susceptibility of rocks.

Magnetic measurements are probably the most rapid, uncomplicated, and inexpensive geophysical observations, and from this point of view there would be much to recommend their use in groundwater investigations. However, the different content of magnetically susceptible minerals in rocks can rarely be correlated with their aquiferous properties, and therefore the cases in which magnetometric methods can make a significant contribution to groundwater prospecting are few. Examples for the useful application of rapid magnetometric surveys are the detection of dikes in country rock concealed under alluvial overburden, detection of fault zones impregnated

88   4 Geophysical Methods

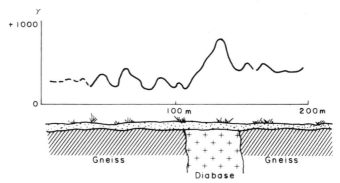

Fig. 4.7 Magnetometric profile across a concealed dike. (After Atlas Copco ABEM AB, AHB 33-15.)

with magnetically susceptible minerals, subsurface extension of basic igneous rocks (basalts), and in some cases, the differentiation between clay and gravel-sand deposits in an alluvial plain (Fig. 4.7).

4.5 GRAVIMETRIC METHODS

Gravimetric methods measure and interpret small anomalies in the force of gravitational attraction exerted by the earth. The unit of measurement, the *gal*, is defined as 1 cm/sec^2 acceleration. The strength of the earth's gravitational field at sea level is 981 gals, and the anomalies of interest rarely exceed 1–2 *milligals* (10^{-3} gals). Modern *gravimeters* (instruments for gravimetric surveys) have an accuracy of ±0.02 mgals; they weigh only 6–12 kg and can be operated by one person.

Observed field data must be corrected in order to eliminate the gravity effect caused by the different distance of each station from the center of the earth (*free air correction*), as well as the effect of crust material between the station level and datum level (*Bouguer correction*). In hilly terrain still another correction (*terrain correction*) is necessary to neutralize the effects of relief features (Fig. 4.8). The application of these corrections requires data on station elevations that must be accurate within ±5 cm in order to be commensurate with the accuracy of gravimeters. Precise topographic work constitutes the most time-consuming and expensive part of a gravimetric survey.

The map that results after corrections have been applied is likely to reflect mainly deep-seated regional structures. Further analysis is required for the separation of gravity effects that are caused by different densities of rocks near the surface, from regional anomalies. The mathematical problem

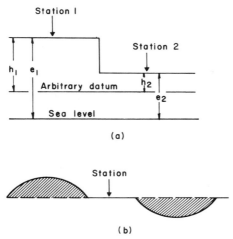

Fig. 4.8 Gravimetric method—corrections of field measurements. (a) *Free-air correction* refers all stations to an arbitrary datum plane: $C_a = +2.867 \times 10^{-2}$ mgal/m. *Bouguer correction* adjusts for slabs of earth material between a station and the datum plane: $C_b = -3.892 \times 10^{-3}\ \sigma$ mgal/m, where σ is the density of the crustal material. The *elevation correction* combines both corrections, taking sea level as datum. For $\sigma = 2.67$ g/cm^3, $C_c = +1.79 \times 10^{-2}$ mgal/m. (b) *Terrain correction* compensates for irregularity of relief near station by theoretically removing hills and filling up valleys to station elevation. (From "Introduction to Geological Prospecting" by Dobrin. Copyright © 1976 by McGraw-Hill, Inc. Used with the permission of McGraw-Hill Book Company.)

of *regional-residual* separation can be solved by graphical and numerical methods. It should be borne in mind, however, that any *result-enhancing* technique also increases the influence of observational errors on the results.

Main sources of error in gravity surveys are (1) errors in determination of station elevation, (2) incorrect calibration of the instrument or unrecognized lack of linearity in its response, (3) incorrect densities used in Bouguer and terrain corrections, (4) improper evaluation of the regional gradient, (5) pronounced irregularity of the bedrock surface, (6) lateral density variations in either the unconsolidated fill or bedrock, and (7) variations of density with depth.

In sedimentary rocks density contrasts are small and there is a wide range of overlap (Table 4.1). The density of one and the same rock type tends to increase with depth and with geologic age. Bulk density is greatly influenced by porosity and therefore low density rock formations can often be correlated with potential aquifers. The density contrast between sediments and igneous rocks is more pronounced. The most appropriate task for the application of gravimetric methods is the detection of unconsolidated fill in buried valleys. A more detailed hydrogeologic interpretation depends on

TABLE 4.1

Density of Selected Rock Types $(g/cm^3)^a$

Rock type	Bulk density			
	Dry		Saturated	
	Range	Average	Range	Average
Stratified glacial drift, including silt, sand, and gravel	1.54–2.12	1.73	1.88–2.40	2.02
Glacial till	1.82–2.19	2.07	2.08–2.36	2.26
Alluvial fill of intermontane basins–undifferentiated clay, silt, sand, and gravel	0.88–2.22	1.63	1.55–2.39	2.02
Recent alluvium	1.53–1.55		1.69–1.97	
Recent silt	1.36		1.86	
Pre-Tertiary bedrock, U.S.	2.04–2.82		2.28–2.82	
Sand (Fort Union sand, Teritiary, Montana, U.S.)	1.79–1.81		2.14	
Dakota Sandstone (Cretaceous, Iowa, U.S.)	1.65–1.76		2.03–2.10	
St. Peter Sandstone (Ordovician, Oklahoma, U.S.	2.28–2.55		2.42–2.59	
Clay (Middendorf clay, Cretaceous, Colorado, U.S.)	1.51		1.93	
Shale (Carlyle shale, Cretaceous, Wyoming, U.S.)	2.00		2.24	
Limestone (Greenhorn limestone, Cretaceous, Wyoming, U.S.)	1.74		2.12	
Chalk (England)	1.53–2.22		1.96–2.40	
Dolomite (England)	2.54		2.63	
Granite	2.52–2.81		—	
Gabbro	2.85–3.12		—	

[a] After Eaton and Watkins (1969) and Dobrin (1976).

the presence of aquiferous and nonaquiferous formations with significantly different densities and on the availability of data from boreholes, including information on the depth of the water table. From the point of view of cost, closely spaced gravimetric and electric resistivity surveys are comparable.

4.6   SEISMIC METHODS

Seismic methods of exploration are based on the observation of the speed of propagation of elastic waves—comparable to sound waves—within the rock formations building up the upper part of the earth's crust. In practice, an artificial shock, created by the detonation of an explosive charge or by other devices, is used as a source of elastic waves. Detectors, called *geophones*, are placed at various distances and in various directions from the point of detonation and connected with a recording instrument to record the arrival time of waves, which have been refracted or reflected back to the surface from various depths.

The *seismic velocity* of rocks depends on their elastic properties. Igneous rocks, in general, have higher seismic velocities than sedimentary rocks, but there is a considerable overlap. Some limestones, for example, show higher values than some granites. Rock formations of older geologic age have velocities higher than younger formations, except in the near-surface weathered zone.

Wave velocities in unconsolidated or semiconsolidated sediments are the result of many geologic factors, among which are depth of burial below the surface, lithology (including grain size distribution, grain shape, degree of cementation, and composition of the cement), confining pressure, degree of saturation, and fluid pressure of the saturant. Rock porosity is a function of some of these factors, and for this reason, velocity and porosity display a very high degree of correlation. But interpretation of results of seismic measurements in quantitative terms of expected rock porosity is possible only in rare cases. The main objective of seismic surveys remains the identification of different wave-velocity layers, determination of their depth and thickness, and their identification with known or assumed stratigraphic units or structural features.

Velocities of compressional (also called longitudinal) waves range from 300–2000 m/sec for loose Quaternary sediments to 4000–5700 m/sec in granite. Some characteristic wave velocities are listed in Table 4.2. The

TABLE 4.2

Compressional Wave Velocities[a]

Rock type	Velocity range (m/sec)
Saturated unconsolidated sediments	1460–4200
Saturated Unconsolidated sediments predominating values	1460–1800
Saturated consolidated rocks	2250
Weakly cemented saturated rocks	1800–3000
Unsaturated, Unconsolidated sediments and soils	80–730
Unsaturated, unconsolidated sediments and soils, predominating values	300–500
Unsaturated, consolidated rocks	1300–5000

[a]After Eaton and Watkins (1969).

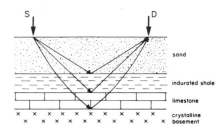

Fig. 4.9 Seismic reflection method. S, shot point; D, detector.

figures show that a sound basis for correlation with geologic data is necessary for the correct interpretation of wave velocities in terms of rock formations.

There are two seismic methods, *reflection* and *refraction*. The reflection method observes waves that are reflected from a buried velocity interface (Fig. 4.9). In a simple two-layer case the travel time between the shot point S and the detector D is easily derived by the application of the Pythagorean theorem:

$$\tau = \frac{L}{v} = \frac{2}{v}\sqrt{z^2 + \left(\frac{x}{2}\right)^2} \tag{4.4}$$

where L is the length of the path traversed by the wave, x the distance shot point-detector, τ the travel time, v the speed of the wave, and z the depth of the interface.

The average wave velocity in the layers above the interface has to be determined by calibration against borehole sections or by indirect methods (Dobrin 1960, Schneider 1973). If the interface is not sharply defined or if it is inclined, interpretation becomes difficult. The depth limit of reflection shooting, several thousand meters, is larger than the depth limits of all the other geophysical methods. Reflection shooting to shallow depths requires the measurement of very short travel times. Modern instruments are capable of providing information from depths as shallow as 30 m.

The principle of the seismic refraction method will be explained by considering a simple two-layer model consisting of an upper layer with a small wave velocity V_1 and a lower layer with a larger wave velocity V_2. The two layers are separated by a horizontal interface (Fig. 4.10). A seismic wave is generated at the *shot point S*, and its arrival is detected by the geophone G at distance X from S.

In an isotropic layer the seismic wave spreads outward in hemispherical wave fronts. Vectors perpendicular to the wave fronts are called *rays*. One set of rays travels near the surface from S to G. Another set travels downward and is refracted into the lower layer in accordance with *Snell's*

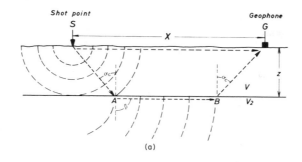

(a)

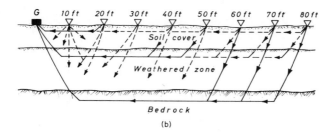

(b)

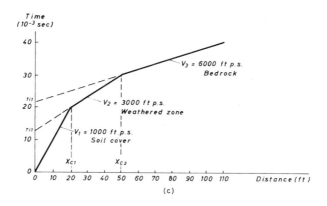

(c)

Fig. 4.10 Seismic refraction method. (a) Refraction of seismic waves in two-layered subsurface, (b) field array of geophone and tamper-blow stations, (c) time–distance diagram of first shock wave arrivals. (Used with permission of Soiltest, Inc.)

law which states: $\sin\alpha/\sin\beta = V_1/V_2$, where α is the angle of the incident ray with the normal to the interface and β is the angle of the refracted ray with the normal. The angle of incidence, for which, according to Snell's law, $\sin\beta = 1$, is termed the critical angle α_c. A ray that is refracted at the critical angle travels along the interface in the lower layer. The interface is therefore subjected to oscillating stresses by two wave fronts, one in the upper layer and one in the lower layer, traveling at the speeds V_1 and V_2, respectively. For reasons that cannot be explained here these stresses create rays that are refracted into the upper layer at the critical angle α_c. Thus, the refracted ray shown in Fig. 4.10 travels from S to A in the upper layer, from A to B in the lower layer, and from B to G in the upper layer.

The recording instrument at G (distance X from S) registers the arrival time of the first wave. Where X is relatively small, the first shock registered pertains to the waves that travel at velocity V_1 through the upper layer. But with increasing distance between the energy source and the detector the refracted waves traveling through the lower layer with velocity V_2 will have overtaken the ones propagated in the upper layer and will be the first to arrive. The distance between the point of wave generation and a point where both waves arrive at the same time is called *critical distance*.

The results of refraction measurements are plotted in the form of time-distance diagrams, with distances on the ordinate and time on the abscissa (Fig. 4.10c). The critical distance is recognized by a break in the graph. The straight line passing through the origin represents the slower waves traveling through the upper layer. The less steeply inclined segment represents the more speedy waves that travel through the lower layer. The intersection between the extension of this line with the time axis (T_i) marks the *intercept time*. The depth of the interface between the two layers (z) can be calculated from the intercept time, the critical distance X_c, and the velocities V_1 and V_2 using the following formula:

$$z = \frac{X_c}{2}\sqrt{\frac{V_2-V_1}{V_2+V_1}} \qquad (4.4a)$$

Similarly, mathematical solutions for multilayer cases are possible as long as the velocity of propagation in each successive deeper layer is greater than the one overlying it.

Figure 4.10 presents the field application of portable refraction seismic equipment, using a tamper type of device for creating shock waves, and a typical first-arrivals time graph displaying two distinct breaks. These are interpreted as topsoil–weathered-rock and weathered-rock–bedrock interfaces, respectively.

The refraction method of seismic exploration postulates that two requirements be fulfilled in the subsurface if it is expected to obtain accurate and significant results of depths of various interfaces:

(1)   The velocity of sound wave transmission in the strata must increase with depth. If it does not, the seismic wave cannot be refracted at the critical angle along the interface between two transmitting layers and be returned to the geophones on the surface. It will be refracted downward and will not return to the surface until an increase in velocity is encountered at another interface at greater depth. Such a situation is called a "velocity inversion."

(2)   The various layers through which the refracted wave travels horizontally must have a thickness that permits transmission of the refracted wave. This thickness is a function of the depth of burial and of the velocity contrast between adjacent strata. If a layer is less than this minimum thickness, the refracted wave will not be transmitted horizontally through that layer, but will traverse the layer, to some lower horizon that will permit the transmission of the refracted wave horizontally Such layers unnoticed on the records are called "blind zones."

Interpretation of refraction seismic data is frequently complicated by the occurrence of velocity inversions and/or blind zones within the overburden. Velocity inversions lead to overestimations of the depth to bedrock. They can be identified, and interpretations can be adjusted, where well logs are available for correlation. The drilling of test holes may be indicated. Special techniques can be used to overcome difficulties resulting from velocity inversions, such as *uphole shooting*, i.e., the observation of seismic waves from detonations in boreholes, and the interpretation of results by the *wave-front plotting* technique.

Depth of interfaces can be defined generally with an accuracy of 10%. The seismic depth of an interface as determined by the refraction method is the average depth over a distance equal to the depth itself.

In addition to vertical changes in velocity, horizontal changes along the line of observation in the loose-rock overburden and in the bedrock may occur. Difficulties in interpretation arising from such changes can often be overcome by reversing the position of the energy source and the detector points.

Refraction techniques tend to smooth out local highs and lows on the bedrock surface. The experience and skill of the geophysicist in choosing the proper distances between shooting points and geophones and, in multichannel equipment, between the different geophones often can resolve such problems. Correlation with well logs is an important aid.

The water table itself is a seismic refraction interface, inasmuch as it abruptly increases the compressional wave velocity, and this factor must be considered in interpretation. Some authors suggested the use of the refraction method to map the water table. Perched water tables may produce velocity inversions and mask underlying layers. They can sometimes be identified by their limited lateral extent.

Seismic prospection equipment consists of three basic elements: a wave-generating device (i.e., a source of energy), a set of detecting instruments called geophones, and an amplifying and recording instrument. The operation technique for refraction surveys differs from that for reflection surveys principally with respect to the shot point-detector separation. In reflection work, this is virtually never greater than the depth to the shallowest reflecting interface expected. In refraction surveys, the separation is usually much greater than the depth to the horizon to be followed.

In shallow refraction techniques, as applied in groundwater investigations, shock waves are created by exploding a small explosive charge, by a sledge hammer, a tamper, or a vibrator inducing in the surface an exactly defined signal of several seconds duration, with a controlled-frequency wave train. The nonexplosive energy sources have, of course, the advantage of greater safety and applicability also in inhabited and built-up areas.

Portability of equipment and ease of operation by small crews (two persons) is essential for use in groundwater investigations. The simplest type of recorders are the one-channel types. The single geophone is set up at a selected point and shock waves are created by hammer blows at different distances and in different directions. This kind of equipment weighs from 4 to 15 kg. The vibrator-type energy sources are relatively heavy, truck-mounted pieces of equipment and are not practicable with the truly lightweight portable apparatus. More elaborate equipment, of the multi-channel type (6, 12, or 24 channels) is also available and is heavier, weighing up to 20 kg without the energy source. With multichannel equipment, arrivals of each shock wave created are recorded simultaneously at different stations.

One complete refraction profile using portable hammer seismic equipment can be completed in about 20 min. Difficult terrain or exceptionally long profiles may require as much as 1 hr. It is quite possible, in a normal working day, to complete 15–20 locations. In some situations, reversed refraction profiles will be required, in others, single-ended profiles will be sufficient. The reversed refraction profile yields continuous subsurface sections of layers of distinct and increasing velocity.

Reflection seismic surveys using single-channel equipment can be conducted at a rate of 15–20 locations per working hour; with a 30 m spacing between observations, 120–160 stations can be completed in a day, corresponding to a coverage of 4–6 km. Difficulties of terrain and access will reduce the efficiency. With 12-channel equipment used in conjuction with explosives or hammer, approximately one-half hour is required for each geophone spread.

Operational and equipment costs for portable seismic equipment are comparable to those for heavier types of electrical resistivity equipment, but are considerably higher than the costs for gravity and magnetic surveys. In groundwater investigations seismic methods are used mainly for mapping the thickness of detritic strata overlying dense bedrock.

4.7   REMOTE SENSING TECHNIQUES

Remote sensing techniques collect data with the aid of airborne or satellite-borne instruments. Airborne magnetometers and aerial photography were mentioned in previous sections (3.1 and 4.9). *Imagery techniques* (Moore and Deutsch, 1975) replace the photographic film by *sensors*, devices that transform the incoming radiation into electric pulses. Each sensor reacts to a specific spectral interval, from ultraviolet to thermal infrared. A *scanning device* rapidly directs the sensors onto successive points on a selected area. The pulses are stored on magnetic tape and then integrated into a mosaiclike digitalized image of the area. For ease of interpretation the digital mosaic is transformed into a black and white or color image.

In satellite imagery the electric pulses are transmitted by radio, thus eliminating the problem of physical transportation. The commercially available *LANDSAT* (land satellite) images represent an area of approximately 80 by 60 m by one point. A complete LANDSAT image covers 34,225 km^2 (i.e., a square 185 by 185 km) and thus makes it possible to correlate features that escape detection on larger-scale aerial photographs.

Thermal infrared imagery by airborne or satellite-borne instruments has found relatively wide application in hydrology, especially for the mapping of submarine springs, which have a different temperature than the surrounding water.

Active remote sensing techniques employ artificial energy sources, such as radar beams. Side-looking airborne radar (*SLAR*) yields pictures even under difficult atmospheric conditions and makes it possible to accentuate topographic and geomorphological characteristics.

The principal advantage of remote sensing techniques is that they provide information from large areas without being hampered by difficulties of access. Satellite imagery also makes it possible to monitor transient phenomena such as floods, snow cover, draughts, volcanic eruptions, etc., since the satellite returns to each position in its orbit at regular intervals (in LANDSAT images the interval is 18 days). These advantages carry little weight in groundwater investigations, except in their most preliminary phases. For work of practical value, access to the particular, relatively small, area of interest must be gained. The investigator should consult available remote sensing information, but the application of remote sensing technique. specifically for groundwater investigations, will probably remain restricted to very few special cases.

4.8   WELL-LOGGING TECHNIQUES

Geophysical well logging (Guyod and Shane, 1969), also called borehole, or downhole, geophysics includes all techniques of lowering sensing devices into a borehole and recording physical parameters that may be interpreted in terms of the characteristics of the rocks adjoining the hole, the fluids contained in the hole and in the rocks, and constructional details of the hole. The sensors applied are, in most cases, electrodes that can serve to measure electrical potential and resistivity, but visual, mechanical, nuclear, acoustic, magnetic, and thermal sensors are also used. Most well-logging techniques are restricted to uncased holes and are therefore applied mainly in conjunction with rotary drilling.

Drilling is generally the most expensive item on the budget of a groundwater investigation. It is essential, therefore, to assure that full advantage be taken of any hole to obtain the most detailed and precise information. Geophysical well logging can help to overcome uncertainties concerning stratigraphic boundaries stemming from imperfect or incomplete formation samples or erroneous drilling records. It can provide, in addition, data on fluid and rock properties that may not be available from routine borehole records. In contrast to other borehole records, which provide discontinuous and subjective observations, geophysical logs provide continuous and objective records that are consistent from well to well and from time to time, and are not dependent on the personal skill and varying terminology of different drillers or geologists. Despite these advantages, well logging cannot be a substitute for routine formation sample collection, because properly taken samples are essential also to the correct interpretation of geophysical logs. This is true especially in the exploration phase of the investigation, when each new hole must be expected to represent a separate subsurface geological and hydrogeologic environment.

The spectrum of information that can be obtained from the interpretation of geophysical well logs includes the exact position of formation boundaries and thickness, identification of thin individual beds, bulk density of the rock, approximate total porosity, effective porosity or permeability, moisture content, approximate salinity of the fluids filling the hole and of the groundwater contained in the formations adjoining the hole, and temperature and movement of fluids in the hole. Quantitative interpretation of log data can provide numerical values for some rock characteristics required in groundwater investigations. Data from geophysical well logs serve also as an aid to the interpretation of surface geophysical investigations. Logging techniques also permit the repeated observation of fluid and rock characteristics in a well, which may change because of pumping, injection, or construction operations (cementation, acidation, etc.).

Accurate information on the vertical distribution and boundaries of aquiferous and nonaquiferous, caving and stable beds permits the preparation of a casing plan with much greater confidence than the driller's or geologist's log alone. The graphic presentation of geophysical logs allows a rapid visual interpretation already at the well site and facilitates taking the right decisions on the continuation of the drilling operations.

Geophysical well logging is an outgrowth of the petroleum industry. Its application in groundwater investigations is still restricted and has not yet attained the scope it merits. One of the reasons is the relatively high cost of well logging. For the logging of wells of more than 200 m depth and the application of the full range of different sensors and techniques, the services of a logging company must be contracted, and charges will be comparable to those paid by the petroleum industry. For depths smaller than 200 m, light, do-it-yourself logging instruments are available. These, however, are designed to register only certain types of logs and do not provide the wide range of data that can be obtained by the more sophisticated loggers. Furthermore, the use of these light loggers requires that personnel trained in their operation and in log interpretation be available to the project.

As in surface geophysical techniques, the data recorded on well logs reflect certain physical properties, which can result from different subsurface conditions. Interpretation of well logs always requires, therefore, geologic background information and experience, in addition to an understanding of the theory of each logging technique. The following review is intended to provide the investigator with the knowledge he may require to use his judgement, but he should leave the planning and performance of the operation and the interpretation of results to specialists, in cooperation with the project geologist.

Logging Equipment

Any well logger consists of three essential components: a sensor, signal conditioners, and a recorder or indicator. The sensor is contained in a probe suspended on a cable by which it is lowered into the hole. The cable serves also to transmit to the probe the required power and to the surface instruments the signal produced by the sensor. Important accessories are a depth indicator and a motor operating the winch over which the cable and probe are moved in the hole. Chart paper or photographic film is moved through the recorder as the probe moves up or down the hole to record the signal obtained from the sensor. Vertical scales, generally in feet per inch, are selected by changing a gear ratio in the recorder.

Electrical Logging

Despite the advent of several other logging techniques, electrical logs remain the most useful and widely applied in groundwater investigations. There are two types of electric logs, the spontaneous potential and the resistivity log. Electric logs can be applied only in uncased holes, or uncased portions of holes, because they are based on the registration of electrical conditions resulting from the contact between the fluid filling the hole (generally the drilling mud), the rock formations adjoining the hole, and the fluids contained in them.

Spontaneous Potential Logs

Spontaneous potential (SP) logs are records of the *natural* potentials developed between the borehole fluid and the surrounding rock material. The electrical spontaneous potential is considered to represent the algebraic sum of the natural earth potentials, electrofiltration potentials (i.e., potentials resulting from the flow of drilling mud into formations surrounding the hole, or the flow of water through porous formations), and electrochemical potentials. The spontaneous potential is measured by lowering a single electrode into the uncased hole. A second electrode, the ground electrode, is located at the surface in a small hole filled with drilling mud. Measurements are obtained from a recording potentiometer, in millivolts. In most formations, the spontaneous potential is due mainly to the electrochemical effect (Fig. 4.11). The electrochemical potential is caused by two electrolytes (in the case of boreholes, the drilling fluid and formation water) of different ionic concentration being in contact through a permeable medium, such as a sandstone, adjoining the hole.

In the case represented in Fig. 4.11, contacts exist at the four interfaces: mud–mud filtrate, mud filtrate–formation (ground-) water contained in the sand, formation water–shale, and shale–mud. The potentials arising at these interfaces cause a current to flow in the mud column filling the borehole, near sand–shale boundaries.

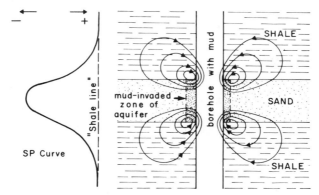

Fig. 4.11 Spontaneous potential currents and SP curve in a sandstone–shale sequence. (After Keys and MacCary, 1971.)

When the formation water is much more saline than the mud, the current follows the paths shown by the arrows, entering the mud column from the shale and moving into the sandstone. At the bed boundary, the current density is maximum and the electrode moving uphole senses a decreasing potential so that a deflection to the negative side of the graph is registered. The maximum negative potential is attained when the electrode is positioned opposite the middle of the sandstone layer and from there the curve is reflected back toward the positive side of the graph. If the formation water is fresh as compared to the mud, the deflection will be to the positive side, because the flow of the currents will be reversed.

SP logs are usually run together with electric resistance or electric resistivity logs and are recorded on the left column, or *track*, of the chart. Reading of the log consists in identifying positive or negative deflections from a recognizable, arbitrary baseline, which represents a permeable or impermeable formation of considerable thickness. Potential logs point out permeable zones, but absolute value of permeability cannot be determined from the SP log alone. Thus the spontaneous potential serves mainly to locate beds of different permeability and their tops and bottoms.

Where the formation water is more saline than the drilling mud filling the hole, the greatest positive deflections correspond to shales and greatest negative deflections to permeable formations such as sands. A "shale line" connecting the greatest positive deflections and a "sand line" passing through the extreme negative deflections are constructed. If the ionic concentrations of the borehole fluid and the formation water are constant throughout the length of the borehole, the shale line and the sand line will generally be parallel to the vertical margin of the log. In aquifers of high

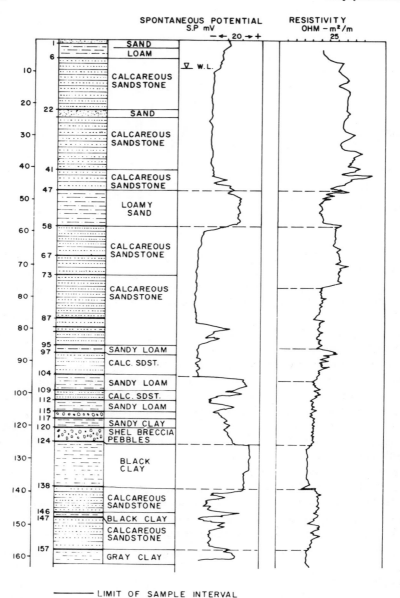

Fig. 4.12 Lithologic and electric log of a groundwater exploration well.

groundwater salinity, and, in some cases, in freshwater aquifers, reading of potentials taking the shale line as a baseline can serve to estimate sand–shale ratios in the layers. The application of this method is, however, limited. For example, where the borehole fluid has a very low resistivity compared with the sand beds, SP deflections opposite sand beds may actually be more positive than those opposite the shales.

The SP log is sometimes used to determine groundwater quality. The method is based on a formula expressing the potential E as a function of the electrochemical activity of the formation water and the mud filtrate:

$$E = K \log \frac{\text{activity of the formation water}}{\text{activity of the mud filtrate}} \qquad (4.5)$$

K is a factor mainly depending on temperature. Chemical activity being for most situations nearly proportional to the electrical conductivity of a solution, the following formula can be applied:

$$E = K \log \frac{\rho_{mf}}{\rho_w} \qquad (4.6)$$

in which ρ_{mf} is the resistivity of the mud filtrate and ρ_w is the resistivity of the water that saturates the permeable formation. This formula can be used, however, only when three conditions are simultaneously satisfied:

(1)   the formation water is very saline;
(2)   sodium chloride is the dominant salt;
(3)   the mud filtrate is relatively fresh and contains no unusual additives.

It is, therefore, possible to identify saline groundwater zones from the SP log, but differences in the salinity of low-concentration groundwater cannot be determined with accuracy. Saline water concentration can be determined with an accuracy of $\pm 10\%$ to $\pm 20\%$, and brackish water concentration within $\pm 100\%$. It has been suggested that where empirical correlations are available in specific freshwater aquifer systems, the method may be applicable, within a certain margin of error. The spontaneous potential log should always be interpreted in conjunction with the electrical resistivity log; the pair of logs interpreted simultaneously provides information not available directly from any one of them alone. For this reason, both SP and resistivity logs are recorded even by the simplest logging instruments (Figs. 4.12, 4.13).

Resistance Logging

Resistance logging consists of measuring the resistance in ohms, of the subsurface between a surface electrode and an electrode introduced into a

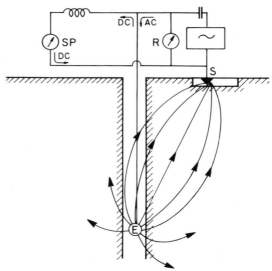

Fig. 4.13 System for recording of spontaneous potential and single-electrode resistance log. ~, alternating current source; S, surface electrode immersed in mud pit; E, down-hole electrode; R, resistance meter; P, potential meter. (After Guyod; in Keys and MacCary, 1971.)

borehole or between two downhole electrodes. These qualitative logging methods are known as single-point, point resistance, or single-electrode systems to distinguish them from the multielectrode systems used for quantitative measurements of resistivity called *resistivity logging*. The resistance logging method is less used than resistivity logging. Its main application is for geologic correlation, to determine bed boundaries and changes in lithology and location of fractures in resistive rocks. The stratigraphic resolution of resistance logs is often superior to that of resistivity logs, especially in formations of low to moderate resistance. Equipment for single-point logging is similar to that used for spontaneous potential logging (Fig. 4.13). Resistance logs are of particular value for the determination of fracture zones, but difficulties may arise in highly resistive formations, such as crystalline rocks.

Resistivity Logging

Multielectrode techniques are used for measuring resistivities in boreholes. Four electrodes constitute the system: two current electrodes, conventionally designated by the letters A and B and two measuring electrodes, designated by the letters M and N (Fig. 4.14).

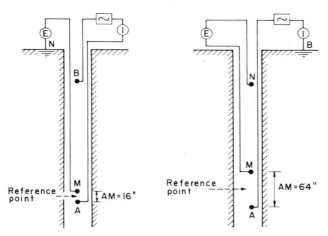

Fig. 4.14 Electrode arrangement for short and normal resistivity logging. $\sim$, alternating current source; E, potential measuring instrument; I, current measuring instrument; A, B, M, N, electrodes. (After Keys and MacCary, 1971.)

A number of electrode arrangements and spacings are used in resistivity logging, each one with its particular characteristics of current penetration into the formations adjoining the hole and power of resolution to identify beds of different thickness. A simultaneous recording and graphic presentation of logs obtained with different arrangements offers the greatest potential for correct and meaningful interpretation (Table 4.3).

In the *normal electrode arrangement*, the effective spacing is considered as the distance *AM*. Most manufacturers have standardized on the *short normal* (*AM* = 16 in.) and the *long normal* (*AM* = 64 in.) arrangement (Fig. 4.14). The short normal arrangement gives good vertical detail and measures an apparent resistivity primarily reflecting the resistivity of the mud-invaded zone of the walls of the hole. The long normal arrangement can sense the average resistivity beyond the invaded zone for a radius of approximately twice the *AM* spacing. Short and long normal curves are useful in the identification of bed boundaries and thicknesses as well as for stratigraphic correlation between different boreholes. Another important application is the interpretation of normal curves for water quality in clastic rocks. A relation between ionic concentration of formation water and the long normal resistivity reading can be established empirically. The method is subject, however, to three conditions: (1) the aquifer must be similar to an ideal porous medium, (2) the aquifer must be of relatively constant porosity and clay content both vertically and laterally, and (3) the apparent resistivities measured by the long normal arrangement must approximate formation resistivities.

TABLE 4.3

Applicability of Electric Logs in Groundwater Investigations[a]

Properties to be investigated				Type of electric log					
	Single point	Short normal	Long normal	Lateral device	Wall resistivity (nonfocused)	Focused guard and laterolog	Micro-focused	Induction	SP
Lithologic correlation	X	X	—	—	—	X	—	X	X
Bed thickness	X	X	—	—	X	X	X	X	X
Formation resistivity (low resistivity muds)	—	—	X	X	—	X	—	X	—
Formation resistivity (freshwater mud)	—	—	X	X	—	—	—	X	—
Flushed zone resistivity	—	—	—	—	X	—	X	—	—
Mud resistivity (in place in hole)	—	—	—	—	X	—	—	—	—
Formation water resistivity	—	—	X	X	—	X	—	—	—

[a]After Keys and MacCary (1971).

The electrical resistivity of a rock is a function of the porosity of the rock, the manner of distribution and interconnection of the pores, the amount of fluid contained in the pores, its salinity, and the temperature of rock and fluid. The ratio between the resistivity of a rock 100% saturated with water (ρ_0) and the resistivity of the water contained in the pores (ρ_w) is called the formation factor (F_f).

$$F_f = \rho_0 / \rho_w$$

Formation factors vary from 3 to 200 for most natural materials. The formation factor is a very useful parameter for the evaluation of groundwater salinity and aquifer porosity in loose granular rocks. If the formation factor can be determined for a certain aquifer, or part of it, long normal resistivity readings on electric logs, providing the bulk rock resistivity values ρ_0, permit determining, within certain limits, the groundwater resistivity. This, in turn, can be interpreted in terms of groundwater salinity.

The procedure consists of three steps:

1. The determination of the formation factor from existing logs and groundwater analyses.

(a) Find fluid resistivity, in ohm-m from the relationship

$$\rho_w = \frac{10,000}{\text{specific conductance (mho-cm)}}$$

or from a graph presenting this relationship (Fig. 4.15).

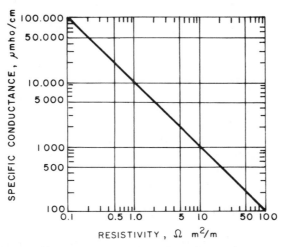

Fig. 4.15 Relationship between resistivity and specific conductance. (After Keys and MacCary, 1971.)

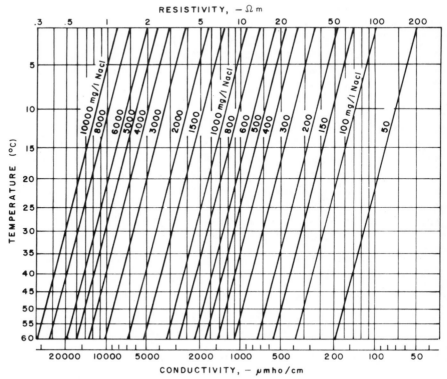

Fig. 4.16 Resistivity and conductivity of sodium chloride solutions at different temperatures. (After Keys and MacCary, 1971.)

(b)   Determine the resistivity of the aquifer, ρ_0 at borehole temperature from the long normal curve. Correct to standard temperature using available graphs (Fig. 4.16).

(c)   Calculate F_f from the relationship $F_f = \rho_0 / \rho_w$.

2. The determination of the relationship between specific conductance and total dissolved solids and chlorine content, both in parts per million, using available graphs or an empirical formula, from groundwater analyses.

3. Determine groundwater quality in the logged well.

(a)   Read ρ_0 for a water-bearing formation from the long normal curve.

(b)   Correct this resistivity value to standard temperature.

(c)   Enter corrected ρ_0 value and F_f value in formula $F_f = \rho_0 / \rho_w$ and solve for ρ_w.

(d)   Find obtained resistivity on the graphs mentioned in step 2 and read off total dissolved solids and chloride concentrations.

One limitation on the accuracy of the method lies in the assumption that the long normal curve directly indicates bulk rock resistivity; in effect, this assumption is acceptable only for thick, fairly homogeneous aquifers. In other cases, corrections are required for borehole diameter, mud resistivity, and depth of invasion of mud filtrate.

Normal resistivity curves have also been used in some cases to determine permeability in clastic aquifers. This method is based on an empirical relationship between permeability and formation factor.

In jointed or vugular rocks, anomalous formation factors may obtain, and for this reason the method should be applied only to loose granular rocks or to rocks that, from the hydrogeologic viewpoint, behave like granular rocks.

Instrumentation consists of a steel mandrel containing the A and M electrodes, suspended on a multiconductor armored cable. The cable armor is used as the current return electrode B and is insulated with a rubber sleeve for 50 ft above the cable head. The voltage return electrode N is a lead sleeve on the end of a rubber-covered wire and is placed in the mud pit. Commercial service tools are about 2.50 m long and have a $3\frac{5}{8}$ in. diameter. They weigh up to 65 kg and a frame or derrick over the hole is needed for logging.

The *lateral electrode arrangement* measures the formation resistivity beyond the mud-invaded zone by use of widely spaced electrodes. The lateral is a deep-looking device and gives best results in beds whose thickness exceeds twice the electrode spacing. Its efficiency is poor in highly resistive rocks.

Three effective electrodes are present in the borehole. The potential electrodes M and N are positioned below the current electrode A. The electrode spacings are measured from current electrode A to the midpoint between electrodes M and N. This distance, called the AO spacing, has been standardized at 18 ft, 8 in. The electrode B is located a remote distance from the A, M, and N electrodes.

The lateral device provides greatest penetration of the formations and as a result the most accurate recording of the resistivity of the formations and their contents. It does not record abrupt deflections at the top and bottom of thick formations because of the wide spacing of the electrodes; therefore it is of limited value for stratigraphic correlations.

The most obvious characteristic of the lateral curve is its lack of symmetry about a given bed. Near thin resistive beds whose thickness is less than the distance AO, the curve may be distorted, shadow peaks and dead zones may show, and apparent resistivities may depart from the actual values. The lateral log is run simultaneously with the short and long normals.

Wall-Resistivity Devices

Wall-resistivity devices measure mainly the resistivity of the mud cake and are used to differentiate beds that have been invaded by the mud from relatively impermeable ones that have not. The type of log recorded by these devices is also known as a *microlog*.

The device consists of three small electrodes, 1-in. apart. The electrodes are mounted in an insulating pad which, pressed against the wall of the hole, shields the electrodes against the short-circuiting effect of the drilling mud filling the hole.

The electrode group provides a *micronormal* curve and a *microlateral* curve. The micronormal curve represents resistivities just beyond the mud cake and thus gives a resistivity that is mostly influenced by formation resistivities. The microlateral curve is affected mainly by the mud cake because it "sees" only $1\frac{1}{2}$ in. into the wall of the hole. The two curves are recorded simultaneously. Micrologs provide fine lithologic detail.

The difference between the two curves for any one formation is the basis for interpretation and is known as the *separation*. It is positive if the micronormal curve extends further to the right than the microlateral curve and negative if the relations are reversed. Positive separation indicates that mud has invaded the formation, which in turn suggests an appreciable degree of permeability. Negative separation indicates that the resistivity of the formation is lower than that of the drilling mud, a rather uncommon circumstance, or that no close contact was formed between the wall of the hole and the electrode pad, a case quite frequent in thick sequences of carbonate rocks. Lack of separation indicates that little or no mud has invaded the formation and suggests little or no permeability.

Induction Logging

Induction logging is the downhole equivalent of the surface electromagnetic methods. An induction device consists essentially of two coils, one for transmitting an alternating current by induction into the formation, and the other for receiving the signal returned from the formation. The method was developed for use in the petroleum industry, to be applied in holes drilled with air or with oil-base nonconductive muds. It can be valuable in groundwater investigations where low-conductivity freshwater mud is used, or where it is intended to log an air-drilled section of a hole above the water table.

Radioactivity Logging

Radioactivity logging techniques are based on the faculty of gamma rays emitted during radioactive decay of unstable isotopes to penetrate high-density materials. Neutrons produced by an artificial source are also used for well logging. They have the ability to penetrate dense material but are slowed in hydrogenous materials, meaning, in practice, fluid-containing porous rocks. The great advantage of radioactivity logs in groundwater investigations lies in the possibility of using them in cased holes. Radioactivity logging techniques include natural gamma logging, gamma spectrometry, gamma-gamma logging, and neutron logging.

Natural Gamma Logs

Natural gamma logs are records of the amount of natural gamma radiation emitted by the rocks adjoining the borehole. All rocks exhibit measurable amounts of natural radioactivity. In general, the intensity of radioactivity in sedimentary rocks increases from low values in evaporites, coarse clastics, and carbonates to high values in fine clastics (Fig. 4.17). The gamma-ray-emitting isotopes responsible for the radioactivity in most rocks are ^{40}K and daughter products of the uranium and thorium decay series. The possibility of correlating some hydrogeologically important rock types

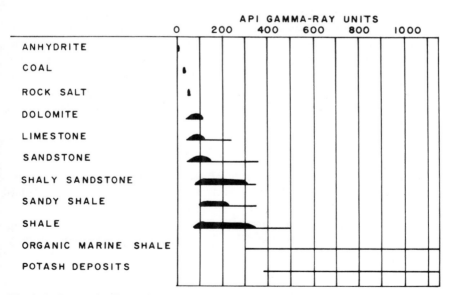

Fig. 4.17 Range of radioactivity of some sedimentary rocks. (From Keys and MacCary, 1971.)

with distinct ranges of natural gamma radiation is based mainly on the much higher gamma activity within sedimentary sequences of rocks containing clay minerals such as clays and shales as compared with most quartz sands, quartzitic sandstones, and carbonate rocks. However, sandstones including much material of igneous origin and fine clastics of volcanic origin may show anomalous high radioactivity. Therefore the successful interpretation of gamma logs depends to a large degree on experience within a given geologic environment.

Probably the most useful application of natural gamma ray logs in groundwater investigations is the identification of clay or shale in sediments and the empirical determination of shale or clay content. The presence of clay as indicated by the gamma log may help to specify total porosity shown by the neutron log in terms of effective porosity, which is of interest in groundwater investigations.

Sensors used in gamma-ray logging are scintillation counters, with pulse amplification and shaping circuits. The radiation is recorded in counts per second, but this has no meaning with respect to the intensity of a field gamma radiation except for a given measuring system. It is necessary therefore to relate counts per second to standards, such as API[1] gamma-ray units, by comparison and calibration with standard gamma-ray sources.

Gamma Spectrometry

Gamma spectrometry is a technique by which the energy distribution of the gamma radiation is analyzed. The energies of emitted gamma rays are characteristic of the isotopes emitting them, and these can therefore be identified. The method seems so far to have found little practical application in groundwater studies. Ratios of natural radioisotopes can be an aid to stratigraphic correlation and to lithologic identification. Another possible use is the identification in liquid wastes and polluted groundwater of characteristic artificial radioisotopes.

Gamma-Gamma Logging

Gamma-gamma logs are records of the intensity of gamma radiation originating from an artificial source installed in the probe, after the radiation has been backscattered and attenuated in the borehole and the surrounding rocks. The gamma-gamma technique is mainly used for lithologic identification and correlation and for the measurement of the bulk density and porosity of rocks.

[1]American Petroleum Institute.

The gamma-gamma probe contains a source of gamma radiation, generally ^{60}Co or ^{137}Cs, and a radiation detector (scintillator crystal) shielded from the source. Degradation of the radiation is due to several processes, of which the Compton scattering effect (elastic collision between a gamma quantum and an atomic electron) is the most significant. The gamma radiation is absorbed proportionally to the electron density of most materials penetrated in logging. Electron density, in turn, is approximately proportional to bulk density of the materials. For this reason, the gamma-gamma log has also been called the density log, and the following equation is applied:

$$\text{Porosity} = \frac{\text{grain density} - \text{bulk density}}{\text{grain density} - \text{fluid density}} \qquad (4.7)$$

Grain density can be derived from laboratory analysis of cores or cuttings, or an average value is assumed such as 2.65 g/cm^3 for quartzite sandstones. Fluid density is assumed to be 1 g/cm^3. If the same lithologic unit is present above and below the water table or if gamma-gamma measurements can be made before and after drawdown, the specific yield of aquifers can be determined by the gamma-gamma log, as the difference between the bulk densities of the saturated and drained sediment. Wide experience with this technique is still lacking and its practicability seems to be rather limited. Specific yields are better determined by hydrogeologic methods.

Neutron Logging

The neutron logging techniques measure the relative intensity of gamma rays emitted from a formation under the influence of neutron bombardment. The neutrons are captured by the atomic nuclei of certain elements. This capture results in gamma rays being emitted, and these are recorded by the probe. The gamma rays induced by this technique are of greater intensity than the natural gamma rays being emitted spontaneously, and therefore the induced radiation can be recorded without interference from the relatively weak natural radiation. Neutrons have no electric charge and lose energy when passing through matter by elastic collision. This process is called *moderation*, and the slowed-down neutrons are described as *thermalized*. The most effective element in moderating neutrons is hydrogen. Because of the great number of hydrogen atoms in the fluid contained in the pore spaces of rocks, the induced gamma radiation provides an indication of the amount of fluid in a rock and—in the saturated zone—also of its porosity. High intensities signify dry, impermeable rocks, whereas low intensities indicate porous, saturated formations. Neutron logs are used therefore mainly for the measurement of moisture content above the water table. Neutron logs, like other radiation logs, can be run in dry and liquid-filled holes and in cased and uncased ones. The most common use of neutron logging is for the monitoring of soil moisture.

There are a number of neutron logging techniques, distinguished by the kind of radiation recorded. Some devices count the *gammaphotons* produced by neutron reaction. The *neutron–thermal neutron* probe responds chiefly to thermal neutrons and the *neutron–epithermal neutron* device mostly to low-energy neutrons. Most neutron logs are *hybrids* and their names indicate the chief type of radiation to which they respond.

Neutron curves showing low values suggest high porosities, though not necessarily high effective porosities, such as are found in shale, shaly sandstone, and sandstone. Medium values are taken to represent shaly carbonate rocks and shaly sandstones, whereas high values suggest low-porosity rocks such as compact carbonate rocks, rock salt, or granite. The greatest benefit from the neutron curve is derived by simultaneous interpretation with the natural gamma curve, which identifies the type of porosity involved. A few specific indications are described below:

(1) Shale is generally indicated by high gamma-ray counts and low neutron values. Black (bituminous) shale is characterized by extremely high gamma-ray values and low values on the neutron curve. Volcanic ash and bentonite in shale sequences cause a similar response.

(2) Sandstones are characterized by minimum values on the gamma-ray curve and low to medium values on the neutron curve. Shaly sandstone is suggested by medium gamma-ray values and medium to low neutron values. Shaly limestone (chalk) produces a similar configuration.

(3) Thin-bedded sandstone and shale record an alternating succession of high and medium values on the gamma-ray curve and alternating unequal low values on the neutron curve. A similar log image is produced by porous carbonate rocks and shales.

(4) Massive carbonate rocks generally register low gamma-ray and high neutron curve values. Carbonate rocks with porous beds show low gamma-ray values and neutron values varying from low to high.

(5) Alternating carbonate rock and shale sequences show unequal low to medium gamma-ray values and irregular high neutron curve values.

(6) Granite and highly radioactive igneous rocks are generally indicated by extremely high gamma-ray curve and neutron curve values.

All logging techniques utilizing an active radiation source require precautionary measures to protect personnel as well as the environment from radiation damage. No radiation-emitting device should be introduced into a borehole unless this has been tested beforehand by a sonde to assure safe recovery of the device. Personnel must be properly protected during all stages of the investigation, and only crews experienced in handling radioactive materials should be allowed to carry out logging operations involving a radiation source.

Acoustic Logs

Acoustic, or sonic, logs are among the more specialized and less commonly applied logging methods in groundwater investigations. They can be visualized, in some sense, as the downhole counterpart of seismic refraction methods. In the petroleum industry their principal use is for the measurement of porosity. A variety called amplitude logging is often applied to locate fractures in a borehole and determine the character of cement bonding between the casing of a hole and the formation.

Acoustic logging devices contain one or two transmitters and one to four receivers. The transmitters consist of a roll of thin magnetostrictive alloy wrapped with a coil of wire. A pulse of current through the wire causes the metal to oscillate with rapid contractions and expansions. The vibrational energy is transmitted through the fluid in the hole to the rock and back through the fluid to the receivers. Frequencies emitted range from 5000 to over 40,000 Hz.

The parameters observed in acoustic logging are (1) interval transit time, which is the reciprocal of velocity, and (2) amplitude, or the reciprocal of attenuation. The continuous acoustic velocity log is a record of transit time (t) of an elastic wave through the media being logged. A detailed description of the types of waves created and of their paths is beyond the scope of this review, and the reader is referred to the specialized literature on this subject (Guyod, 1969).

The continuous acoustic velocity log is now employed mostly to obtain a measure of rock porosity in open holes, though the method has been applied also in cased holes with 40–50% cement bonding. The calculation of rock porosity is based on the *time average equation*:

$$\frac{1}{V_r} = \Delta t = \frac{n}{V_f} + \frac{1-n}{V_m} \tag{4.8}$$

where Δt is the interval transit time in seconds per unit of distance, n equals porosity (fraction); V_f is the velocity of signal in fluid in units of distance per second; V_m is the velocity of signal in matrix in units of distance per second; V_r is the velocity of signal in rock in units of distance per second. The equation derives from the consideration that the path of the acoustic pulse through saturated porous rock consists of two velocities in series, V_f

and V_m. The length of the path in the fluid is equal to the porosity (n) and the length of the path in the rock matrix is equal to ($1-n$).

Approximate porosity can be determined from the acoustic log by a graphical method (Welex, 1968). This method can be applied, however, only for aquifers having uniformly distributed primary porosity. In rocks with secondary porosity due to vugs and fractures, the method can lead to erroneous results, because first-arrival signals will not show the influence of the large secondary fluid-filled openings. On the other hand, the effect of secondary porosity on the various elastic wave parameters can be used to locate fracture zones near wells (Walker, 1962). Acoustic logs can also serve to determine the cement bond behind well casing and to identify lithologic units causing seismic reflections.a

Caliper Logging

The caliper log presents the average diameter of the borehole at various depths. Its main applications are to correct other logs for hole diameter effects and to provide lithologic information, stratigraphic correlation, and the location of fractures and other openings. Caliper logs are also useful as aids to correct construction of wells.

Caliper sondes consist of devices, such as arms, bow springs, or pads, capable of sensing the wall of the hole. Averaging of the hole diameter is achieved by recording the diameter rather than the radius of the hole at a given depth. The arm-type device is more sensitive than the bow spring device. Caliper logging tools are available also for small loggers.

Temperature Logging

Temperature logs are continuous records of the temperature in the borehole. They are used, in the first place, for testing the effectiveness of cementations, but also to appraise some hydrologic phenomena, such as points of entrance and movement of water of different temperature in the hole. Whether the geothermal gradient can be determined from a temperature log depends on the movement of fluid in the hole. Under completely static conditions—a very rare case in water wells—the temperature of the fluid can be assumed to be in equilibrium with the rocks forming the walls of the hole, but in holes with a vigorous flow there may be no temperature gradient at all. Geothermal gradients are generally steeper in rocks with low permeability than in rocks with high permeability. It has been suggested that this relationship could be used to appraise magnitude of permeability from geothermal data. Temperature logs are also used to identify infiltrating waste or recharge water of a temperature differing from the temperature of the natural groundwater. Fluid temperatures in the borehole are needed also for the interpretation of resistivity logs.

Apart from the straightforward temperature log, there is the differential temperature log, which offers the possibility of discerning temperature differences over a fixed depth interval. Instruments include either two sensors spaced some distance apart (one to several feet) or one sensor and an electronic memory that permits comparing the temperature actually measured to the temperature observed at a selected previous time. The device is set at zero in a reference temperature gradient in the borehole, and changes from this gradient are recorded as deflections from a baseline on the log.

If it is desired to obtain both temperature and differential temperature logs, both should be run simultaneously and prior to other logs, because the introduction of any tool into the hole will disturb the temperature stratification of the fluid column, so that repeat runs will not give as adequate a log as the first one.

Fluid Conductivity Logging

The purpose of fluid conductivity logging is to obtain a record of the vertical distribution of chemical water quality in the borehole. The log is obtained by a sensor consisting of two closely spaced electrodes; the voltage drop of an alternating current between the electrodes permits the determination of the borehole fluid's conductivity. Fluid conductivity is expressed as the reciprocal, resistivity, in ohm-meters, when it is intended to use the data obtained in the interpretation of resistivity logs. Conductivity is registered in micro-mhos per centimeter equaling 10,000 divided by the resistivity in ohm-meters. Running a temperature log simultaneously with the fluid conductivity log permits the most accurate conversion of the values obtained to resistivity or conductivity at standard temperature (see Fig. 4.16).

A relation between total dissolved solids and specific conductance can often be established empirically and thus a rapidly applicable tool for the observation of total groundwater salinity in boreholes becomes available. The concentration of the different ions in groundwater, however, cannot be recognized from conductivity. One of the most common uses of the fluid conductivity logs is the determination of freshwater–saltwater interfaces in wells.

Fluid Movement Logging

The observation of natural or induced flow within a borehole is a useful tool in well construction and groundwater investigations. Devices used to determine vertical and horizontal flow velocities in boreholes are impeller current meters, thermal current meters, and various systems based on the observation of the movement of injected tracers.

This logging method is applied to identify, in wells open to various aquifers with different heads, zones of passage of water from one aquifer to another, and to locate main contributing zones in secondary porosity aquifers. Most fluid movement logging observes vertical flow. Techniques for measuring horizontal flow have been developed (Moser, 1972; Klotz, 1977). Logs with the most commonly used impeller-type current meter are run with the sensor device moving up and down the hole at a relatively constant speed. The rotation of the impeller sends pulses to the recorder, where they are integrated. A fluid movement log run in a stagnant column of water would show a straight trace both in the up and down direction. Where vertical flow occurs, deflections in opposite directions are recorded on the up and down trip. With a moving current meter, rates of flow can be detected that are too small to affect the instrument when it is in a stationary position.

Tracer techniques are recommended in cases of extremely low flow speeds.

The sensitivity of the current meter can be greatly improved by using inflatable packers to force most of the flow through the instrument.

Thermal current meters contain a heating element located between two thermistors in a small-diameter tube. The amount of heating registered is inversely related to the fluid velocity through the tube. The apparatus must be calibrated empirically. Flow velocities observed range from 0.5 to 25 m/min, with errors of not more than 0.15 m/min at low velocities and 0.30 m/min at high velocities.

FURTHER READINGS

Alger, R. P. (1966). Interpretation of electric logs in fresh-water wells in unconsolidated formations. *Soc. Prof. Well Log Analysts, 7th Annu. Logging Symp., Tulsa, Okla. Trans.* pp. CC1–CC25.

Bennet, G. D., and Patten, E. P., Jr. (1960). Borehole geophysical methods for analyzing specific capacity of multi-aquifer wells. *U.S. Geol. Surv., Water-Supply Pap.* No. 1536-A, 1–25.

Boschart, R. A. (1969). Ground electromagnetic methods. *Min. Groundwater Geophys., Proc. Can. Centennial Conf. Min. Groundwater Geophys.* pp. 67–80.

Botezatu, R. (1971). Sur la nature de certaines anomalies gravimetriques dans les régions a dépots carbonates epais de Roumanie. *Acta Geol. Acad. Sci. Hung.* **15**(1/4), 351–356.

Brown, D. L. (1971). Techniques for quality-of-water interpretations from calibrated geophysical logs, Atlantic coastal area. *Ground Water* **9**(4), 25–38.

Burke, K. B. S. (1969). A review of some problems of seismic prospecting for groundwater in surficial deposits. *Min. Groundwater Geophys., Proc. Can. Centennial Conf. Min. and Groundwater Geophys.* pp. 569–579.

Burke, K. B. S. (1973). Seismic techniques in exploration of Quaternary deposits. *Geoexploration* **2**(4), 207–231.

Carpenter, G. C., and Bessarab, D. R. (1964). Case histories of resistivity and seismic ground water studies. *Ground Water* **2**(1), 22–25.

Carroll, R. D. (1966). Rock properties interpreted from sonic velocity logs. *J. Soil Mech. Found. Div., Proc. Am. Soc. Civ. Eng.* **92**(SM2), Pap. No. 4715, 43–51.

Cartwright, K. (1974). Tracing shallow groundwater systems by soil temperatures. *Water Resour. Res.* **10**(4), 847–855.

Collet, L. S. (1969). Resistivity mapping by electromagnetic methods. *Min. Groundwater Geophys. Proc. Can. Centennial Conf. Min. Groundwater Geophys.* pp. 615–625.

Croft, M. G. (1971). A method of calculating permeability from electric logs. *Geological Survey Research, 1971: U.S. Geol. Surv., Prof. Pap.* No. 750-B, B265–B269.

Dobrin, M. B. (1976). "Introduction to Geophysical Prospecting." McGraw-Hill, New York.

Doll, H. G. (1949). Introduction to induction logging and application to logging of wells drilled with oil-base mud. *J. Pet. Technol.* **1**, 148–162.

Doll, H. G. (1951). The laterolog, a new resistivity logging method with electrodes using an automatic focusing system. *Trans. Am. Inst. Min. Met. Eng.* **192**, 305–316.

Eaton, G. P., and Watkins, J. S. (1969). The use of seismic refraction and gravity methods in hydrogeological investigations. *Min. Groundwater Geophys., Proc. Can. Centennial Conf. Min. Groundwater Geophys.* pp. 544–568.

Flathe, M. and Homilius, J. (1973). Geophysik. *In* "Die Wassererschliessung," by H. Schneider, pp. 201–313. Vulkan-Verlag, Essen, 1973.

Flathe, M., and Homilius, J. (1969). Interpretation of geolectric resistivity measurements for solving hydrogeological problems. *Min. Groundwater Geophys., Proc. Can. Centennial Conf. Min. Groundwater Geophys.* pp. 580–597.

Ginzburg, A., and Levanon, A. (1976). Determination of a saltwater interface by electric resistivity soundings. *Bull. IASH* **21**(4), 561–568.

Guyod, H., and Shane, L. E. (1969). "Geophysical Well Logging. Vol. 1: Logging—Acoustical Logging." Hubert Guyod, Houston, Texas.

Heigold, P. C., Gilkeson, R. M., Reed, P. C., and Cartwright, K. (1978). Mapping aquifer transmissivity by surface electrical soundings. *EOS, Trans. Am. Geophys. Union* **59**(4), 280. (Abstr.)

Heiland, C. A. (1946). "Geophysical Exploration." Prentice-Hall, Englewood Cliffs, New Jersey.

Hempen, G. L. (1978). Detection of solution features in karst terrain; *EOS, Trans. Am. Geophys. Union* **59**(4), 221. (Abstr.)

Huntley, D. (1978). On the detection of shallow aquifers using thermal infrared imagery. *Water Res. Resear.* **14**(6), 1075–1083.

Ibrahim, A. and Hinze, W. J. (1972). Mapping buried bedrock topography with gravity. *Ground Water* **10**(3), 18–23.

Issar, A., and Levanon, A. (1974). The use of geophysical methods in hydrological investigations in Israel. *Bull. IASH.* **19**(2), 199–217.

Johnson, D. M., and Stewart, M. T. (1978). Resistivity study of the coastal discharge of a carbonate aquifer. *EOS, Trans. Am. Geophys. Union* **59**(4), 280. (Abstr.)

Keller, G. V., and Frischknecht, F. C. (1966). "Electrical Methods in Geophysical Prospecting." Pergamon, Oxford.

Keller, G. V., and Frischknecht, F. C. (1969). Application of resistivity methods in mineral and ground water exploration. *Min. Groundwater Geophys., Proc. Can. Centennial Conf. Min. Groundwater Geophys.* pp. 109–122.

Keys, W. S. (1968). Well-logging in groundwater hydrology. *Groundwater.* **6**(1), 10–18.

Keys, W. S. and MacCary, L. M. (1971). Application of borehole geophysics to water resources investigations. In "Techniques of Water Resources Investigations of the United States Geological Survey," Book 2, Chap. E1. U.S. Gov. Print. Off., Washington, D.C.

Klotz, D. (1977). "Berechnung der Filtergeschwindigkeit der Grundwasserströmung aus Tracerverdünungsversuchen in einem Filterpegel," Rep. R149. Ges. Umwelt und Strahlenforsch. G. M. B. H., Munich, Germany.

Lennox, D. M., and Carlson, V. (1969). Integration of geophysical methods for groundwater exploration in the prairie provinces, Canada. *Min. Groundwater Geophys., Proc. Can. Centennial Conf. Min. Groundwater Geophys.* pp. 517–535.

Linck, C. J. (1963). Geophysics as an aid to the small water well contractor. *Ground Water* **1**(1), 33–37.

Lynch, E. J. (1962). "Formation Evaluation." Harper, New York.

Malvik, O., Burmaster, R. F., and Sharp, J. M. (1978). Geophysical delineation of buried river valley aquifers in North-Western Missouri. *EOS, Trans. Am. Geophys. Union* **59**(4), 221. (Abstr.)

May, P. R. (1968). Gravimetric estimation of depth to aquifers in the Hatzeva area, Arava valley, Israel. *Isr. J. Earth Sci.* **17**(1), 30–43. Weizman Science Press, Jerusalem.

Merkeland, R. H., and Kaminski, J. T. (1972). Mapping ground water by using electrical resistivity with a buried current source. *Ground Water* **10**(2), 18–25.

Moore, G. K., and Deutsch, M. (1975). ERTS imagery for ground-water investigations. *Ground Water* **13**(2), 214–226.

Moser, H. (1972). Verwendung von kuenstlich zugegebenen radioaktiven isotopen zur Messung der Geschwindigkeit und Richtung von Grundwasser. *Gas, Wasser, Abwasser* **52**, 157–173.

Norris, S. L. (1972). The use of gamma logs in determining the character of unconsolidated sediments and well construction features. *Ground Water* **10**(6), 14–21.

Orellana, E. (1961). Criterios erroneos en la interpretacion de sondeos electricos. *Rev. Geofis.* **20**, 207–227.

Page, L. M. (1969). The use of the geoelectric method for investigating geologic and hydrologic conditions in Santa Clara county, California, *J. Hydrol.* **7**(2), 167–177.

Patten, E. P., Jr., and Bennet, G. D. (1963). Application of electrical and radioactive well logging to ground water hydrology. *U.S. Geol. Surv., Water-Supply Pap.* No. 1544-D.

Richard, B. H., Lillie, J. T., and Daju, R. A. (1978). Gravity studies of the Hanford Reservation, Washington. *EOS, Trans. Am. Geophys. Union* **59**(4), 221. (Abstr.)

Sabins, F. F. (1978). "Remote Sensing, Principles and Interpretation." Freeman and Co.

Schlumberger Well Surveying Corp. (1958). "Introduction to Schlumberger Well Logging," Schlumberger Doc. No. 8. Houston, Texas.

Schlumberger Well Surveying Corp. (1966). "Log Interpretation Charts." Houston Texas.

Schwartz, F. W., and McClymont, G. L. (1977). Application of surface resistivity methods. *Ground Water* **15**(3), 197–202.

Spangler, D. P, and Libby, F. J. (1968). Application of the gravity survey method to watershed hydrology. *Groundwater* **6**(6), 21–26.

Stallman, R. W. (1963). Computation of groundwater velocity from temperature data. *U.S. Geol. Surv., Water-Supply Pap.* No. 1544-M, H36–H46.

Stewart, M. T. (1978). Gravity survey of a deep buried valley system. *EOS, Trans. Am. Geophys. Union* **59**(4), 281. (Abstr.)

Strange, W. E. (1969). The use of gravimeter measurements in mining and groundwater exploration. *Min. Groundwater Geophys. Proc. Can. Centennial Conf. Min. Groundwater Geophys.* pp. 46–50.

Tripp, A. C. (1978). Electromagnetic and resistivity sounding profiling in groundwater exploration. *EOS, Trans. Am. Geophys. Union* **59**(4), 221. (Abstr.)

von Seggern, David (1967). Electromagnetic mapping of Hawaiian lava tubes. *Hawaii Univ. Water Resour. Res. Cent., Tech. Rep.* No. 8.

Walker, T. (1962). Fractive zones vary acoustic signal amplitudes. *World Oil* **154**(6).

Wallace, D. E. (1970). Some limitations of seismic refraction methods in geohydrological surveys of deep alluvial basins. *Ground Water* **8**(6), 8–13.

Ward, S. H. (1969). Airborne electromagnetic methods. *Min. Groundwater Geophys., Proc. Can. Centennial Conf. Min. Groundwater Geophys.* pp. 86–108.

Welex—A Division of Halliburton Service (1968). "Charts for the Interpretation of Well Logs," Welex Bull. A 133. Houston, Texas.

Worthington, P. F. (1976). Hydrogeophysical equivalence of water salinity, porosity and matrix conduction in arenaceous aquifers. *Ground Water* **14**(4), 224–232.

Wyllie, M. R. J. (1963). "The Fundamentals of Well Log Interpretation." Academic Press, New York.

Zohdy, A. A. R., Eaton, G. P., and Mabey, D. R. (1974). "Application of Surface Geophysics to Groundwater Investigations." Book D in the series Techniques of Water Resources Investigation. U.S. Geol. Survey, U.S. Gov. Print. Off., Washington, D.C.

CHAPTER

5

Drilling for Exploration
and Water Supply

5.1 DRILLING TECHNIQUES

The excavation of a deep narrow hole with vertical walls poses three major problems:

(a) The rock has to be disintegrated into pieces ("cuttings") of manageable size;

(b) The cuttings have to be removed from the hole;

(c) The vertical walls have to be prevented from collapsing.

These problems are solved in different ways by the two principal drilling methods, *percussion* (*cable tool*) and *rotary* drilling. There are also a number of variants, such as *reverse circulation*, for relatively shallow boreholes with very large diameters, *air rotary* drilling for small diameter boreholes above the saturated zone, and others. For a detailed discussion of well-drilling techniques that is beyond the scope of this text the reader is referred to Further Readings. The relative merits of the two principal methods are compared in Table 5.1.

The factors that have to be considered in the selection of a drilling method are

(1) the expected depths of the holes to be drilled,

(2) the number of holes,

TABLE 5.1

Comparison of the Two Principal Drilling Methods

	Percussion drilling	Rotary drilling
Speed of drilling	Around 3–15 m per shift[a]. Speed rapidly decreases at depths exceeding 200 m.	In hard rock formations 15–30 m per shift, in soft formations up to 150 m per shift[a].
Depth limit	Nominal, 500 m and more. Practical, in water well drilling, about 300 m.	Any depth practically required in water well drilling.
Diameter	Maximum diameter about 26 in.; 12–16 in. can be drilled even by medium sized rigs. However, frequent reductions of diameter may be necessary in order to stabilize the hole by a casing.	Drilling starts normally with $5\frac{7}{8}$ in. diameter. Larger diameters are obtained by subsequent reaming. For large-diameter holes heavy rigs are required. Long sections can be drilled without reducing diameter.
Technical complexity	Simple procedures. Work can be interrupted without endangering the hole. Casing of various diameters must be at hand, and casing program is difficult to establish in advance.	Complex procedures. Interruption of work may endanger hole. In desert locations provision of water for drilling fluid may be difficult and costly. Casing program can be established in advance.
Geologic information	Relatively large cuttings from hard rocks, but fines may become suspended in water. Mixing with caved-in particles from uncased parts of hole possible.	Size of hard-rock cuttings is 2–4 mm. Fines become emulsified in the drilling mud. Mixing of samples may occur because of the recirculation of the drilling fluid or of some caving. Electric logs and/or core samples are usually necessary.
Hydrologic information	Changes of water level are immediately noted. Water samples can be obtained by bailing periodically during drilling.	During drilling, hole must be filled with drilling fluid. Its sudden disappearance indicates the presence of very permeable formations. Otherwise, little or no hydrologic information can be obtained before the well is cleaned.[b]
Cleaning and development of borehole	With aquifers containing loose sand, backwashing, swabbing, surging, etc., may be necessary. Otherwise the borehole is easily cleaned and developed.	The "mud cake" adhering to the walls of the hole and mud that penetrated into the aquifer are often difficult to clean out. Treatment with mud-dispersing agents and prolonged surging and swabbing may be required.

[a] A shift is a working period of about 8 hr duration.
[b] This so-called loss of circulation depends also on the viscosity of the drilling fluid.

(3) the specific purpose of the holes (production, exploration, observation),

(4) the properties of the rock formations,

(5) available drilling rigs and accessories,

(6) cost,

(7) technical competence of the personnel and reputation of the drilling contractor, and

(8) availability of repair and other services and the general level of the technical infrastructure in the region.

The rated capacity of the rig should always exceed the expected depth of drilling. Percussion rigs are preferable when only a few boreholes have to be drilled, to relatively shallow depths, in sparsely settled areas. Rotary rigs are preferable when a large number of holes has to be drilled or when depths exceeding 300 m are required. For a large drilling program the publication of a national or even international tender to obtain the most suitable equipment at the best price can be considered. When only a few boreholes are planned, the rig will have to be selected from locally available equipment.

5.2   THE SELECTION OF WELL SITES

Drilling sites for water supply purposes are selected on the basis of hydrogeologic and planning considerations. Hydrogeologic criteria should take precedence in any relatively unknown area, and in areas where localized geologic features such as a fault, or a gravel lens, make it necessary to pinpoint the well site. In areas underlain by a well-known extensive aquifer in which depth, thickness, permeability, and water quality vary but little from place to place, decisions can be made mainly according to planning criteria.

Experience shows that in small projects the hydrogeologist is well advised to propose a definite site even if rather similar conditions can be expected over a certain area, instead of leaving the choice to the client.

The following hydrogeologic items of information must be specified for any proposed drilling site:

(1) *The depth, below ground, of the top of the aquifer*. Information is usually derived from geologic maps and cross sections and from geophysical measurements. If a geophysical measurement made at the well site contradicts previous assumptions, the site is doubtful and should be reevaluated, or, if possible, an inexpensive, small-diameter pilot hole should be drilled.

(2) *The depth, below ground, of water level.* In an unexplored area the approximate position of the water level may be inferred from the regional base level of drainage (the sea, a major stream, or a lake), or from a nearby natural outlet through which the aquifer presumably drains. In areas at high elevations efforts are usually concentrated on finding a perched aquifer that may exist above some impervious layer. In such a situation considerations regarding the base level of drainage are irrelevant. Reliable information can be obtained only by drilling down to the impervious layer in the hope of locating a sufficiently thick saturated section. A small-diameter exploration borehole may be advisable for this purpose. In areas where the elevation of the water level is known from other wells, predictions are, of course, easily made.

(3) *The depth of drilling.* In a thick aquifer the depth of drilling must be specified so that a sufficiently long screen can be inserted. A generous estimate should be adopted, leaving some margin for the uncertainty inherent in all hydrogeologic predictions. In a thin aquifer the well site has to be carefully chosen so as to make sure that the saturated portion of the aquifer enables a reasonable discharge and trouble-free operation of the pump. Drilling should be carried down to the bottom of the aquifer.

(4) *The sequence and properties of the rock layers penetrated by the well.* It is of particular importance to identify loose layers prone to caving, excessively hard layers, layers where very heterogeneous material will be encountered such as talus, and, in the case of rotary drillings, zones where loss of circulation is expected.

(5) *Indications regarding any factors that may adversely affect water quality.* If contamination from the surface is feared or if low-quality water is expected in the strata overlying the aquifer, allowance should be made for the eventual cementation of parts of the borehole.

(6) *The possibility of dynamic interference with any neighboring well.* This factor is easy to evaluate by estimating the transmissivity of the aquifer on the basis of data from these wells.

A typical dilemma that is often encountered in Israel and seems to be fairly universal is sketched below (Fig. 5.1).

(1) A well drilled into the known alluvial aquifer at location A will be in the middle of the irrigated area, its depth will not exceed 80 m, the initial water level will be only 15 m below ground. A serious disadvantage of this location is the small aquifer thickness, which will cause discharge to decline when the water level drops during drought years or after a period of intensive exploitation. If the well is to be used also for drinking water supplies, the likelihood of pollution by organic wastes constitutes an additional adverse factor.

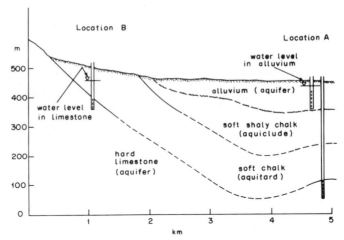

Fig. 5.1 Alternative borehole locations.

(2) A well drilled into a known limestone aquifer at location B near the outcrop area promises a more abudant and more reliable water supply. The disadvantages of this alternative are the cost of drilling to a depth of 150 m and the cost of constructing a conveyance facility to the area of demand; the water level at 40 m depth, which makes pumping more costly; and the inconvenience of servicing a well at some distance.

(3) A well drilled into the deep, confined part of the limestone aquifer at location A will necessitate drilling to an estimated depth of 470 m. The initial water level is expected to be shallow, and an abundant, dependable water supply is expected at this location.

The cheapest alternative, in terms of investment funds, is obviously a shallow well at site A. A client who finds it difficult to raise the required investment will have to be satisfied with this choice despite its hydrologic disadvantages. A more affluent client should be prepared to make a rational choice between alternatives (2) and (3).

A deep well at site A requires an investment for deep drilling; site B requires an investment for drilling to a moderate depth plus construction of a conveyance facility. Operating costs are cheaper at site A because of the lower pumping lift and because of its more convenient location. Since, in the long run, operating costs weigh more heavily than the one-time investment, site A will probably turn out to be more attractive in economic terms. However, the crucial factor that has to be considered is the reliability of hydrologic predictions at sites A and B, respectively. In particular, it is necessary to make sure that the limestone stratum at site A is really encountered at the expected depth, that it constitutes an extension of the limestone aquifer known to exist near location B, and that it is similar to it in respect to permeability and water quality. Hence, for a final decision, geophysical work is required, and a small-diameter exploration borehole may be suggested to dispel any lingering doubts.

The preceding examples refer to the location of a single well for water supply purposes. The *regional investigation* of groundwater resources requires a well-planned drilling campaign. The primary purpose of the campaign is to find out all relevant information on the aquifers in the region. A secondary purpose is, frequently, to provide urgently needed water supplies in certain locations. The simplest approach, drilling boreholes according to an arbitrarily defined mesh, is advisable only in small, geologically simple areas. For example, 100 boreholes would be required to cover an area of 1000 km² with a mesh 10 by 10 km. Even with this relatively large number of boreholes, crucial information can be missed.

A *scientifically planned* drilling campaign must be based on working hypotheses regarding prospective aquifers, their extent and distribution in the region, and their probable hydrologic regime. It may call for a dense spacing of boreholes in some areas and much wider spacing in others. The campaign should include small-diameter exploration boreholes as well as large-diameter boreholes, because only these can provide tangible proof for the existence of exploitable groundwater and the necessary data for the adequate planning of a supply system. Geophysical measurements during the campaign are necessary for the selection of drilling sites and for the calibration and updating of geophysical work in the light of knowledge acquired from new holes. Arrangements must be made for the continuous evaluation of new data acquired from boreholes and for the updating of existing concepts (see Section 5.6).

In the initial stages of exploration, efforts should concentrate on the most promising sites. Quite apart from their practical value, early successess enhance the investigator's authority and enable him to pursue subsequent stages of the work in a systematic manner. Once some success has been achieved, more doubtful sites may be tested. Reluctance to take calculated risks retards progress. The investigator who is too hesitant may have only successes to his credit, but he may also have missed some excellent opportunities.

For the exploration of problematic sites less expensive small-diameter exploration boreholes should be considered. Sometimes it is proposed to drill a slim hole with a view of widening it to an exploitable diameter if positive indications are obtained. This course of action looks attractive because it seems to reduce the investment sunk in "unproductive" drilling.

Under favorable circumstances this may be true, but generally the procedure is more expensive, in terms of rig time, than drilling a new borehole at the required diameter. Failures must be carefully analyzed. If this is not done, the same error may unknowingly be committed again and again.

The regional program should include boreholes for testing negative indications, such as the suspected existence of saline water at the bottom of a very thick aquifer, the doubtful supply potential of an aquitard, and others. The damage that plausible but unproved assumptions can do will be illustrated by a few examples from Israel.

Large parts of the confined carbonate aquifer in central Israel were for a long time considered as practically unexploitable because drilling to a shallow depth below the confining layer yielded brackish water, and it was assumed that water quality was bound to become worse with depth. When deep boreholes were eventually drilled, it became apparent that salination occurs at the contact with confining marly layers and that the rest of the aquifer with a thickness of about 700 m contains excellent water.

An aquitard composed of Eocene chalk southeast of Tel Aviv was assumed to be exploitable because a few very ancient shaft wells in the area yielded moderate discharges, and it was assumed that modern methods of exploration and drilling could easily repeat these results, or even improve on them. Exploratory drilling showed, however, that the ancient wells had been dug with consummate skill at the very few locations where karstic solution phenomena rendered the chalk more permeable. These ancient successes could not be repeated elsewhere and eventually the whole aquitard had to be written off as a source of water supply.

Drilling in the mountainous terrain near Jerusalem and in Galilee was long delayed because of the preconceived notion that the regional water table could be expected only near Mediterranean sea level, far too low for economic exploitation. Deep exploratory drilling showed eventually that the water table, controlled by structural and stratigraphic features, is situated at much higher elevations and that excellent producing wells can indeed be drilled in suitable locations.

In conclusion, the following seven rules for the planning of a drilling campaign are proposed:

(1) Formulate working hypotheses concerning the most promising drilling sites.

(2) Drill the first few holes in locations that promise early success.

(3) Regard small-diameter exploration holes as investment into the acquisition of knowledge, not as unproductive drilling.

(4) Analyze failures and draw the necessary conclusions.

(5) Do not accept "obvious" but ill-documented notions that are current in the area without subjecting them to the test of drilling.

(6) Have the courage to substantiate all assumptions, including disagreeable ones.

(7) Arrange for the continuous evaluation and feedback of all the information acquired by drilling, whether successful or not.

5.3 DESIGN CRITERIA FOR PRODUCTION BOREHOLES

The diameter of the well must be wide enough to accommodate a pump of the required size, at a depth that exceeds by a few meters the foreseeable lowermost pumping water level.

When the depth of pump setting is determined, allowance must be made for the expected drawdown during operation, for seasonal fluctuations, and for regional decline of the water table that will occur when the aquifer is fully exploited. Restrictions on the technically feasible depths of pump settings imposed by inadequate casing diameters may eventually create a constraint on the exploitation of the aquifer, since well owners may insist that the water table should never be lower than the pumps in their wells, regardless of hydrologic criteria. Therefore a generous option for the depth of pump setting should be provided for in the diameter specifications.

The pump aggregate should be suspended vertically in the well without touching the casing. Therefore the casing itself must also be as vertical as possible. The recommended difference between the diameter of the pump and the diameter of the casing is 2–4 in., the larger figure becoming mandatory when the depth of the pump setting exceeds 100 m below ground. In order to ensure verticality of the casing, the borehole diameter should be at least 4 in. larger than the casing diameter. For example, if a 12-in. pump with a discharge of 400 m^3/hr is to be installed, a 16-in. casing is required, and the diameter of the borehole should be 20 in.

The well screen that enables the water to flow into the well should be installed below the pump setting, since the highly turbulent flow that occurs near the pump may erode the aquifer. The frictional losses of energy caused by the well screen (well losses, see Section 6.8) depend on the size of the individual holes and on the total area of screen openings. When the aquifer contains fine, loose material that must be prevented from being drawn into the well, a filter with very fine holes or a gravel pack is required in spite of the considerable energy losses involved. The total area of the well screen is given by diameter $\times \pi \times$ length. Hence, other factors being equal, the diameter of the screen plays a role in well performance. The highest percentage of openings per unit of screen surface is about 30% and is achieved by screens made of wire wound in spiral fashion around supporting rods. Perforated or louvered pipes are cheaper and sturdier, but their open surface area is generally 10% or less.

Water level measurements are carried out in the annular space between the pump and the casing. The installation of a very-small-diameter pipe ($\frac{1}{4}$ in.) is recommended. Water level measurements are indispensable not only for the purpose of hydrologic investigations but also for monitoring the technical condition of the well and the pumping equipment. When eventually the energy consumption of the equipment increases, the trouble may be due to a decline of the water level, to the clogging of the screen, or to the deterioration of the pump aggregate. If the water level can be measured, it is easy to diagnose the cause of the trouble without dismantling any part of the pump or the borehole (see Section 6.8).

The *annular space* between the casing and the walls of the hole may permit the entrance of pollutants from the surface or of loose material from the strata above the screen. In wells tapping confined aquifers, losses of water to overlying strata and even uncontrollable seepages around the casing may occur. Backfilling of the annular space with clay should be insisted on, and in some cases, cementation may be necessary.

5.4 DESIGN CRITERIA FOR OBSERVATION BOREHOLES

An observation borehole has to accommodate measuring devices, must facilitate withdrawal of small quantities of water, and must allow periodic cleaning of the screen. The upper casing is usually 4–8 in. in diameter and the diameter of the screen is 2–6 in. Observation holes with a diameter of 2 in. or less may do service for temporary purposes, such as interference tests, but they are easily damaged and almost impossible to repair. It is important to make sure that the screen is in good hydraulic contact with the aquifer. Rotary drilling of observation wells should be done only with clean water or very thin mud, since it is difficult to clean mud from a small-diameter hole. The condition of the screen should be tested at regular intervals by bailing the hole or pumping it with compressed air and observing water level recovery.

The water in the upper, cased section of the borehole interchanges very slowly with the water in the aquifer, even when the screen is open. In order to obtain a water sample for quality determination, the hole must first be bailed or pumped until a quantity of water equal at least to the volume of water in the well has been withdrawn. Submerged measuring devices such as conductivity cells must be lowered into the screened part of the hole.

The annular space between the casing and the hole should be cemented or at least backfilled with a clay-sludge so as to make sure that observations in the hole really refer to the strata they are intended to represent.

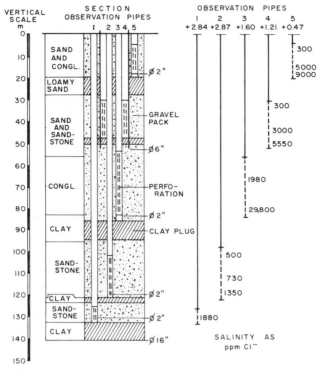

Fig. 5.2 Multiple-pipe observation well. (After Mandel, 1965.)

Sometimes separate observations in a number of vertically superimposed subaquifers are required. A schematic design for a multiple observation hole is shown in Fig. 5.2. Frequently, however, it is more expedient to drill a number of separate observation wells to different depths, starting with the deepest one.

5.5   SAMPLE COLLECTION DURING DRILLING

In percussion drilling, samples are taken from the material bailed from the bottom of the hole. The depth intervals between bailings are measured on the steel cable. The samples are regarded as representative of the interval drilled between bailings, but some material from higher strata may be admixed because of caving. In rare instances the driller may have thrown foreign material into the hole to facilitate drilling. The influence of caving can be minimized by following the bit closely with a temporary casing. The addition of foreign material should be noted in the driller's diary; for safety the material used for this purpose should be easily distinguishable from the native strata in the hole.

Hard rock samples from percussion drilling are of a fair size if the driller knows his job and uses a sharp bit. Soft material tends to form a sludge with water and may thus escape collection. However, some of it usually sticks to the bit, where it can be scraped off. The driller should be instructed to take samples at regular intervals, say every 3 m and whenever a change in formation is noticed. The samples are laid out on a plank for drying and the depth interval each one represents must be immediately and clearly marked. The supervising hydrogeologist should collect the samples on his visits to the site, note in his diary their preliminary description together with the information received from the driller and, finally, collect the samples for further analysis and safekeeping.

In rotary drilling the cuttings are continually brought to the surface by the drilling mud. The size of hard rock samples is usually around 2–4 mm; fine components become mixed with the mud and cannot be separated from it. The samples are taken to be representative of the simultaneously re-corded depth of drilling, although this is not quite correct, because it takes some time for the sample to travel from the bottom of the hole to the surface. In deep wells corrections have to be applied for this time lag. Admixture of material from higher strata is frequently caused by the circulating drilling mud and by cavings. A representative of the investigator, the *well sitter*, who should always be present at a site of rotary drilling, collects samples at depth intervals of about 5 m, prepares their preliminary description, and puts them into sample boxes for future detailed analysis.

It is frequently difficult to deduce correctly the nature and sequence of the natural strata from an examination of the rotary drill samples alone. For reliable correlations a geophysical well log is almost always necessary, and in important parts of the hole, *core samples* may have to be taken with the aid of a *core barrel*. However, this procedure is costly in terms of rig time, since it involves dismantling and reassembling the entire drill stem twice in succession.

The *storage* of the expected large number of samples has to be organized in advance. Individual samples are often preserved in bags made of plastic, paper, or cloth. This method looks attractive because bags are easily obtained and they do not take up much space. However, a large number of bags makes an untidy heap, necessitating much shifting in order to get at the ones that are needed for inspection. Then each bag has to be opened, and after inspection of the sample it has to be closed again. After repeated handling, the bags become torn, spillage occurs, and labels are lost or become illegible.

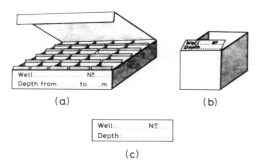

Fig. 5.3 Borehole sample box. (a) Cardboard box for storing formation samples, (b) interior cardboard box with flap, (c) detail of flap.

A much better storage method uses cardboard boxes of standard size, 20 by 20 cm approximately (see Fig. 5.3), each one containing 25 cardboard cells 4 by 4 cm large. The designation of the well and the depth interval of the samples are marked on a flap attached to each cell. Each box is used for keeping samples from one well only. The code number and location of the borehole as well as the total depth interval of samples in the box are clearly marked on its side. The boxes are tidily arranged on shelves so that their content can be read off without handling. Small pieces of core samples are accommodated in the same way; only large core samples that one wishes to preserve intact have to be stored separately. A reference in the appropriate cell shows where the complete core is to be found.

The complete collection of samples should be kept at least until the project of investigations is terminated. The samples will be needed for correlation and reexamination, even though it may seem that they have already been described in all possible detail. The question of what to do with the samples arises when the project is terminated. Future investigators, employing different methods of analysis or pursuing different aims, may be able to derive important information from material that seems to have outlived its utility. The best course of action is to transfer the whole collection to an appropriate permanent organization, such as a geologic survey or research department. If this cannot be done, at least a few of the most characteristic items of the collection should be kept by the contractor or the client.

5.6   THE BOREHOLE SECTION (WELL LOG)

A *borehole section* is a verbal or graphic description of the borehole. The description may emphasize one or several characteristics, such as technical

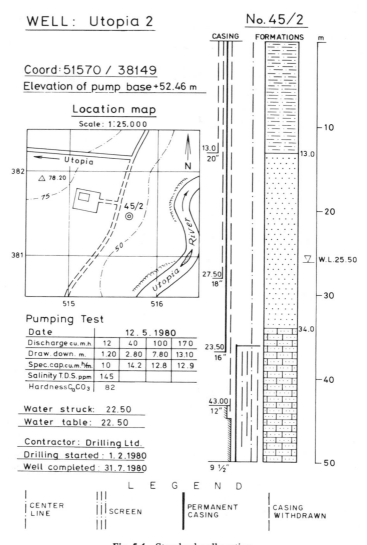

Fig. 5.4 Standard well section.

construction of the borehole, the geologic section, the results of geophysical measurements in the borehole, etc.

The *standard borehole section* (Figs. 5.4 and 5.5) conveys at a glance all the practically important features of the borehole, such as location and elevation, a rough geologic description, data on the technical construction, depth of water level when first measured, specific discharge during the first

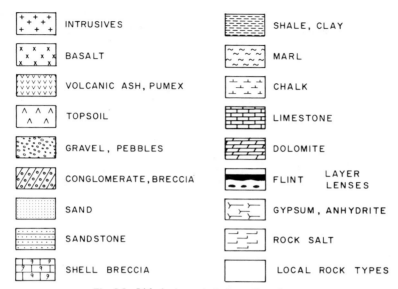

Fig. 5.5 Lithologic symbols for well section.

pumping test, etc. The section will be consulted when a change of the pump setting or deepening of the well is being planned, when the screen has to be cleaned, when the driller of a particular well must be identified and found for consultation, and for many similar purposes. The standard section should be drawn on transparent paper by the hydrogeologist who supervised the drilling. As long as his memory is still fresh, he can easily accomplish this task on the basis of his notes and perhaps referral to the driller's journal. When the job is unduly delayed, it becomes quite difficult to locate, decipher, and correlate items of information from "ancient" handwritten notebooks. There is also the danger that some notes may be irretrievably lost.

The *composite interpretive log* gives a detailed description of all geologic data. The log is prepared on the basis of a laboratory examination of the samples under a stereoscopic microscope with concurrent reference to geophysical well logs and the speed of penetration log. A restricted vocabulary of terms in a fixed sequence must be used for the verbal descriptions and a graphic representation is drawn on the same log form, side by side with the verbal one. The description includes lithologic characteristics, identification of microfossils, size and shape of the particles, hardness and porosity (from geophysical logs and drillers observations), and sometimes also the statistical distribution of various components in a sample (Maher, 1959).

The disadvantage of the composite interpretive log is the time required for its preparation. During a drilling campaign it is important to have reasonably detailed well logs soon after the completion of a number of holes since the information is needed to decide on subsequent drilling sites. Simplified shorter procedures focus attention on a few selected parameters that are deemed to be of particular relevance. This, of course, may introduce an element of personal judgment. The descriptions are usually given in verbal form only, thus saving the labor of drawing a meticulous graphic representation on the same sheet.

5.7 ORGANIZATION AND SUPERVISION OF A DRILLING CAMPAIGN

The following personnel are usually involved:

Investigator in charge ⎫
Geologist(s)   ⎪
Planning engineer(s)   ⎬   Usually on the investigator's staff
Well sitters   ⎪
Draftsmen   ⎭
Drillers   ⎫
Geophysicists   ⎪
Suppliers of other   ⎪
    services, such as   ⎬   Usually contractors
    Well logging   ⎪
    Chemical laboratory work ⎪
    Precise leveling   ⎭

All the data and technical specifications necessary for drilling at a specific site are collected and evaluated by a hydrogeologist, who may be aided by geophysicists, junior geologists, etc. The formal proposal for drilling is then discussed in the *drilling committee*, and authorization for drilling is eventually given through the *authorization for drilling* form (Fig. 5.6). This procedure ensures that the hydrogeologic problems of each proposed borehole are thoroughly discussed and that hydrogeologic assumptions and technical specifications are unequivocally presented and communicated to all concerned.

While drilling is in progress, each borehole has to be frequently visited and supervised by a hydrogeologist, preferably the one responsible for the selection of the site. The driller is required to keep a technical drilling diary and to take formation samples at specified intervals. Definition and description of the samples are carried out by the supervisor or by a person

AUTHORIZATION FOR DRILLING

Serial No. ..16......Date of issue.....March 15/72....Date of expiry...Sept. 15/72........

Location Ekvelt. 530. m. N. of. trigpoint. Ek/79. Purpose....Irrigation...................

Expected Section :

Surface to. 12 m. Alluvial. soils. gravel......from. 12.....to.25. m.. Sandstone.......

from..25.....to...60 .m.. Marly. Chalk...........from 60.......to.110. m. Chalk.and.herd.Cherts

from..110....to..175 .m.. herd. Limestone........from. ~~~~.to.~~~~~~~..............

Water will be struck at..110. m.m,   Static W'Level at 28 .m .below. surface...............

Specific disch..30......cum/hr/m,   Water Qual..110 .ppm .Chloride. ,. 270 .ppm. .TDS.......

Basis for predictions. Memo. by. H. Naor. dated. 28.. Feb. 1972...........................

Drilling Specifications :

Surface to...55 .m. 16". Casing.................from..55.....to...110 m.. 12" Casing.....

from. 110....to..175 .m.. 12". Screen..........from. ~~~~.to...~~~~~~~.....

from. ~~~~..to...~~~~~.................from. ~~~~.to..~~~~~~~.....

Additional instructions. Drilling .beyond. 175. m .only .according. to. written .instruction.

....

Administrative - Legal

Permission to drill on site... Agreement. with. landowner,. see. document. Ek/GB/17. of. March: 3/72

Site was shown to driller on.... March. 14/72........and marked by.. Heap. of. stones. and. staff

Proposer of well	Driller	Chairman Drilling Committee
H. Naor	*Z. Tivona*	*E. Ortega*
H. Naor	Z. Tivona	E. Ortega

Fig. 5.6 Authorization for drilling form.

authorized by him. Many drillers were trained to prepare their own sample description. These are by no means a substitute for description by a competent geologist.

If drilling progresses at a very rapid pace (i.e., in the case of drilling, by rotary rig) and whenever drilling enters a critical phase, the permanent presence of a *well sitter* at the site is required. The well sitters should be junior geologists or engineers (perhaps students in their last years of study), who thus acquire valuable practical experience. The well sitter collects the samples, gives a preliminary description of them, keeps an eye on the progress of drilling, and immediately notifies the supervisor when unexpected findings are encountered.

Each new borehole has to be developed by drawing mud and fine, loose particles from the part of the aquifer adjoining the screen. *Development procedures*, such as *plunging, jetting,* or *surging with air*, or simply intermittent pumping (Anon., 1966) have two aims: to ensure that the well produces clear water and to attain the largest possible specific discharge.

After development, a step drawdown and recovery test is carried out by provisional equipment in order to determine specifications for the permanent pumping aggregate, and a water sample is taken for complete chemical analysis. These operations, which may take one or two weeks, should be budgeted as an integral part of the drilling operation, since otherwise they may be stinted of funds and performed in a slipshod way.

Pending the installation of the permanent pumps the well has to be capped; an access pipe is left for water level observations and is marked by some clearly visible sign for easy identification in the field. Frequently it is advisable to surround the well with heavy obstacles as a safeguard against accidental damage by vehicles or farm machinery.

The drilling campaign is supervised by the *drilling committee*. Its regular members should be the investigator in charge as chairman, the hydrogeologists on the investigator's staff, a planning engineer, a representative of the driller, and other personnel as required by the topics to be discussed. When the campaign is in full swing, the committee should meet weekly or at least biweekly. The decisions of the committee are formulated by the chairman, without putting them to a formal vote, and summed up in a short, written resume.

The agenda of each meeting encompasses as a matter of routine the following items:

(1) *Progress of drilling on each site*. The driller's representative reports on the state of drilling, progress made, and difficulties encountered since the last meeting of the committee. His report is followed by a discussion and the relevant conclusions concerning the continuation of the work are formulated by the chairman.

(2) *Discussion of proposals for new boreholes*. Proposals for new boreholes are presented and after a discussion it is decided whether additional investigations (such as more detailed geologic surveys, geophysics, etc.) are necessary, or whether the proposal is accepted, deferred, or rejected. Problematic drilling sites may necessitate the preparation of a written memorandum by the proposer.

(3) *Authorization for the drilling of new boreholes*. Final authorization should be given solely on the standard *authorization for drilling* form that summarizes all the requisite information, apportions responsibilities, and

shows that all the necessary steps, prior to drilling, have been carried out (Fig. 5.6). The form authorizes the chairman to order drilling as specified, but it does not automatically compel him to do so. Thus the chairman reserves final power of decision, especially as regards financial arrangements and priorities.

A wise chairman will prepare a sufficient number of authorized drilling sites well in advance so that available rigs are always fully utilized, but he will avoid authorizing too many boreholes, the actual drilling of which is uncertain. Above all, he will keep a tight control on the drilling budget and inform the drilling committee whenever budgetary or other constraints make it necessary to modify the drilling program considerably.

FURTHER READINGS

Anderson, K. E. (1967). "Water Well Handbook," 2nd ed. Scholin Bros. Print. Corp., St. Louis, Missouri.

Anonymous (1966). "Ground Water and Wells." E. E. Johnson, Inc, St. Paul, Minnesota.

Anonymous (1968). "Manual of Water Well Construction Practices." Oregon Well Contractors Assoc., Portland.

Anonymous (1977). "Ground Water Manual." U.S. Dep. Inter., Bur. Reclama., U.S. Gov. Print. Off., Washington, D.C.

Burt, E. M. (1970). "Well Development: A Part of Well Completion; Principles and Application of Groundwater Hydraulics Conference." Michigan State Univ., East Lansing.

Campbell, M. D., and Lehrs, J. H. (1973). "Water Well Technology." McGraw-Hill, New York.

Coulter, A. W. and Gurley, D. G. (1971). "How to Select the Correct Sand Control System for Your Well," Repr. Pap No. SPE-3177. Soc. Pet. Eng. AIME, New York.

Gibson, U. D., and Singer, R. D. (1971). "Water Well Manual," Agency for International Development, Washington D.C.

Helweg, O. J. (1976). Fibonacci search for high-yield well sites. *Groundwater* **14**(2), 78–81.

Huisman, L. (1972). "Groundwater Recovery." Macmillan, New York.

Legette, R. M. (1950). Prospecting for groundwater geologic methods. *J. Am. Water Works Assoc.* **42**, 945–946.

Maher, J. C. (1959). The composite interpretive method of logging drill cuttings. *Oklahoma Geol. Surv., Guideb.* **8**.

Mandel, S. (1965). The design and instrumentation of hydrogeological observation networks. IASH publ. No. 68, 413–424.

Schneider, H. (1973). "Die Wassererschliessung." Vulkan Verlag, Essen.

Thomas, R. G. (1978). Principles of search techniques for hydrology. *Groundwater* **16**(4), 264–272.

Turk, G. (1977). Two-dimensional searches for high-yield well sites. *Groundwater* **15**(4), 267–275.

6

Pumping Tests

6.1 CONFINED AQUIFER TESTS

The nonequilibrium well formula (Theis, 1935) describes the spread of a cone of depression from a pumped well into the aquifer (Fig. 6.1). The derivation of the formula is based on the following, highly idealized assumptions: (1) The aquifer is *confined, homogeneous, isotropic,* and *infinite* (i.e., the boundaries are so far distant that their influence is not felt during the test). (2) The well is *fully penetrating*; it is drilled down to the base of the aquifer and perforated through its entire saturated thickness. (3) Before pumping starts, the water level is horizontal and constant in time. (4) The discharge of the pumped well remains constant during the test. (5) The well is infinitely narrow (*linear sink*). (6) Water is released instantaneously from storage when the hydraulic head is lowered.

Under these conditions the drawdown in an observation well at a distance r from the pumped well is given by

$$s = \frac{Q}{4\pi T} W(u) \qquad (6.1a)$$

where u is defined by

$$u = \frac{S}{4T} \frac{r^2}{t} \qquad (6.1b)$$

The well function $W(u)$ is defined by the infinite series

$$W(u) = -0.5772 \cdots - \ln u + u - \frac{u^2}{2 \times 2!} + \frac{u^3}{3 \times 3!} - \cdots \qquad (6.1c)$$

140

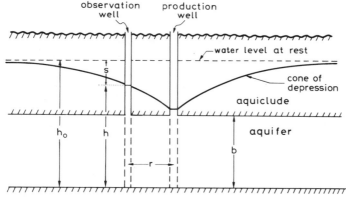

Fig. 6.1   Confined aquifer—cone of depression around a fully penetrating well.

where $s = h_{(0)} - h_{(t)}$ is the drawdown, $h_{(0)}$, $h_{(t)}$ are the elevations of the water level above an arbitrary reference datum before and during pumping, respectively, $T = Kb$ is the transmissivity, K the hydraulic conductivity, b the thickness of the aquifer, Q the discharge of the well, S the storativity, r the distance from pumping well to observation well, and t the time since pumping started.

The term r^2/t in Eq. (6.1b) substitutes a time series of drawdowns measured in one observation well for a spatial picture of drawdowns (the *cone of depression*) at a given time. The utility of the well function stems largely from this property.

The *type curve*, a plot of log $1/u$ versus log $W(u)$, is shown in Fig. 6.2. This way of defining the free variable makes the time increase from left to right in accordance with convention.

When a sequence of water level measurements in one or several observation wells is available, the aquifer parameters T and S can be extracted from Eq. (6.1a) by a *curve fitting method*. A plot of log t/r^2 versus log s is drawn on the same scale as the type curve on transparent paper and then matched as closely as possible against the type curve, keeping the coordinates of both sheets parallel. Any point on the matched curves is then selected and marked by a needle stuck through both sheets of paper. The coordinates of *the match point* are as follows: on the plot of observations, t/r^2, s; on the type curve, $1/u$, $W(u)$. T and S are determined from the values of the coordinates with the aid of Eqs. (6.1a) and (6.1b).

A short record of data from one observation well can almost always be fitted against some part of the type curve with reasonable accuracy, even if the actual situation strays very far from assumptions (1)–(6), thus leading to

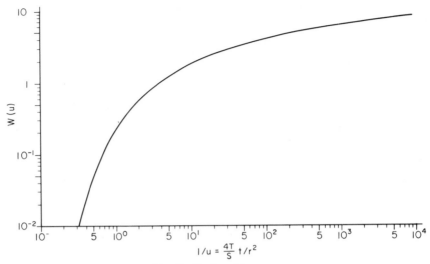

Fig. 6.2 Confined aquifer type curve.

spurious results. Deviations from the theoretical assumptions are more easily spotted when a long record of data, preferably from several observation wells, is available (see Section 6.12).

Another method uses the *logarithmic approximation* of the well function (Jacob, 1950). The variable u decreases with time and the infinite series of Eq. (6.1c) eventually converges toward the sum of its first two terms. For example, for $u=0.01$, $W(u)=4.0379$, whereas the sum of the first two terms is 4.024.

Substitution of the logarithmic approximation in Eq. (6.1a) yields

$$\text{if} \quad u \leqslant 0.01, \qquad s \approx \frac{2.30Q}{4T} \log \frac{2.25Tt}{Sr^2} \qquad (6.2a)$$

where the numerical constant has been subsumed into the logarithmic term and the natural logarithm has been replaced by the decimal one.

The semilogarithmic plot s versus t/r^2 is a straight line (see Fig. 6.3). Transmissivity is determined by measuring the slope of this line with the t/r^2 axis. One log cycle has, by definition, unit length; hence

$$\Delta_t s = \frac{2.30Q}{4\pi T} \qquad (6.2b)$$

where $\Delta_t s$ = change of s over one log cycle.

For the computation of storativity the line is extrapolated to zero drawdown, thus defining a point with the coordinates

$$t/r^2 = \left(t/r^2 \right)_0 \qquad \text{and} \qquad s=0$$

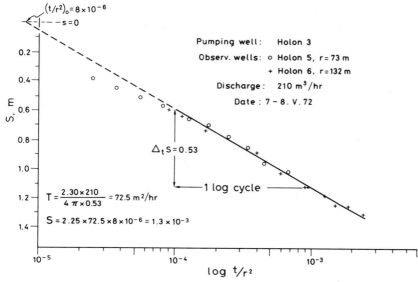

Fig. 6.3   Interpretation of pumping test by logarithmic approximation.

Since s can become zero only when the argument of the log term in Eq. (6.2a) is 1, it follows that

$$S = 2.25T(t/r^2)_0 \qquad (6.2c)$$

The measured depths of the water level may be substituted for the drawdowns, thus saving computations.

This method of interpretation is less laborious than curve fitting. Failure of the data to plot linearly reveals deviations from the theoretical assumptions. However, the mere fact that the plot of measurements from a single observation well defines a straight line does not constitute a guarantee against spurious results.

In a confined aquifer u can be expected to become sufficiently small after a relatively short period of pumping, since storativity is in the neighborhood of 10^{-4}. In thick phreatic aquifers (see Section 6.2) prohibitively long pumping tests may be required to justify the use of this formula.

6.2   PHREATIC AQUIFER TESTS

In a phreatic aquifer most of the water is released from the void space in the cone of depression by relatively slow gravity drainage. Because of this *delayed yield*, storativity determined by the test steadily increases from a small initial value to a limiting value, the effective porosity (Neuman, 1972).

The time drawdown plot of a very long test tends to have a wriggly shape (Fig. 6.13) because of the initial increase and eventual decay of the delayed yield. A rather complicated method of interpreting such a curve is cited by Walton (1970). Alternatively, the largest value of S, obtained by fitting the last few observations of a long pumping test against the Theis type curve, may be taken as indicative of the specific yield.

Unfortunately, a controlled pumping test can rarely be kept going for more than a week, and it is doubtful whether the specific yield thus obtained is applicable to computations involving several months or a year. For example, in the coastal aquifer of Israel the largest value of S, obtained from pumping tests of 10 days duration, is 0.17. Digital calibration of the aquifer based on seasonal (twice yearly) water level maps and on very accurate data of groundwater abstraction yielded values between 0.25 and 0.30.

A *phreatic aquifer* is termed *thick* when the drawdown is only a small fraction (say, less than 10%) of the saturated thickness. Such an aquifer is similar to a confined one, inasmuch as the saturated thickness may be regarded as constant during pumping. Therefore the Theis method may be employed to determine reliable values of transmissivity.

In a *thin phreatic aquifer* the thickness of the saturated section—and with it, transmissivity—changes considerably during the pumping test. As a consequence, drawdowns increase more than logarithmically with time and more than linearly with discharge.

According to Bentall (1963), the initial transmissivity of the aquifer can be determined by the Theis method, if corrected drawdowns are substituted for actually measured ones. The correction formula is

$$s' = s - s^2/2b(t) \qquad (6.3)$$

where s' is the corrected drawdown that would be observed in an equivalent confined aquifer, s is the observed drawdown, and $b(t)$ is the thickness of the saturated portion of the aquifer at the time of observation.

This formula is applicable only when the aquifer has been pumped long enough to establish quasi-steady-state conditions of flow (see following section).

6.3   STEADY-STATE FORMULAS

Steady-state methods stipulate that pumping must be continued until the water levels in the pumping and observation wells become constant in time. In an infinite aquifer a rigorously steady state cannot be attained but it is possible to define a *quasi-steady state* that justifies the application of these formulas. The steady-state formula for a confined or thick phreatic aquifer with two observation wells is

$$h_2 - h_1 = s_1 - s_2 = \frac{Q \ln r_2/r_1}{2\pi T} \tag{6.4}$$

where r_1, r_2 are distances of observation wells from the pumping well and h_1, s_1; h_2, s_2 are steady-state water level elevations and drawdowns.

Equation (6.4) may be derived by expressing s_1 and s_2 with the aid of Eq. (6.2a). It follows that $h_2 - h_1$ and hence also the gradient $(h_2 - h_1)/(r_2 - r_1)$ become independent of time as soon as the logarithmic approximation becomes justified. It should be noted, however, that this is true only for the gradient, not for the individual values h_1 and h_2, which continue to decrease with time. Therefore a *quasi-steady state* justifying the application of steady-state formulas is reached when the water level gradient in the tested region declines approximately parallel to itself, and this happens as soon as the logarithmic approximation becomes valid.

In order to judge whether a steady-state formula is applicable one has to carry out a time series of water level observations and to plot them on a semilog graph. However, in this case it is preferable to apply a nonsteady-state method that uses all the data, instead of relying only on a few selected water level measurements.

A steady-state formula applicable to a *thin phreatic* aquifer is

$$K = \frac{Q \ln r_2/r_1}{\pi\left(h_2^2 - h_1^2\right)} \tag{6.5}$$

where h_2 and h_1 are the elevations of the phreatic water levels measured above the horizontal base of the aquifer.

Equation (6.5) is sometimes adapted to observations in the pumping well only by writing Eq. (6.5) as

$$K = \frac{Q \ln r_e/r_w}{\pi\left(h_0^2 - h_w^2\right)} \tag{6.6}$$

where r_e is the *radius of influence*, the minimum distance at which the water level is not changed by pumping, r_w is the *effective radius* of the well (the distance from the center of the well at which Darcy's law becomes valid), h_0 is the initial water level, and h_w the water level measured in the pumping well.

It will be noted that h_w refers to a region of turbulent flow where Darcy's law is not valid, that r_w is not necessarily identical with the design diameter of the well, and that the radius of influence cannot strictly be defined. At best one may refer to a distance where the influence of pumping becomes "practically" negligible, which is, however, anybody's guess. Because of these curious features the use of Eq. (6.6) is not recommended.

6.4 PARTIALLY PENETRATING WELLS

A partially penetrating well (Fig. 6.4) forces the flow lines to converge vertically toward the screen, thus causing larger drawdowns than a fully penetrating one. In the vicinity of the well the flow pattern has the symmetry of a rotational ellipsoid; with increasing distance from the well it approaches cylindrical symmetry.

The steady-state flow pattern has been analyzed by Muscat (1937). Bentall (1963) gives correction procedures for the conversion of actually measured drawdowns to those that would be measured in a fully penetrating well, assuming steady-state flow. A type curve procedure for pumping tests in partially penetrating wells that are open at the base of the aquifer has been proposed by Walton (1970).

Drawdown formulas for the nonsteady state in a confined isotropic aquifer have been developed by Hantush (1961), who concludes

(1) The Theis formula can be used if $r \geqslant 1.5b$ (r is the distance between pumping and observation well and b the aquifer thickness) or if the observation well is fully penetrating.

(2) Regardless of the location of the wells and the space portions of their screens, the time drawdown curves will approach the slope of fully penetrating conditions when $t \gg b^2 S / 2T$.

Thus a pumping test in a partially penetrating well may yield a good approximation of transmissivity if the observation well is at a sufficiently large distance or if pumping is continued for a sufficiently long time. It is obvious that in an unknown area the application of these criteria may be rather hazardous.

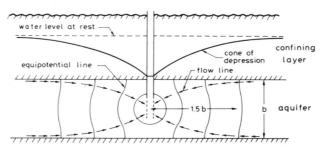

Fig. 6.4 Flow toward partially penetrating well in confined aquifer.

6.5 VERTICAL ANISOTROPY

Sedimentary and alluvial aquifers tend to be anisotropic, the major axes of permeability being directed along the bedding planes and the minor axis at right angles to them. In uniform aquifers horizontal permeability is about one order of magnitude larger than the vertical one; in thinly stratified aquifers (e.g., lacustrine or deltaic sediments) anisotropy may be much more marked.

The flow net in such an aquifer can be obtained from an isotropic flow net by a transformation of scales (DeWiest, 1970):

$$x' = x \sqrt{\frac{K_v}{K_h}} \qquad (6.7)$$

where x is a distance on the horizontal axes; K_v, K_h are vertical and horizontal permeabilities, respectively; and x' is the same distance on the transformed horizontal axes. The isotropic flow net with flow lines and equipotential lines intersecting at right angles is drawn on a scale distorted according to Eq. (6.7) and then replotted to true scale.

Vertical anisotropy increases the drawdown in a pumping well and enlarges the effect of partial penetration so that it becomes negligible if

$$r \geqslant 1.5b \sqrt{\frac{K_h}{K_v}} \qquad (6.8)$$

6.6 EFFECTS OF AQUIFERS WITH BOUNDARIES

An aquifer limited on one side by an impermeable *barrier boundary* is illustrated in Fig. 6.5a. The flow pattern in the aquifer half plane can be computed by assuming that the aquifer is infinite and that the *image well* shown in the figure operates simultaneously with the real one (Lang, 1960). The drawdown in an observation well is obtained by the addition of the drawdowns caused by the real and the image well, respectively. If the aquifer is limited by a *recharge boundary* (ideally, a freshwater lake with constant water level), the image well is assumed to recharge water and the influence caused by it is reckoned negatively.

In a pumping test the presence of a nearby boundary makes itself felt by a change of slope in the time drawdown plot (Fig. 6.5b). During the early part of the test only the influence of the real well is felt, during the later part the influence of the more distant image well is being added. The two parts are separated by the pronounced kink in the semilog plot. The drawdown(s)

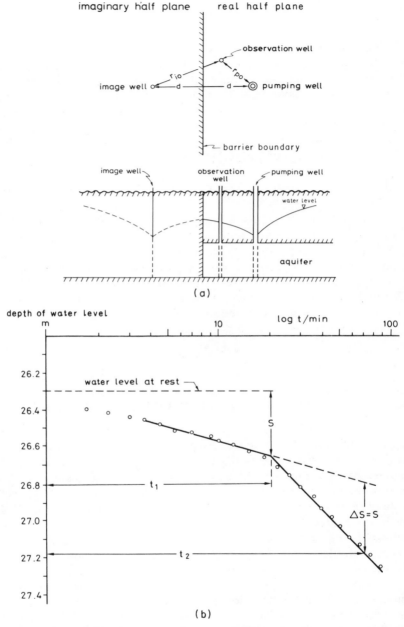

Fig. 6.5 (a)   Aquifer with one barrier boundary, (b)   determination of single barrier boundary. $t_1 = 20$ min, $t_2 = 70$ min, $r_{p0} = 86$ m. Distance of image well from observation well is $r_{i0} = \sqrt{70/20} \times 86 = 160.9$ m.

and the incremental drawdown Δs are given by

$$s = \frac{2.30Q}{4\pi T} \log \frac{2.25T}{S} \frac{t_1}{(r_{po})^2} \qquad (6.9a)$$

$$\Delta s = \frac{2.30Q}{4\pi T} \log \frac{2.25T}{S} \frac{t_2}{(r_{pi})^2} \qquad (6.9b)$$

if $\Delta s = s$,

$$r_{pi} = \sqrt{t_2/t_1}\, r_{po} \qquad (6.10)$$

where s is the drawdown due to the real well, Δs the incremental drawdown due to the image well, t_1, t_2 are the time intervals for which s equals Δs, r_{po} is the distance between pumping and observation well, and r_{pi} the distance between pumping and image well.

The effect of multiple boundaries may be represented by constructing one image well across each boundary, images of each image well across all the other boundaries, etc., until the distances of the secondary images become so large that their influence is negligible. However, in practical applications one or, at most, two boundaries are all one can hope to identify by a pumping test.

Partial boundaries, like the edge of a confining layer separating two aquifer zones with strongly contrasting storativities, or the dividing line between two parts of the aquifer with strongly contrasting transmissivities, may cause similar effects in the time drawdown plot, but these cannot be interpreted by the method of images. Caution and reference to geologic data are strongly advisable when the interpretation of such a test is attempted.

6.7 LEAKY AQUIFERS

Figure 6.6 shows an aquifer, overlain by an aquitard, which, in turn, is overlain by a phreatic aquifer. Several varieties of such leaky aquifers have been investigated (Hantush, 1956, 1960). Only the simplest case will be referred to. The assumptions are (1) the elastic storativity of the aquitard is negligible as compared to the one of the semiconfined aquifer; (2) the water table in the phreatic aquifer remains practically constant throughout the test; and (3) the flow of water is vertical in the aquitard and horizontal in the aquifer.

When the well is pumped, water is diverted from the elastic storage of the semiconfined aquifer, and the cone of depression thus formed induces leakage through the aquitard from the constant potential source (the phreatic aquifer) above it. Eventually, when the cone of depression spreads out far enough, all the water is diverted from seepage and a steady state is reached.

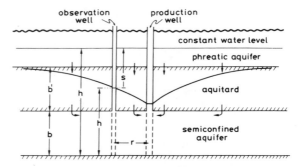

Fig. 6.6 Flow toward well in leaky aquifer.

The drawdown in an observation well is given by

$$s = \frac{Q}{4\pi T} W(u, r/B) \tag{6.11}$$

where $B = \sqrt{T/(K'/b')}$, K'/b' is the *seepage factor*, k' the vertical permeability of the aquitard, and b' the thickness of the aquitard.

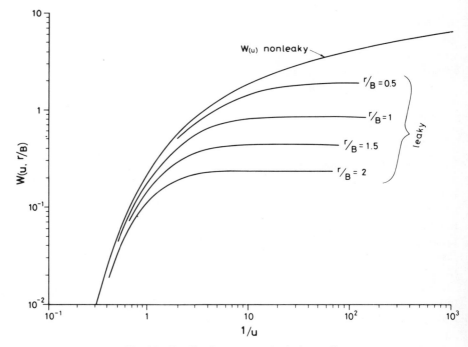

Fig. 6.7 Family of type curves for leaky aquifer.

The family of well functions $W(u, r/B)$ has been tabulated (Walton, 1970). A few type curves of the family are shown in Fig. 6.7. The horizontal portions of the curves indicate that a steady state is eventually attained.

An extension of the curve-matching procedure outlined in Section 6.1 enables the determination of the aquifer parameters when a time series of observations from observation wells is available. For each well the plot of observations, log t versus log s, is drawn; the curves are matched against the family of type curves; and T and S are determined by Eqs. (6.1a) and (6.1b). Then the values of r/B are noted from the matching type curves and the seepage coefficient k'/b' is determined from the definition of B [Eq. (6.11)]. If b' is known, k' can be computed.

When only one observation well is available it is often difficult to identify correctly the matching type curve. Two or more observation wells facilitate the procedure, since the observations from each well match a different type curve.

6.8   STEP DRAWDOWN TESTS FOR THE DETERMINATION OF WELL LOSSES

The drawdown in a pumping well reflects turbulent flow in the well and in its immediate vicinity and laminar flow in the aquifer (see Fig. 6.8). It is approximately given by the equation

$$s = s_{\text{lam}} + s_{\text{turb}} \approx \frac{2.30Q}{4\pi T} \log \frac{2.25Tt}{Sr_{\text{w}}^2} + CQ^\nu \tag{6.12}$$

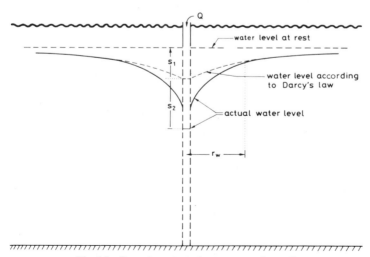

Fig. 6.8   Drawdown in and near a pumping well.

where r_w is the effective well radius inside which the flow becomes turbulent, v, C are parameters related to turbulent flow ($v>1$) and s_{lam}, s_{turb} are components of the drawdown resulting from laminar and turbulent flow, respectively.

Step drawdown tests enable the determination of the well losses (s_{turb}), which depend to a certain extent on the construction and development of the well. The theory of step drawdown tests assumes that the parameter v equals 2 and that the well is pumped at different discharge rates Q_1, Q_i, Q_n for equal time intervals, say about one hour, at each rate, care being taken to let the water level fully recover between successive periods of pumping. Under these conditions Eq. (6.12) becomes

$$s_i \approx DQ_i + CQ_i^2 \qquad (6.13a)$$

where s_i is the drawdown caused by the discharge Q_i

$$D = \frac{2.30}{4\pi T} \log \frac{2.25Tt}{Sr_w^2} \qquad \text{(for } t=\text{const.)}$$

hence

$$s_i/Q_i \approx D + CQ_i \qquad (6.13b)$$

The slope of the plot Q_i versus s_i/Q_i indicates C.

In practical work it is desirable to eliminate time-consuming recovery periods and to avoid the frequent starting and stopping of the pump aggregate. The standard procedure is, therefore, to pump the well continuously and to change the discharge rate, stepwise, at equal time intervals Δt. Under these conditions the drawdown at the end of the second step is

$$s(2\Delta t) \approx \alpha Q_1(\log \beta \Delta t + \log 2) + \alpha(Q_2 - Q_1)\log \beta \Delta t + CQ_2^2 \quad (6.14a)$$

where $\qquad\qquad \alpha = 2.30/4\pi T, \beta = 2.25T/Sr_w^2.$

$$s(2\Delta t) = \alpha Q_1 \log 2 + DQ_2 + CQ_2^2 \qquad (6.14b)$$

The net drawdown, corrected for the influence of pumping at the previous rate Q_1, is given by an expression identical to Eq. (6.13b), namely,

$$s_{net} = DQ_2 + CQ_2^2 \qquad (6.14c)$$

Net drawdowns are determined by the graphic procedure shown in Fig. 6.9 and then plotted in order to obtain the linear relation.

The discharge of pumping installations can be varied only within certain limits by throttling the outlet pipe or by changing the rotational speed of the motor. These technical difficulties make it almost impossible to obtain more than four sufficiently distinct discharge rates. The plotted points often show

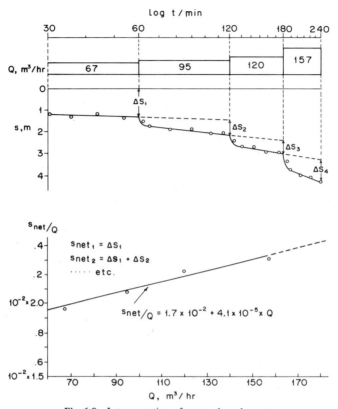

Fig. 6.9 Interpretation of a step drawdown test.

considerable scatter because of the many approximations that are involved in the theoretical derivation and, sometimes, because the well develops during the test itself.

In spite of this shortcoming, step drawdown tests are of great value in the following situations: (1) The optimal permanent pumping aggregate has to be specified on the basis of test pumping with a temporary pump, and it is necessary to predict the drawdown that will occur when the rated capacity of the permanent aggregate exceeds the maximum discharge during test pumping. (2) The discharge of a well declines, and one wishes to find out, without dismantling the installation, whether this is due to the deterioration of the pumping aggregate or of the screen. (3) When a well is developed by acidation, swabbing, etc., a step drawdown test before and after the development will measure the increase of hydraulic efficiency that has been obtained. (4) Several wells are drilled in the same aquifer according to different designs and one wishes to evaluate the merits of different well designs.

6.9 SINGLE WELL DRAWDOWN TEST

The drawdown as a function of time is observed in the well pumped at a constant discharge. The slope of the linear plot s versus $\log t$ enables the determination of transmissivity according to Eq. (6.2a). Storativity cannot be determined since the effective well radius r_w is not known.

Single well drawdown tests are difficult to carry out in practice. During the first few minutes the outlet pipes are still empty, the pump works against a very small pressure, and its actual discharge is much larger than the rated discharge. Therefore the initial part of the test during which the main portion of the drawdown occurs cannot be interpreted. Later on water levels tend to jump erratically because of minor variations of discharge that instantaneously change the nonlinear drawdown component. Additional adverse factors are the noise and the vibrations that accompany pumping and place a strain on the observer.

6.10 SINGLE WELL RECOVERY TEST

The well is pumped for 2 hr or more; then pumping is stopped and the recovery of the water level is observed. Stoppage of pumping is represented mathematically by the assumption that the well continues to be pumped at a constant rate and that, from the time of stoppage onward, injection of water is carried out into the same well at an equal rate, so that the imagined injection cancels the imagined continued pumping (Fig. 6.10).

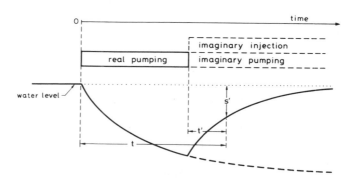

Fig. 6.10a Single well recovery test.

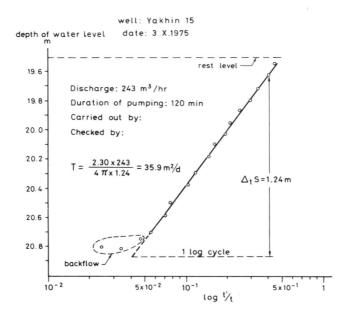

well: Yakhin 15
date: 3.X.1975
depth of water level

Discharge: 243 m³/hr
Duration of pumping: 120 min
Carried out by:
Checked by:

$$T = \frac{2.30 \times 243}{4\pi \times 1.24} = 35.9 \, m^2/d$$

$\Delta_t S = 1.24 \, m$

1 log cycle

backflow

rest level

Fig. 6.10b   Interpretation of single well recovery test.

Pumping causes a drawdown; injection causes *upconing* (drawdown with inverted sign). When both processes are expressed by the logarithmic approximation [Eq. (6.2a)] and combined, the following formula results:

$$s' = \frac{2.30Q}{4\pi T} \log t/t' \tag{6.14}$$

where s' is the residual drawdown after the pump has been stopped, t the time since pumping started, and t' the time since pumping stopped (for the definition of symbols see also Fig. 6.10a).

The slope of the linear graph s' versus $\log t/t'$ enables the determination of T. In practical work it is convenient to plot the depths of water levels instead of drawdowns and to plot t/t' so that the line ascends and is thus distinguishable from a drawdown graph (see Fig. 6.11). This test is rather insensitive to fluctuations of discharge during pumping, and it is easier to carry out than a single well drawdown test.

When pumping is terminated, the water in the pump column rushes back into the well and causes a sudden rise of the water level. After a few minutes the disturbance dies down and regular recovery according to Eq. (6.14) starts. The disturbed water levels may be corrected by applying the formula of the slug test [Eq. (6.15b)], putting V equal to the volume of water in the

HYDROLOGIC   PUMPING   TEST

Sheet No...*1*...

of...*4*...Sheets

Type..*Recovery*.Obs.Well..~.....Pumped Well.*Hedar 17*. Distance,..~.... ▪

Test Started*3/5/67 08*.Test Ended*3/5/.13*. Observer *M. Zuckmir*.....

Time	W&Level Depth	Disch.	Space for Computations				Remarks
3/5/67 07 50	13. 57	0					
08 00	13.56	0					
08 10	13.56	0					
08 15	—	2.5 cum/ min		*av. discharge*			*Pump started*
08 20	16.79	2.1 cum/ min		*126 cum/hr*			
08 30	16.93	''					
09 30	17.15	2.1 cum/ min					
10 35	—	''	*t* *min*	*t'* *min*	*t'/t*		
11 15	17.25		180	0	0		*Pump stopped*
11 19	13.75	0	184	4	0.022		*Backflow*
21	13.90		186	6	.032		*from*
23	13.98		188	8	.042		*column*
30	13.91		195	15	.077		
35	13.87		200	20	0.10		
40	13.84		205	25	0.122		
45	13.82		210	30	0.143		
50	13.80		225	35	0.155		
55	13.79		220	40	.182		
12 05	13.76		230	50	.217		
12 10	13.75		235	55	.234		
15	13.74		240	60	0.250		

Fig. 6.11   Standard work sheet for pumping tests.

ascending pipe. However, in most cases a sufficient number of measurements can be made after the disturbance has died down.

Irregularities in the recovery graph may be caused by partial penetration, by the presence of complete or partial boundaries, such as the edge of a confining layer, and by changes in the value of phreatic storativity during the time of recovery.

6.11   SINGLE WELL BAILER AND SLUG TESTS

Assume that a volume of water is quickly withdrawn by a bailer from a fully penetrating well. The residual drawdown in the vicinity of the well is (Ferris *et al.*, 1962):

$$s' = \frac{V}{4\pi T} \exp\left(\frac{-r^2 S}{4Tt} \right) \tag{6.15a}$$

where V is the volume of water instantaneously withdrawn, r the distance of the observation well, t the time after bailing, and s' the residual drawdown after bailing.

Inside the bailed well with the small radius r_w

$$\frac{r_w^2 S}{4Tt} \approx 0, \qquad \exp\left(-\frac{r_w^2 S}{4Tt} \right) \approx 1$$

and Eq. (6.15a) becomes

$$T \approx \frac{V}{4\pi s' t} \tag{6.15b}$$

This equation shows a simple way to estimate the transmissivity in a well that has just been drilled and where the rig is still in place.

The bailer is lowered into the well and left there for a few minutes until the water level resumes its initial position. The electrode of an electrical wire is placed at a certain predetermined position s', say 20 cm, below the water level at rest. Then the bailer is quickly but carefully withdrawn, without smashing the electrode and with a minimum of spilling. The time t that elapses between the moment when the bailer detaches itself from the water level (this event is accompanied by a smacking noise) and the moment when the water level renews contact with the electrode is measured with the aid of a stopwatch. The volume V is determined from the outside dimensions of the bailer, and Eq. (6.15b) is applied. The procedure works best in a confined aquifer with small transmissivity. In a phreatic aquifer the conditions for which Eq. (6.15b) is derived may not be applicable. If T exceeds a value of about 250 m²/day, recovery is too quick for accurate time measurements.

Another procedure is to bail the well continuously during, say, 30 min and to observe the subsequent recovery of the water level. In this case the volume of water withdrawn is equated to a pumping discharge Q and Eq. (6.14) is applied. The procedure works well when the water level is shallow so that quick bailing is possible.

In a slug test a small volume of water is quickly poured into the well. The water level rises and its subsequent sinking is observed. Equation (6.15b) is applied with s' indicating the residual rise of the water level.

An ingenious method uses a closed metal cylinder filled with gravel or scrap metal to make it heavy. Rapid insertion of the cylinder is equivalent to a slug test. When the rest level has been reestablished, the cylinder is suddenly withdrawn, this action being equivalent to one cycle of bailing. The procedure is less messy than the bailing or pouring of water.

Bailer and slug tests are only of indicative value. They are often employed during drilling in an aquitard in order to find out whether conditions are favorable for the construction of an at least marginally useful well or whether the borehole has to be abandoned.

6.12   TECHNICAL PROCEDURES

One of the first items in the work program for a regional investigation should be single well tests of the drawdown, recovery, and step drawdown types. It may happen that some tests defy interpretation in terms of hydrologic parameters, but they yield at least reliable data on the specific discharge (discharge/drawdown) of the wells; they may furnish valuable qualitative information (Fig 6.12), and they enable the selection of sites for more elaborate tests. The drawdown phase should last 2–4 hr, even though significant water level changes may be observable only during part of this time. Short pumping periods are followed by a quick recovery of the water level and render the subsequent recovery test less accurate.

After pumping has been stopped, the water level is monitored at frequent intervals as long as a significant trend of recovery can be observed. As a rule of thumb, one may reckon that significant recovery lasts about half as long as the preceding pumping phase, much less if transmissivity is large. A final measurement should be made after a time equaling the duration of the pumping phase. If, after this time, the water level remains significantly below the original rest level, the aquifer penetrated by the well is probably surrounded by less permeable strata. Such a situation is often met in alluvial aquifers that are composed of lenses of gravel and sand surrounded by silt and clay.

The step drawdown test is carried out after the recovery period. The whole sequence of tests may take 8–14 hr. When these tests are completed, aquifer tests involving one or several boreholes are carried out in selected locations. A test of this kind may take 12 hr to several days. Existing wells should be used wherever possible. Costly observation boreholes should be drilled only as a last resort.

The frequency of water level measurements should be adjusted so that a significant change, say 1 cm, occurs between two successive readings. When changes occur rapidly, the measurements must be effected as quickly as possible, at 1 min intervals and even quicker. Slow changes may be sufficiently well monitored by readings at 10 min and even longer intervals. In this case each measurement should be repeated twice in quick succession, in order to minimize errors.

At least ten significant water level measurements should be effected during a test. Five points without scatter uniquely determine second-degree curvature (quadratic equation). If the test is interpreted by a curve fitting method, five points will indicate only a zero approximation, and at least ten points will be needed to ensure a reasonably accurate fit, especially when the curvature is weak and scatter is noticeable. If a linear plot is expected, it often happens that a straight line can be fitted only to a part of the points, whereas another part shows marked curvature, because of deviations from the postulated conditions. When at least ten points are available, the linear part is more likely to be discerned.

Theoretical derivations postulate that a steady state of flow (ideally, a state of stagnation) is disturbed only by the test procedure. Under field conditions the so-called rest levels may either rise or fall or undergo cyclic variations in response to diurnal changes of barometric pressure or to tides. There may also be erratic noises caused, for example, by pressure waves emanating from traffic on a highway.

Background trends are taken into account by observing the trend before and after the test and by interpolating hypothetical rest levels for the test period. Drawdowns are then reckoned from these interpolated rest levels. This procedure becomes, however, doubtful when the background trend is of the order of magnitude of changes caused by the test itself.

Ideally one should monitor the rest levels before and after the test for a period equaling the test time, but this can rarely be done. The common practice is to observe the rest levels during about $\frac{1}{2}$ hr before and after a single well test, and during several hours before and after a longer test involving several boreholes. The technician who carries out the test should understand at least the basic principles of groundwater hydraulics, should be able to operate pumping equipment, and should be a resourceful person capable of overcoming hitches that have to be expected in field work. He will gain a better insight into his work if he also plots and interprets some tests under the supervision of a fully trained hydrologist. However, even a very well-trained worker should confine his attention to instrument readings only, as long as field work is in progress. Very few people are capable of mixing observations and computations without getting confused in the process.

The essential equipment of the observer consists of two calibrated electrical wire instruments (one for use and one as a spare), a steel tape for recalibrating the wire if necessary, a stopwatch or at least a watch with a second hand, a flashlight for work at night, a supply of standard work sheets (Fig. 6.11), a clipboard, and pencils. A competent observer will keep the field sheets reasonably clean and legible, obviating the need to copy them. All computations of time intervals, drawdowns, discharges, etc., are done on the original field sheets after the observations have been completed. The data are then plotted on a standardized format and their interpretation is marked on the graph. Finally, the graphs are filed in the folder of the appropriate well. Generally, the field sheets may be discarded. They should be kept only when it is intended to reinterpret the test by a different method.

6.13   INTERPRETATION OF IRREGULAR TEST GRAPHS

The investigator does not always know beforehand whether the aquifer he studies is confined, leaky, or phreatic; whether the existing wells are fully or partially penetrating; etc. Under these circumstances he can only plot his

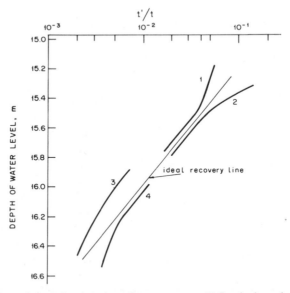

Fig. 6.12 Irregular graphs of single well recovery tests. (1) Barrier boundary, or contact of rising water level with confining layer. (2) Leaky aquifer, or recharge boundary. (3) Thin aquifer, or partially penetrating well in vertically anisotropic aquifer. (4) Partially penetrating well, or edge of confining layer.

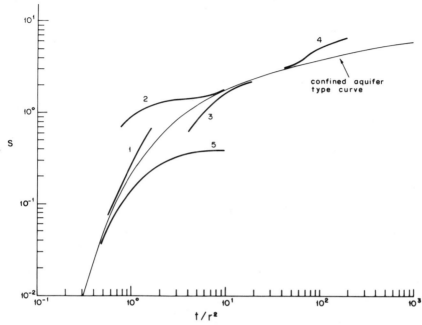

Fig. 6.13   Irregular graphs of tests with one observation well. (1) Thin phreatic aquifer. (2) Thick phreatic acquifer. (3) Partially penetrating well. (4) Barrier boundary. (5) Leaky aquifer, or recharge boundary.

tests in the standard way. An irregular graph (i.e., a semilog graph that does not plot linearly or a log–log graph that cannot be matched to the Theis type curve) indicates more complex conditions, provided, of course, that the irregularities are not due to faulty field procedures.

Figures 6.12 and 6.13 show the indications that can be obtained from such graphs. In almost all instances several interpretations are possible. The most likely one has to be found by reference to geologic data and to well logs.

6.14   MAPPING OF AQUIFER CONSTANTS

The data obtained from a campaign of pumping tests should be mapped and thus checked for consistency with other hydrogeologic data, before they are used for computations or, as initial values, for aquifer calibration. Mapping problems arise almost exclusively in connection with transmissivity. The storativity of an aquifer is usually represented by two values only,

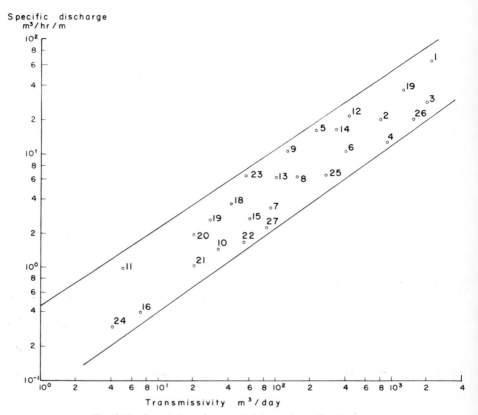

Fig. 6.14 Correlation of transmissivity and specific discharge.

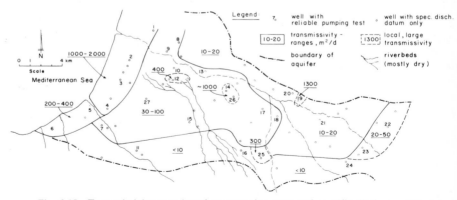

Fig. 6.15 Transmissivity map based on pumping tests and specific discharges (Western Mesaoria, Cyprus). (After Arie and Zomenis, 1968.)

phreatic and confined storativity, respectively. The relatively small lateral variability of each value can usually be neglected.

For a single-layered, nonhomogeneous aquifer such as river alluvium, the following procedure is suggested (Figs. 6.14, 6.15). A graphic correlation of transmissivity and specific discharge is drawn and the values of transmissivity in locations where only specific discharge is known are read off from the graph. Values of specific discharge that were obtained with minimum discharge and, therefore, with minimum well losses are preferable for this purpose. Care must be taken to check each value against the well log and the relevant part of a geologic section and to eliminate doubtful data from badly constructed wells. All transmissivity values thus obtained are then penciled into a well location map and areas of approximately equal transmissivity are delineated, taking into account the subsurface structure of the aquifer.

A different procedure is suggested for aquifers consisting of several fairly homogeneous layers separated by impermeable strata, such as, for example, a sandstone shale complex (Fig. 6.16). Each layer may be assumed to have a constant permeability so that lateral changes of transmissivity reflect mainly changes of aquifer thickness. The permeability of each

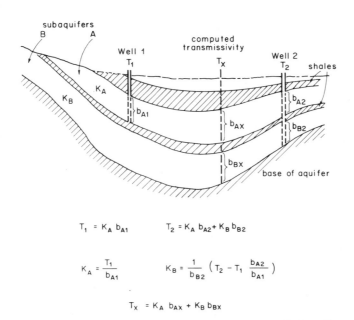

$$T_1 = K_A b_{A1} \qquad T_2 = K_A b_{A2} + K_B b_{B2}$$

$$K_A = \frac{T_1}{b_{A1}} \qquad K_B = \frac{1}{b_{B2}} \left(T_2 - T_1 \frac{b_{A2}}{b_{A1}} \right)$$

$$T_x = K_A b_{Ax} + K_B b_{Bx}$$

Fig. 6.16   Mapping of transmissivity in homogeneous stratified aquifer.

subaquifer is determined from tests in suitable boreholes. Total transmissivity values are then synthetized at selected locations of geologic cross sections and finally transferred to a map.

FURTHER READINGS

Bentall, R., ed. (1963). Methods of determining permeability, transmissibility and drawdown. *U.S. Geol. Surv., Water-Supply Pap.* 1536-I.

Boulton, N. S., and Streltsova, T. D. (1975). New equations for determining the formation constants of an aquifer from pumping test data. *Water Resour. Res.* **11**, 148–153.

Bouwer, H., and Rice, R. C. (1978). Delayed aquifer yield as phenomenon of delayed air entry. *Water Resour. Res.* **14**, 1068–1074.

Cooley, R. L., and Cunningham, A. B. (1979). Consideration of total energy loss in the theory of flow to wells. *J. Hydrol.* **43** No. 1/4, 287–311.

Dagan J. (1967). A method for determining the permeability and effective porosity of unconfined anisotropic aquifers. *Water Resour. Res.* **3**, 1059–1071.

DeWiest, R. J. M. (1970). *"Geohydrology."* Wiley, New York.

Ferris, J. G., Knowles, D. B., *et al.* (1962). Groundwater hydraulics. *U.S. Geol. Surv., Water-Supply Pap.* 1536-E.

Hantush, M. S. (1956). Analysis of data from pumping tests in leaky aquifers. *Trans., Am. Geophys. Union* **37**, 702–714.

Hantush, M. S. (1960). Modification of the theory of leaky aquifers. *J. Geophys. Res.* **65**, 13713–13725.

Hantush, M. S. (1961). Drawdown around a partially penetrating well. *ASCE Hydraul. Div.* July **61**, pp. 83–98.

Jacob, C. E. (1950). Flow of groundwater. *In* "Engineering Hydraulics," (Rouse H., ed), Wiley, New York.

Kirkham, D. (1959). Exact theory of flow into a partially penetrating well. *J. Geophys. Res.* **64**, 1317–1372.

Kruseman, G. P., and Ridder, N. A. (1970). Analysis and evaluation of pumping test data. *Int. Inst. Land Reclam. Improv., Neth., Bull.* No. 11.

Lang, S. M. (1960). Interpretation of boundary effects from pumping test data. *J. Am. Water Works Assoc.* **55**, 356–364.

McElwee, C. D., and Yukler, M. A. (1978). Sensitivity of groundwater models with respect to variations in transmissivity and storage. *Water Resour. Res.* **14**, No. 3, 451–459.

Muskat, M. (1937). "The Flow of Homogeneous Fluids through Porous Media." McGraw Hill, New York. Second printing, Edwards Brothers, Ann Arbor, Michigan (1946).

Neuman, S. P. (1972). Theory of flow in unconfined aquifers considering delayed response of the water table. *Water Resour. Res.* **8** 1031–1045.

Neuman, S. P. (1974). Effect of partial penetration on flow in unconfined aquifers considering delayed gravity responses. *Water Resour. Res.* **10**, 303–312.

Stallman, R. W. (1971). Aquifer test design, observation and data analysis. *In* "Techniques of Water Resources Investigations," Book 3, Chap. B1. U.S. Geol. Surv., U.S. Gov. Print. Off., Washington, D.C.

Streltsova-Adams, T. D. (1978). Well hydraulics in heterogeneous aquifer formations. *Adv. Hydrosci.* **11**, 357–423.

Theis, C. V. (1935). The relation between the lowering of the piezometric surface and the rate and duration of a well using groundwater storage. *Trans. Am. Geophys. Union* **35**, 917–936.

Walton, W. C. (1970). "Groundwater Resource Evaluation." McGraw-Hill, New York.

Walton, W. C. (1978). Comprehensive analysis of water table aquifer test data. *Groundwater* **16**, 311–317.

Walton, W. C. (1979). *Progress in analytical groundwater modelling. J. Hydrol.* **43**, No. 1/4, 149–157.

Weeks, E. P. (1969). Determining the ratio of horizontal to vertical permeability by aquifer test analysis. *Water Resour. Res.* **5**, 196–214.

7

Water Level Measurements, Hydrographs, and Water Level Maps

7.1 ACCURACY OF WATER LEVEL MEASUREMENTS

The *depth below ground* of the water level is the distance between a fixed, clearly marked *measuring point* on the well casing or the pump base and the water level in the well. Measurements can be effected by four principal types of instruments: *wetted tape, electrical wire, bubble gauge*, and various *registering instruments*.

In the *wetted tape* method, one end of a calibrated steel tape is smeared with chalk over the length of about 1 m. Then a weight is attached to this end and the tape is lowered into the borehole to such a depth that the chalked end becomes immersed in water. The depth below ground of the water level is the length of tape between the sharp mark that the water leaves on the chalk and the point on the tape held against the measuring point. The position of the water level must be known beforehand with an accuracy of, say, ± 0.5 m, or it has to be located by trial and error. A skilled observer can effect measurements reproducible within ± 0.1 cm. The procedure is, however, rather tiring, especially when repeated measurements at depths exceeding 20 m have to be made. Another disadvantage of the method is that broken pieces of tape may become wedged between the casing and the pump and cause damage when the pump has to be pulled.

Electric wire instruments consist of a calibrated, insulated wire with a blank electrode at one end. When the electrode touches the water, an electrical current supplied by a flashlight battery passes through the wire, the water, the metal casing of the well, and an amperemeter, which serves as indicator. A variant of this instrument uses a twin wire with a bulb containing a metallized float at its lower end. The circuit is closed when the float rises and touches the exposed ends of the twin wires. This type is useful for measurements in wells without a metal casing.

Electric wire instruments enable readings reproducible within ± 0.3 cm if measurements are carried out in quick succession in one and the same well by one and the same instrument. It is, however, difficult to keep the wire precisely calibrated, therefore the error of a large number of measurements in different wells is unlikely to be smaller than ± 2 cm. At depths exceeding 100 m the wire becomes difficult to handle and stretching may become a serious source of error.

Very deep water levels are more conveniently measured by a *bubble gauge*, which incorporates a permanently installed pipe and a manometer. The water is driven out from the pipe by compressed air and the maximum pressure that can thus be attained indicates the length of the water column originally in the pipe. If the depth of the lower end of the pipe is known, the depth of water level can be calculated. The accuracy of the instrument depends mainly on the calibration of the manometer. Readings reproducible within a ± 5-cm margin are about the best that can be expected, although in theory greater accuracy is feasible. A constant source of error is introduced when the pressure pipe is bent during installation, so that its length does not correspond to the depth of the lower end. This type of instrument has the advantage of being unaffected by the thick layer of oil that is often present where oil-lubricated pump aggregates are installed.

The accuracy of *registering instruments* is limited by the necessity to downscale the records so that they can be accommodated on a chart of convenient size. Simple instruments of this type are also hamstrung by mechanical losses in the transmission mechanism. The records can usually be read with an accuracy of 2–5 cm.

More modern devices, such as pressure transducers, have not found routine application. Under favorable conditions, geoelectrical resistivity measurements roughly indicate the depth of a phreatic water table, but accurate water level measurements can be effected only in wells. Altogether the state of the art is curiously archaic. A nineteenth-century technician would feel at home with most of the instruments currently in use.

The *elevation of the water level* (above mean sea level or above any other reference datum) is obtained by subtracting the depth below ground of the water level from the elevation of ground level. Ground elevations can be measured rather quickly and cheaply with the aid of *barometric altimeters*. The accuracy of this method is, however, only ± 2 m at best and barely suffices for rough, approximative work. Water level maps should be based on measurements in *precisely leveled wells*. A skilled sureyor usually carries the *precise leveling datum* from a *benchmark* to a point near the well, and it is up to the hydrologist–technician to carry the datum from there to the actual measuring point on the well. Even with careful work the cumulative error at this point is likely to be ± 3 cm.

The accuracy of data on water level elevations depends on the accuracy of the hydrologic instruments and of the precise leveling. Under optimal conditions errors can probably be kept as low as ± 5 cm, but under the usual field conditions and when semiskilled technicians are employed, errors of ± 10 cm are more likely.

The required accuracy of water level measurements can be judged by the following considerations.

The main purpose of water level observations is to determine gradients that are generally about 3 m/km (0.003). If such a gradient is to be determined with 10% accuracy by measurements in two boreholes at a distance of 1 km from each other, the error of each measurement must be less than 15 cm. Smaller gradients are frequently met, and greater accuracy is often desirable. It follows that the accuracy of water level measurements required for quantitative interpretation more or less corresponds to the limits of the technically feasible accuracy.

At the outset of the investigation, water levels should be measured in all accessible wells at monthly intervals. The measured well itself and neighboring wells that may interfere with it must be at rest for at least 12 hr before the measurements are made. The work may be done in installments by measuring each day wells that can be shut down, provided only that each well is measured at, approximately, monthly intervals. These observations should be supplemented by campaigns of simultaneous water level measurements in the whole area carried out once or twice yearly, at a time when almost all wells can be shut down.

All data should be transferred as soon as possible from the technicians' notebooks onto filing cards (see Section 15.1) and kept in this form for all future references. On the basis of a few months' records, redundant or unreliable observation wells may be weeded out. The remaining wells, or at least a selected number of them, must be precisely leveled for the purpose of drawing water level maps.

The observation network for the permanent monitoring of the aquifer may consist of a still smaller number of exploited wells supplemented by specially constructed observation boreholes. The relevant criteria are discussed in Chapter 14.

7.2   WATER LEVEL HYDROGRAPHS

Water level hydrographs are useful for the simple, visual interpretation of water level data, for judging the reliability of data from a given observation point, and as a preliminary step, for the drawing of water level maps. The scale of the hydrograph should enable the representation of data with significant accuracy, and for the sake of manual interpolation, it should be chosen so that the resulting curve is neither very steep nor very flat. If the hydrographs are drawn on the basis of monthly water level observations, suitable scales are as follows: horizontal (time), 1 month = 1.5 cm; vertical (water levels), 0.1 cm on paper = 2 cm in nature. When only depth of water level data are available, the vertical scale is inverted so that it increases from top to bottom, corresponding to the intuitive picture of a rising and falling water level. When the well is, eventually, precisely leveled, this scale is easily converted into absolute water level elevations.

The visual examination of hydrographs presenting the record of several years may yield the following indications (Fig. 7.1): (1) Water levels fluctuating around a constant mean indicate a state of hydraulic equilibrium that is usually associated with a stable hydrologic situation. However, the

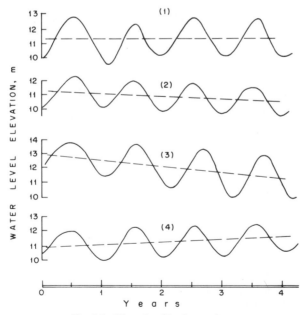

Fig. 7.1   Water level hydrographs.

mere existence of a hydraulic equilibrium provides no guarantee against the eventual influx of low-quality water (see Section 13.1). Therefore this conclusion should be taken with a grain of salt. (2) Decreasing mean water levels associated with a constant or decreasing amplitude of yearly oscillations suggest diminished natural replenishment, which may be caused by drought years, by changes of surface cover (e.g., urbanization), or by the diversion of river flow from the area. (3) Decreasing mean water levels accompanied by increasing yearly oscillations are the result of intensified groundwater abstraction. (4) Steadily rising water levels can usually be traced back to return flows from irrigation or from urban effluents or to climatic causes. (5) When an aquifer is exploited on a sustained yield basis, the immediate effects should be as under (3) and after a number of years a new equilibrium state as under (1) should be reached. However, this development may take a long time. It will probably not become apparent during the two or three years that are usually allotted to an intensive investigative effort.

It should be emphasized that the above indications do not prove the existence of a certain situation. They provide only hints and have to be corroborated in each case by additional lines of evidence.

7.3   WATER LEVEL MAPS

Water level maps should show elevations of the water level for a certain month or season of a specific year, undisturbed as much as possible by ongoing abstraction or replenishment.

Quantitative work requires large-scale maps in the range of 1 : 100,000 to 1 : 20,000 on which distances and hence gradients can be accurately measured. It is assumed, of course, that the density of observation wells justifies maps on this scale. The interpolation of contour lines between widely distant observation wells is a poor substitute for measurements.

Estimates of the depth of water level at points of interest (e.g., at new well locations) are easily obtained by the comparison of a water level contour map with a topographic map. Sometimes maps representing the depths of water levels are drawn for planning purposes.

When water level maps are drawn, the following procedures should be adhered to:

(1) Approximately undisturbed conditions correspond to the periods of maximum and minimum water levels that are easily determined from the water level hydrographs of the area.

(2) A month within such a period is selected. The water level in this month is read off from each one of the hydrographs and marked on the well location map.

(3) Contour lines that can most easily be picked out on the map are the first to be drawn.

(4) Less obvious contour lines are then inserted by linear interpolation.

(5) Sharp wriggles in a contour line should be drawn only when they are supported by a number of observations.

(6) Isolated discrepant data are always suspect. They may be due to measurements in an insufficiently recovered exploitation well, to a faulty leveling datum, to the erroneous inclusion of a well tapping a different aquifer, or to some other error. Such points should be surrounded by a closed line, marked with a question mark, and not be used for interpolating other lines (Fig. 7.2).

(7) Spurious data are more easily spotted and accuracy increases when a number of maps are drawn for successive periods.

(8) Generally, the drawing of water level contour lines demands a certain amount of judgment. Blind reliance on linear interpolation procedures is out of place.

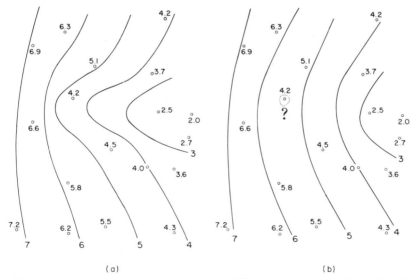

(a)   (b)

Fig. 7.2 Preparation of a water level map. (a) Water level contours obtained by linear interpolation, (b) water level contours obtained by applying judgment.

Experience shows that the transmissivity of an aquifer tends to be inversely related to the steepness of water level gradients. Small gradients of the order 1:2000 to 1:500 are almost always associated with very good aquifers, gradients in the neighborhood of 1:100 indicate a poor aquifer, and still steeper gradients, 1:20 or more, are usually found in aquitards.

The remarkable correlation between water level gradients and transmissivity is probably due to two causes: (1) Groundwater usually flows through large cross-sectional areas, so that the flux per unit area is small. Hence relatively steep gradients occur only when transmissivity is poor. (2) In the rare instances where large fluxes do occur, loose particles are dragged into the pore space and the permeability of the aquifer gradually diminishes. Thus a water level contour map gives a rather reliable qualitative indication of aquifer characteristics even when no additional information is available.

FURTHER READINGS

Auriol, J., and Canceill, M. (1974). Constitution de fichiers de mesures de niveaux piezo-metriques periodiques. *Bull. BRGM, Sect.* 3 No. 1.

Garber, M. S. and Koopman, F. C. (1968). Methods of measuring water levels in deep wells. *In* "Techniques of Water Resources Investigations," Book 8, Chap. A. U.S. Geol. Surv., U.S. Gov. Print. Off., Washington, D.C.

Heath, R. C. (1976). Design of groundwater level observation well programs. *Groundwater* **14**(2), 71–77.

Mandel, S. (1965). Design and instrumentation of hydrogeological observation networks. *IASH Publ.* No. 68, pp. 413–424.

U.S. Geological Survey (1976). "Design of Groundwater Level Observation Networks," Open file report prepared in cooperation with hydrological service of Israel, No. 84, E-7, pp. 76–165. U.S. Gov. Print. Off., Washington, D.C.

CHAPTER

8

Interpretation and Utilization
of Spring Flow

8.1 DEPLETION CURVE ANALYSIS

Consider a perennial spring in a region with seasonal rainfall issuing through a well-defined outlet (a karstic spring in the Mediterranean area may be taken as a prototype). The groundwater system feeding the spring is only vaguely known, but several years' records of spring discharge on weekly or monthly basis are available. The problem is to interpret these records in order to obtain quantitative information on the groundwater system and to predict spring discharges.

The spring and the groundwater system feeding it can be simulated, very roughly, by the *unicell model*, a tank with vertical walls filled with sand or some other porous material and provided with a spout above its bottom (Fig. 8.1). The sand is saturated with water to a certain depth and the discharge issuing from the spout is observed. The relation of the unicell model to the natural prototype is shown in Fig. 13.1 (Section 13.1). The errors introduced by the extreme simplification will be discussed at the end of this section.

For the dry weather flow of a spring fed from a thick aquifer we obtain from the model

$$\text{if} \quad d \gg h, \quad h + d \approx \text{const} = b \tag{8.1}$$

$$V(t) = ASh(t) \tag{8.2}$$

$$Q(t) = KbCh(t) \tag{8.3}$$

$$Q(t) = -\frac{dV}{dt} \tag{8.4}$$

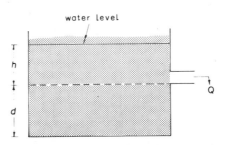

Fig. 8.1   Unicell model for the simulation of spring flow.

where $h(t)$ is the elevation of the water level above the outlet, V the volume of water stored above the outlet, d the aquifer thickness below outlet, A the base area of tank, S, K are the storativity and permeability, respectively, and C is a dimensionless parameter representing the flow pattern.

The elimination of $h(t)$ from Eqs. (8.2) and (8.3) and of $V(t)$ from Eqs. (8.4) yields

$$V(t) = \frac{AS}{KC} Q(t) = t_0 Q(t) \tag{8.5}$$

$$Q(t) + t_0 \frac{dQ}{dt} = 0 \tag{8.6a}$$

$$Q(t) = Q_0 \exp\left(-\frac{t}{t_0}\right) \tag{8.6b}$$

$$\log Q(t) = \log Q_0 - \frac{1}{2.30} \frac{t}{t_0} \tag{8.6c}$$

where t_0 is the depletion time and Q_0 the initial discharge.

The following information can be extracted from these equations:

(1) The depletion time t_0 is easily read off from the plot of dry weather discharges on a semilogarithmic scale, $\log Q$ versus t (Fig. 8.2).

(2) If the discharge at any time during the dry weather period is known, future dry weather discharges can be predicted with the aid of Eq. (8.6c).

(3) The slope of the depletion line between two given discharges Q_1 and Q_2 characterizes the groundwater system feeding the spring. Changes of slope from one year to the next shows that the system is being interfered with. A steepening slope indicates groundwater abstraction from the aquifer. A flattening slope indicates replenishment during the supposedly dry season, because of return flows from irrigation or urban effluents or because of seepage from surface water reservoirs (Fig. 8.2). In rare cases the change is caused by catastrophic occurrences that modify the aquifer, such as earthquakes.

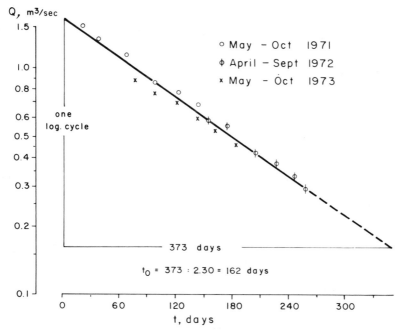

Fig. 8.2 Construction and interpretation of a depletion line.

(4) The *live reserves* of groundwater (above the level of the outlet) that maintain spring flow at any given moment are equal to $Q_t t_0$.

(5) Aquifer replenishment between the end of one dry season and the beginning of the next one is easily computed by Eq. (8.5) and the principle of continuity

$$AR = Q_2 t_0 - Q_1 t_0 + \int_{t_1}^{t_2} Q \, dt \qquad (8.7)$$

where R is the replenishment (LT^{-1}), A the replenishment area of the spring (L^2), t_1, t_2 are the instance of time at the end of one dry season and the beginning of the next one, respectively, and Q_1, Q_2 the spring discharges at t_1 and t_2, respectively.

(6) Estimates of A, S, and h derived from geologic considerations should yield, by Eq. (8.2), a volume of live reserves approximately equal to the volume computed by Eq. (8.5). Estimates of replenishment derived from the assumed replenishment area and from climatic data should be approximately equal to the figure computed by Eq (8.7). Large discrepancies indicate the need for a reevaluation of the accepted hydrogeologic concepts regarding the area.

The depletion of a thin aquifer is simulated by assuming that the spout is at the bottom of the tank and that therefore aquifer thickness is a function of time.

$$d=0, \quad h=h(t) \tag{8.8}$$

$$Q(t) \approx KCh^2(t) \tag{8.9}$$

This yields by combination with Eqs. (8.2) and (8.4)

$$Q(t+\Delta t) = \frac{Q(t)}{(1+\Delta t/t_0)^2} \tag{8.10}$$

$$V(t) = Q(t)t_0 \tag{8.11}$$

The depletion time t_0 is determined by computing the ratios $Q_{(t+\Delta t)}/Q_t$ for successive time intervals Δt and averaging the resulting values. These equations are sometimes used for predicting the dry weather flow of a river fed from a shallow alluvial aquifer (Werner and Sundquist, 1951). They are rarely applicable to perennial springs.

In practical applications the depletion line is put together from a semilogarithmic plot of all available sequences of dry weather flow data, each sequence being identified by a distinctive symbol (Fig. 8.2). The purpose of this procedure is to weed out spurious data, to detect anomalies (see below), and to obtain a line extending over the largest possible range of discharge values. The logarithmic scale must be chosen so that the entire range of data can be plotted with significant accuracy. If commercial semilog paper does not fulfil this requirement, graph sheets have to be drawn by hand. Where a computerized plotter is available, the easiest procedure is to draw the whole hydrograph, ascending and descending limbs, on an appropriate semilog scale, and to synthesize the depletion line from the straightline parts of the descending limbs.

Empirical depletion lines are often composed of two linear segments with different slopes (Fig. 8.3). This property may be due to one or several of the following causes: (1) diversion of water upstream from the gauging station; (2) vertical variability of the product $A \times S$, which, in the unicell model, is assumed to be constant; (3) delayed runoff (*interflow*) entering the spring via the soil mantle; (4) two underground reservoirs draining through the same spring. Such a "two-reservoir model" is often encountered in fissured and karstic rocks where the wide flow channels drain more quickly than the porous rock matrix.

A line with two different slopes can be represented as the sum of two component lines with the constants Q_{01}, t_{01}, and Q_{02}, t_{02}, respectively (Mero, 1958). In practical applications it is sufficiently accurate, and much less laborious, to compute the live storage and recharge only from the

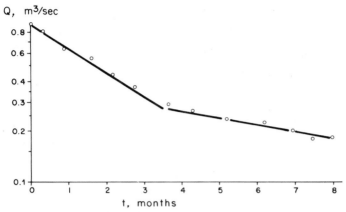

Fig. 8.3   Depletion line with two different slopes.

segment that yields the larger volume, usually the one with the larger depletion time.

Depletion lines that seem to be composed of three or more segments or that show curvature at variance with Eq. (8.10) defy interpretation.

8.2 THE UTILIZATION OF SPRING FLOW

The art of diverting spring flow was perfected already in times of remote antiquity (Forbes, 1964). Urban centers of the Roman Empire were supplied with springwater through elaborate aqueducts. In the eastern Mediterranean area springwater was often used to drive small water turbines attached to millstones before being diverted for domestic consumption and for irrigation. In the highlands of Persia insignificant seepages were developed into large artificial springs by excavating long subterranean galleries, the so-called ghanats. Similar methods of diverting spring flow were universally employed until the present century. The situation changed only when the introduction of turbine pumps attached to diesel or electric motors made it possible to obtain significant discharges from deep drilled wells.

Today it is frequently more convenient or efficient to divert the water directly through wells from the aquifer feeding the spring. The circumstances under which this alternative should be resorted to are

(1) When a spring issues through diffuse seepages from swampy ground. It is easier to drill a few boreholes then to search for original spring outlets below a thick layer of debris and mud.

(2) When the spring is situated at a large distance from centers of demand and when boreholes can be located near them.

(3) When spring discharge exceeds demand during some periods— seasons or years— and shortages occur during other periods. In this case diversion of groundwater can redress the temporal imbalance of water supply.

(4) When springwater is of low chemical quality because of some localized influx of saline water and the water in the aquifer is usable.

Two case histories from Israel illustrate these points (for locations see Fig. 2.7).

The aquifer feeding the Yarkon and Tanninim springs (Section 2.4) is exploited by boreholes situated near centers of demand, all along the mountain border. Yearly groundwater abstraction through boreholes approximates the average annual discharge of the springs in the natural state, but the entire quantity of water is made available in accordance with the demand curve, (Mero, 1963) and in the case of the Tanninim spring, freshwater has been substituted for saline discharges. Overexploitation can be practiced during limited periods (Section 14.2). As a consequence, however, the Yarkon spring has practically dried up, and the discharge of the Tanninim spring has declined to less than half of its original value.

The Na'aman spring in Galilee is fed from a karstic carbonate aquifer and discharged, in the natural state, about 40 MCM/yr of brackish (1700 ppm TDS) water. Salination of groundwater occurs in the vicinity of the spring, probably because of an influx of seawater. Wells situated in the hill country to the east of the spring divert now approximately 40 MCM/yr of freshwater. As a safeguard against the intrusion of saline water into the aquifer, the wells are operated so that a small trickle of saline water continues to discharge from the spring (Mandel and Mero, 1961). Furthermore, the salinity of groundwater is monitored by samples from operating wells and in a few observation wells. The scheme has been operated successfully for more than 15 years.

In this case the advantages are the substitution of freshwater for the brackish spring discharge and the provision of about 80% of the annual quantity during the hot summer months in accordance with the demand curve. These advantages are, however, bought at the price of pumping water from wells and through pipelines to the users.

FURTHER READINGS

Abd El Al, I. (1967). Statique et dynamique des eaux dans les massifs calcaires Libano-Syriens. *Chron. Hydrogeol.* No. 10, pp. 75–94.

Anderson, M. G., and Burt, T. P. (1980). Interpretation of recession flow. *J. Hydrol.* **46**, No. 1/2, 89–101.

Atkinson, T. C. (1977). Diffuse flow and conduit flow in limestone terrain in the Mendip hills (England). *J. Hydrol.* **35**, 93–110.

Berkaloff, E. (1967). Limite de validité des formules courantes de tarissement de débit. *Chron. Hydrogeol.* No. 10, pp. 31–41.

Burdon, D. J. and Safadi, C. (1963). Ras El Ain, the great karst spring of Mesopotamia. *J. Hydrol.* **1**, 58–95.

Castany, G. (1965). Quelques debits des sources remarkables. *Chron. Hydrogeol.* No. 7, pp. 85–86.

Castany, G. (1967). Introduction a l'étude des courbes de tarissement. *Chron. Hydrogeol.* No. 10, pp. 23–30.

Forbes, R. J. (1964). "Studies in Ancient Technology." Brill, Leiden, Netherlands.

Forkasiewicz, M., and Paloc, H. (1967). Le régime de tarissement de la foux de la vis. *Chron. Hydrogeol.*, No. 10, pp. 58–73.

Jenkins, C. T. (1970). Computation of rate and volume of stream depletion by wells. *In* "Techniques of Water Resources Investigations," Book 4, Chap. D1. U.S. Geol. Surv., U.S. Gov. Print. Off., Washington, D.C.

Karanjac, J., and Altug A. (1980). Karstic spring recession hydrograph and temperature analysis; Olimpinar dam project, Turkey. *J. Hydrol.* **45**, No. 3/4, 203–217.

Mandel, S., and Mero, F. (1961). Planned exploitation of the aquifer feeding the Na'aman spring. *Proc. Athens Symp. Groundwater Arid Zones. IASH Publ.* No. 57, pp. 645–650.

Mero, F. (1958). "Hydrological Investigations of the Na'aman Spring Region," Publ. No. 45. TAHAL, Water Plann. Isr., Tel Aviv.

Mero, F. (1963). Application of groundwater depletion curves in analysing and forecasting spring discharges influenced by well fields. *IASH Publ.* No. 63, pp. 107–117.

Tison, G. Jr. (1960). Courbe de tarissement, coefficient d'écoulement et permeabilité du bassin. *IASH Publ.* No. 51, pp. 229–243.

Werner, P. W., and Sundquist, K. J. (1951). On the groundwater recession curve for large watersheds. *IASH Publ.* No. 33, pp. 202–212.

CHAPTER
9

Geochemical Methods

9.1 CHEMICAL ANALYSES

Only short recapitulations of a few chemical concepts are included in this section and in Section 9.3. The reader who needs to recall college chemistry is advised to consult texts on the subject (see Further Readings).

When minerals are dissolved in water, their molecules tend to dissociate into *ions*, electrically charged atoms or groups of atoms (*radicals*) that are separated by water molecules. *Cations* carry positive charges, *anions* negative ones. The number of charges, always an integral figure, is also called the *valence* of the ion. In natural waters there occur mainly *univalent* and *bivalent* ions. The water itself tends to dissociate into the *ion pair* H^+ and OH^-, hydrogen ion concentration being measured as pH. The tendency to dissociate changes from substance to substance and the degree of dissociation actually attained depends on the nature and concentrations of all the solutes.

Standard chemical analyses of water usually report three cations, Ca^{2+}, Mg^{2+}, $Na^+ + K^+$ (combined); three or four anions, HCO_3^-, SO_4^{2-}, Cl^-, NO_3^-; and other characteristics, such as pH, total dissolved solids (TDS), electrical conductivity (EC), temperature (T^0), and *hardness* (the property of the water to form unsoluble compounds with soap). More detailed analyses report potassium separately from sodium, fluoride, bromide, silicium (usually as nondissociated SiO_2), dissolved gases (by their molecular formulas), iron (usually as Fe^{3+}) and boron (see Table 9.2). Various trace elements such as Cu, Zn, Cd, and As are analyzed when their influence on water quality is deemed important.

The standard format of presentation assigns one, ionic or molecular, formula to each element, except oxygen and hydrogen, whereas, in reality, the same element may be distributed among several dissolved species (see, for example, the carbonic species, Section 9.3). However, for most practical purposes, the standard format of presentation is sufficiently accurate.

Concentrations may be expressed either as weight of constituent per unit volume of water [e.g., *milligrams per liter (mg/liter)*] or as weight of constituent per unit weight of water [e.g., *milligrams per kg (parts per million=ppm)*]. The two units are related by the formula

$$ppm = \frac{\text{mg/liter}}{\text{specific weight of the water}} \tag{9.1}$$

The difference between ppm and mg/liter is negligible in usable waters but becomes significant in brackish waters with 7000 or more TDS and in thermal waters.

The unit of weight commonly used in chemical computations is the *milliequivalent (meq)* defined by

$$1\,\text{meq} = \frac{\text{formula weight of the ion}}{\text{number of charges on the ion}} \times \text{mg} \tag{9.2}$$

where formula weight (dimensionless) is the sum of the atomic weights of all atoms comprising the ion.

This presentation has the advantage that it indicates the *combining weights* of ions that may form a salt. Thus, in round figures, 1 meq of $Ca^{2+}(20/2=10$ mg) may combine with 1 meq of $Cl^-(35/1=35$ mg) to form 45 mg (1 mmole) of $CaCl_2$. Concentrations of nondissociated compounds should be expressed in *millimoles*, as above, but the term *meq* is frequently also used in this case. The corresponding units of concentration are the *meq/liter* and the *meq/kg*. They are interchangeable where normal, usable freshwaters are concerned.

Natural waters are electrically neutral; the combined concentrations of cations must be equal to the combined concentrations of anions when both are expressed in meq/liter. The accuracy of an analysis can be checked by the fraction

$$\frac{\text{sum of cations (meq/liter)} - \text{sum of anions (meq/liter)}}{\text{sum of all ions}} \times 100$$

$$= \text{reaction error } (\%) \tag{9.3}$$

Errors of less than 5% may be due to the neglect of rare ions and to normal experimental error. A reaction error in excess of 5% throws doubt on the analysis. Systematic errors caused by faulty instruments or by reagents at faulty concentrations can be detected by analyzing standard samples provided by the *U.S. Geological Survey*.

9.2 CHEMICAL FIELDWORK

Several parameters change rapidly when a water sample is withdrawn and must be measured in the field. *Temperature measurements* are conveniently carried out in a vacuum flask (thermos). Electrical thermometers are most suitable because they allow quick readings, but any type of thermometer may be used, provided it is calibrated to 0.5 Celsius (°C). The conversion formula from degrees Fahrenheit to Celsius is

$$T_C = 5/9(T_F - 32) \approx \frac{T_F - 32}{2} \tag{9.4}$$

Specific electrical conductivity (EC), the reciprocal of specific resistivity, is measured in micromhos per cm (1 micromho $\times$ cm^{-1} = 10^{-6} ohms^{-1} cm^{-1}). EC is a function of ion concentrations. Approximate ranges of EC values are

Distilled water	0.5–5.0 micromhos/cm
Rainwater	5.0–30 micromhos/cm
Fresh groundwater	30–2,000 micromhos/cm
Seawater	45,000–55,000 micromhos/cm
Brines	100,000 and more micromhos/cm

For freshwater free of suspended solids, the following approximate relations hold:

$$\text{TDS (ppm)} \approx 0.65 \times \text{EC (micromhos/cm)} \tag{9.5a}$$

$$\text{TDS (meq/l)} \approx 0.01 \times \text{EC (micromhos/cm)} \tag{9.5b}$$

EC measurements are often substituted for more laborious techniques (1) for the determination of TDS, either by the above approximate relation or, with greater precision, by the derivation of an empirical correlation between EC and a few values of TDS determined by drying and weighing a few samples from the same batch; (2) for the quick checking of a large number of samples (in this case EC measurements make it possible to pick out samples that deviate from the average so much that they warrant detailed attention), and (3) for the measurement of the freshwater–seawater interface in an observation well (see Chapter 15).

pH is defined as the negative decimal logarithm of hydrogen ion concentration. For example, pure water at 25°C contains $10^{-7.00}$ g/liter of

H^+ ion; its pH is 7.00. pH values generally range between 6.5 and 8.5, depending on the dissolved constituents, and to a lesser degree on temperature.

A *pH meter* measures the electromotive force between a glass electrode, made of special glass, and a reference electrode of constant potential. The glass electrode is immersed in the water and the reference electrode is in contact with the water only through a *salt bridge*, usually a slightly porous plug saturated with a solution of KCl. In modern instruments both electrodes are integrated into one bulb. The electrometer is connected to the bulb by a sheathed cable minimizing the influence of stray electric fields. Instrument readings have to be corrected for temperature with the aid of a table or graph that should be supplied with each instrument. Good portable instruments allow readings reproducible within the range of 0.05 pH. Rapid changes of pH may be brought about by the escape of dissolved CO_2 or of some other volatile component, or they may be caused by temperature changes. A great deal of dexterity is often required to effect readings that reflect natural conditions reasonably well.

The *redox potential* (Eh) measures the tendency of the water to oxidize or to reduce dissolved constituents. Eh meters measure the potential difference between an inert metal electrode made of platinum or gold and a reference electrode of constant potential. Readings are made in millivolts. For reliable measurements contact with air must be avoided and the electrode, which tends to become coated with foreign material, must be kept uncontaminated. These conditions are difficult to fulfill.

Ion-sensitive electrodes are similar in principle to pH electrodes. Essentially, they measure the combined concentrations of univalent or bivalent ions and give reliable readings only at low concentrations.

Portable chemical field sets make it possible to carry out rough chemical analyses under field conditions.

The *correct collection and storage of water samples* for laboratory analysis is important. Plastic bottles holding about 150 cm^3 are most suitable for this purpose; larger samples are required only for the determination of trace elements. As a safeguard against contamination the bottles should be flushed with distilled water and closed before being taken to the field. For sample taking, the bottle should be flushed with the water to be sampled and then filled and tightly closed, leaving only a small air bubble below the stopper. A sturdy label should indicate date and hour of sampling, location and nature of the source of water, information on the conditions under which the sample was taken (e.g., after pumping for 1 hr at a discharge of 250 m^3/hr), and the name of the person who collected the sample. The samples must be stored in a cool, shaded place and analyzed not later than one week after collection.

9.3 GROUNDWATER CONSTITUENTS

Chloride (Cl^-). The dominant source of chloride is the ocean, with approximately 19,400 ppm Cl^-. Circulating groundwater picks up chloride by the following mechanisms:

(1) Tiny airborne salt crystals (mainly $NaCl$) are dissolved in rain or settle on the ground and are subsequently dissolved. In Israel, rainfall contains 1–25 ppm chloride derived partly from evaporated sea spray and partly from airborne desert dust.

(2) Residual saline waters are flushed from rocks. The residual water may either be connate with the rock or reflect a phase of oceanic transgression subsequent to rock deposition, or an ancient terminal lake. In many aquifers this mechanism causes an increase of salinity with depth and in the vicinity of fine-grained rocks.

(3) In desert regions saline waters and even salt layers are formed near evaporating surfaces and subsequently flushed out by ascending groundwater (see Section 2.7).

(4) In coastal aquifers fresh groundwater mixes with the heavier seawater at the interface.

Chloride does not enter into ion exchange processes. Chloridic salts precipitate from solution only at concentrations exceeding that of seawater. Because of this *conservative* property (i.e., the tendency to remain in solution), chloride is a reliable indicator of hydrologic processes.

Decreasing chloride concentrations show that freshwater enters the aquifer. Increasing concentrations can be caused by several processes: (1) Mixing with more saline water, (2) solution of solid salt from the rock, and (3) concentration of chloride by evapotranspiration from a very shallow water table.

In a well-flushed aquifer the small concentrations of chloride that stem from airborne salts may serve as data for estimating natural replenishment (Section 12.4). In mixed waters chloride faithfully reflects the mixing ratio of the end members (Section 9.6).

Bicarbonate (HCO_3^-). Carbonate minerals such as calcite and dolomite are only sparingly soluble in pure water but form bicarbonate compounds in water containing carbon dioxide.

$$CaCO_{3(c)} + H_2O + CO_{2(aqu)} = Ca(HCO_3)_2 \qquad (9.6a)$$

$$Ca(HCO_3)_2 \rightleftarrows Ca^{2+} + 2HCO_3^- \qquad (9.6b)$$

where the subscripts (c) and (aqu) refer to solid and dissolved compounds, respectively.

Simultaneously, carbon dioxide reacts with the water.

$$CO_{2(aqu)} + H_2O = H_2CO_3 \rightleftarrows H^+ + HCO_3^- \rightleftarrows 2H^+ + CO_3^{2-} \qquad (9.7)$$

The concentration of each one of the *carbonic species* $CO_{2\,(aqu)}$, HCO_3^- and CO_3^{2-}, reflects the *ionic equilibrium* of all solutes in the water (Garrels and Christ, 1965; Hem, 1970). In chemical analyses the carbonic species are usually lumped together and reported as HCO_3^-.

Water in equilibrium with calcite and atmospheric carbon dioxide, which constitutes about 0.03% of the atmosphere, should contain approximately 60 ppm HCO_3^-. The concentrations actually observed in carbonate aquifers are 300–450 ppm HCO_3^-. The additional carbon dioxide necessary to generate such waters may stem from the biologic activity of plant roots, from the oxidation of organic matter included in the soil and in the rock, from volcanic exhalations, and from various chemical reactions. Opinions differ from author to author and from place to place, but measured data are scarce.

Saturation of a water with respect to calcite is indicated by the saturation pH, which can be computed with the aid of the equilibrium concept mentioned earlier (Hem, 1970; Matthess, 1973). If the saturation pH is larger than the measured one, the water is undersaturated with respect to calcite; if it is smaller, precipitation will occur sooner or later. Waters in carbonate aquifers are sometimes undersaturated, although they have been in contact with carbonate minerals for a very long time. The decrease of pressure that accompanies pumping from a certain depth below water level is likely to cause a decrease of dissolved carbon dioxide and to render the water more saturated with calcite than it originally was. Furthermore, magnesium can remain in solution at a higher pH than calcium. (For this reason only calcitic veins are found in carbonate rocks, even if the rock itself is a dolomite.) Therefore the above method tends to overestimate calcite saturation of water in the aquifer.

The state of saturation in respect to calcite is of interest to engineers. Undersaturated water, containing an excess of carbon dioxide, may corrode pump impellers and pipes, and strongly supersaturated water will reduce the diameter of pipes by calcitic incrustations. The optimum desired by engineers is slight supersaturation that deposits a thin film of calcite and protects the pipe from corrosion. In many installations this optimum is maintained by aeration.

Sulfate (SO_4^{2-}).   The major source of sulfate in freshwater is evaporites, mainly gypsum ($CaSO_4 \times 2H_2O$). Other sources are airborne sulfate compounds originating from the sea and from dust, gaseous sulfur oxides produced by the combustion of fossil fuel and washed down by rainfall, decaying organic matter, volcanic exhalations, and the weathering products of some magmatic rocks. Concentrations in excess of about 30 ppm SO_4^{2-} in groundwater suggest contact with gypsum-bearing rocks. The maximum concentration in fresh groundwater is 1360 ppm SO_4^{2-}; higher concentrations may be reached in saline waters because of the presence of other ions.

SO_4^{2-} is not appreciably affected by adsorption or ion exchange processes. Precipitation may occur only at concentrations in excess of 1360 ppm. Reduction usually produces H_2S. However, H_2S may also stem from the decay of organic matter or from volcanic exhalations. The mere presence of this compound does not necessarily indicate reduction of sulfate minerals. Theoretically, sulfate concentrations may also be diminished by the precipitation of the sparingly soluble compounds $BaSO_4$ and $SrSC_4$, but barium and strontium are so rare in the rocks associated with groundwater that this process is unlikely to occur at any significant rate.

Nitrate (NO_3^-). Nitrate is the most common representative of the nitrogen species, NO_3^-, NO_2^-, NH_3, and NH_4^+ in groundwater. Small concentrations of nitrogen compounds occur in rainwater. They originate from the oxidation of atmospheric nitrogen by electric discharges and from the combustion of fossil fuel.

The major source of nitrogen in groundwater is organic matter that is oxidized by aerobic bacteria in the following sequence: organic compounds $\rightarrow NH_3$ (gaseous ammonia) $\rightarrow NH_4^+$ (ammonium ion) $\rightarrow NO_2^-$ (nitrite ion) $\rightarrow NO_3^-$ (nitrate ion). In the absence of oxygen, anaerobic bacteria may reduce nitrate to nitrite, gaseous ammonia, and eventually even molecular nitrogen. The gaseous components of the nitrification and denitrification sequences may escape; the nitrite ion is strongly adsorbed to clay minerals. Therefore nitrogen compounds are the least conservative of all common groundwater constituents.

Relatively large NO_3^- concentrations, in excess of, say, 20 ppm, and any increase of nitrate concentrations in the course of time point toward pollution by organic matter. Man-made sources of nitrate pollution are agricultural fertilizers, urban effluents, solid waste disposal, and concentrations of livestock. Sometimes the mere lowering of the water table may expose organic matter, such as bog deposits, to air and thus induce nitrogen pollution. This factor has to be anticipated wherever aquifers containing seams of peat or lignite are intensively developed.

Calcium and magnesium (Ca^{2+}, Mg^{2+}). The calcium and magnesium, so-called *earth alkaline* metals, enter into groundwater by the dissolution of carbonate minerals in water containing carbon dioxide. Another major source of calcium is the dissolution of gypsum ($CaSO_4 \times 2H_2O$). Concentrations are indicative of aquifer lithology: Traces to about 30 ppm are characteristic to magmatic aquifers, up to 100 ppm are common in sedimentary terrains, up to 300 ppm occur in carbonate aquifers, and up to 600 ppm are found in aquifers containing gypsum or in contact with gypsum layers. Calcium and magnesium are susceptible to ion exchange with sodium and vice versa.

Sodium and potassium (Na^+, K^+).   Sodium and potassium, the so-called *alkaline metals*, occur in large concentrations, about 26,000 ppm each, in magmatic rocks. Potassium is strongly absorbed by clay minerals and therefore relatively scarce in groundwater and in most natural waters. In the ocean, concentrations are 10,560 ppm Na^+ and 380 ppm K^+.

Groundwater pollution by sodium chloride is the unavoidable by-product of human activity, such as return flows from irrigation and disposal of industrial and urban wastes. The process usually takes the form of a very slow "salt creep" and may remain masked for a long time by the noise inherent in salinity data of groundwater. Intensive groundwater abstraction creates water level depressions with little or no outflow and thus accentuates the process.

Fluoride (F^-).   The source minerals of fluoride occur in igneous, metamorphic, and sedimentary rocks. Fluoride compounds are also a common constituent of volcanic exhalations.

In freshwater the concentration of fluoride generally remains below 1 ppm, but much higher concentrations are sometimes found in very soft water. Fluoride is an important constituent of drinking water because it is taken up by the human body and incorporated into teeth and bones. Excessive fluoride concentrations, however, are toxic.

Bromide (Br^-).   Ocean water contains about 65 mg/liter Br^- and is the main source of bromide. Bromide is an important constituent of brines that are depleted of chloride because of precipitation of NaCl. Dead Sea water, for example, contains 5112 mg/liter Br^-. In fresh groundwater bromide concentrations are usually insignificant. When salination occurs the bromide–chloride ratio may serve as an indicator of the source of salinity.

Boron (B).   The sources of boron are igneous minerals, volcanic exhalations, and some highly concentrated brines. The range of concentrations as follows: in freshwater, generally less than 1 ppm; in ocean water, about 4.6 mg/liter, in oil brines and thermal waters, 10–100 mg/liter and more. Little is known about the dissolved species of this element. Boron concentrations in excess of 4 ppm are sometimes encountered in fresh groundwater of thermal origin. Such waters are destructive to plant growth.

Iron (Fe).   The primary sources of iron are dark magmatic minerals. In sedimentary strata iron occurs in its ferrous (bivalent) form, as ferric (trivalent) hydroxide or oxide, and in a mixed ferric–ferrous form. Ferrous iron is a common constituent of bog and swamp deposits, lignites, and coal. Groundwater in contact with such strata frequently contains 1–10 ppm

Fe^{2-}. When the water is exposed to air, the iron rapidly oxidizes, the water turns dark, and ferric iron precipitates in the form of floccules of $Fe\,(OH)_3$ that are difficult to remove. For this reason even minute amounts of iron in water are undesirable.

Manganese (Mn).   Manganese is widely distributed in rocks and soils, though it is less abundant than iron, with which it is closely associated. Even minute amounts of manganese in water are objectionable, for the same reason as with iron.

Silicium (Si).   Silica species in groundwater are derived from the dissolution of igneous minerals and of their weathering products. They do not readily dissociate into ions but occur mainly in the form of undissociated molecules. Dissolution, precipitation, and the transformation of amorphous into crystalline silica are very slow processes. Therefore waters that are, theoretically, supersaturated with silica are fairly common. The range of silica concentrations in groundwater is about 1–40 ppm SiO_2, the higher part of the range being associated with igneous rock aquifers and with waters of a thermal origin.

9.4   CHEMICAL PROCESSES OCCURRING IN GROUNDWATER

Dissolution and Precipitation

The *solubility* of a substance is the maximum amount that can be dissolved in unit weight of water under given conditions of temperature and pressure. A *saturated* solution contains this maximum amount, an *undersaturated* solution tends to dissolve more of the substance, and a *supersaturated* solution tends to precipitate the substance in solid form or—in the case of gases—to exhale it, until saturation is reestablished. Generally the solubility of minerals increases with temperature and is practically unaffected by pressure, whereas the solubility of gases decreases with temperature and increases with pressure. The solubility values of a few substances in pure water are shown in Table 9.1.

Theoretical insight into the behavior of aqueous solutions is gained through the application of *thermodynamic laws*. Two important conclusions from the *theory of aqueous solutions* are as follows:

(1) In a complex solution, such as groundwater, where several solutes interact with each other, the solubility of each mineral depends on the nature and concentrations of all dissolved constituents.

TABLE 9.1

The Solubility of Various Substances in Pure Water

Substance	Solubility in pure water (mg/liter)	Temperature of water (°C)
$CaCO_3$ [a]	13.2	16
$MgCO_3 + 3H_2O$	970	12
NaCl	264,000	20
KCl	255,800	20
$MgCl_2$	353,000	20
$CaCl_2$	427,000	20
$CaSO_4$	2,040	20
$MgSO_4$	300,000	20
Na_2SO_4	160,200	20
K_2SO_4	99,100	20
NaBr	475,000	20
KBr	394,000	20
$CaBr_2$ [a]	588,000	20
H_e [b]	1.7	0 at atmospheric pressure
N_2	28.8	0 at atmospheric pressure
O_2	69.45	0 at atmospheric pressure
NH_3	1000	0 at atmospheric pressure
CO_2 [b]	3346	0 at atmospheric pressure

[a] After Taussig (1976).
[b] After Matthess (1973).

(2) The minerals that may precipitate from a complex solution are not necessarily identical with the minerals originally dissolved. In other words, the chemical composition of a precipitate is determined by chemical reactions between dissolved constitutents, not by their origin.

More information on this subject can be found under the key words *law of mass action, ionic equilibria,* and *solubility product* in texts on the chemical composition of water and on physical chemistry.

The theory of aqueous solutions is an indispensable tool for the study of very saline waters where complicated solution–precipitation reactions are likely. Normal, usable groundwater may be saturated only with respect to calcite and can, therefore, be investigated by the simpler methods that are discussed in Section 9.5.

Adsorption and Ion Exchange

Cations are strongly attracted by the negative charges that prevail in the crystal lattices of many minerals, especially clay minerals. The thin layer of ions thus adsorbed frequently reflects antecedent geologic conditions. For example, sodium may have been adsorbed during sediment deposition from the sea or during a later phase of flooding by seawater. When these adsorbed sodium ions come in contact with water rich in calcium ions, the latter are exchanged by the former and the water gains sodium while losing calcium (softening effect). The inverse effect is often observed when a coastal aquifer is invaded by seawater. In this case water in the zone of mixing may become enriched in calcium and depleted in sodium so that these two constituents no longer reflect the mixing ratio of seawater and freshwater. Other exchange reactions occur mainly under laboratory conditions or in very saline waters.

Adsorption and ion exchange proceed until a thermodynamic equilibrium between the water and the reacting mineral is reached. At this point the exchange capacity of the mineral can be said to be exhausted. However, under natural conditions and within the relatively short period of measurements the exhaustion of exchange capacity is never observed.

Mixing

The mixing of groundwater bodies with different chemical composition is brought about by two physical processes, *diffusion*, resulting from the thermal motion of molecules and ions, and *hydrodynamic* dispersion, caused by flow through a network of interconnected channels.

Differences of specific density may either induce or impede mixing. An example of the former case is the mixing of relatively light thermal waters with an overlying, colder, and heavier water body. An example of the latter case is the seawater–freshwater interface in coastal aquifers.

Oxidation, Reduction

A cation is said to become *oxidized* if its valence increases because of the loss of an electron. The decrease of valence caused by the gain of an electron is called *reduction*. The reduction of one constituent is always accompanied by the oxidation of another one, whereas oxidation either results from reaction with free oxygen or accompanies the reduction of another constituent. Many oxidation–reduction reactions are speeded up by the biologic activity of microorganisms.

Three reactions of this type frequently occur in groundwater: *nitrification* and *denitrification* (Section 9.3); oxidation of sulfides to sulfates and the reduction of sulfates to molecular sulfur and to H_2S; and oxidation of bivalent iron to trivalent iron (Section 9.3.).

Membrane Effects

Osmotic diffusion may occur where a clay layer separates freshwater from saline water. The influence of membrane effects on water quality is little documented and probably insignificant where fresh groundwater is concerned.

9.5   THE INTERPRETATION OF CHEMICAL DATA

In order to obtain hydrogeologic information from chemical data it is necessary to reconstruct the path of *geochemical evolution*, i.e., the sequence of processes through which the water acquired its chemical composition. Since each analysis can be explained by several different paths of evolution, the most plausible path has to be selected on the basis of hydrogeologic evidence. In other words, chemical data cannot be interpreted without reference to geohydrologic data or assumptions.

The interpretation of brines is difficult because many processes including precipitation intervened in their formation. Fresh groundwaters are undersaturated in all but a few minerals (see Section 9.4), and it is justified to assume that, in this case, dissolution from the aquifer is the dominant process. Hence the interpretation of chemical data from fresh groundwater is comparatively simple. The following working procedure is suggested:

(1) Disregarding the minor mineral content of rainwater, assume that the major constituents were picked up by dissolution from the aquifer and estimate, on the basis of this assumption, the chemical composition the water is expected to have.

(2) Identify significant discrepancies between the prediction thus derived and the chemical analyses at hand.

(3) Identify significant changes of chemical composition along the flow path, with depth, and in time.

(4) Formulate hypothetical explanations for the observed discrepancies and changes.

(5) Find hydrogeologic evidence to support these hypotheses. For example: If mixing is postulated, two identifiable end members must be in hydrologic contact somewhere in the region. If ion exchange is assumed, contact with exchange minerals has to be demonstrated.

(6) Introduce corrections for the precipitation of calcite and/or gypsum if concentrations are sufficiently high.

(7) Explain the presence and concentrations of minor constituents, such as NO_3, H_2S, F, Si, and support the explanations by hydrogeologic evidence.

The value of this procedure stems from the unsuspected hydrogeologic features it is likely to indicate. The investigator has to decide whether the hydrologic problems thus brought to light merit a more detailed investigation or whether a plausible, though not completely proved, explanation suffices for the practical purpose at hand. Indications that can be obtained from several common groundwater constituents have been discussed in Section 9.4. Additional technical aids for the interpretation of groundwater analyses, followed by a table of chemical data (Table 9.2), are listed below.

The *ionic formula* ranks anions and cations separately, expressed in meq/liter, in the order of decreasing magnitude; for example:

$$HCO_3^- > SO_4^{2-} > Cl^-$$
$$Ca^{2+} > Mg^{2+} > Na^+$$
Carbonate water

$$Cl^- > SO_4^{2-} > HCO_3^-$$
$$Na^+ > Ca^{2+} > Mg^{2+}$$
Chloridic water

The dominant anion identifies the large geochemical group to which the water belongs. The ranking order of the other ions indicates more detailed characteristics, which have to be explained with reference to actual concentrations and to hydrogeologic data. Theoretically, 36 permutations of constituents are possible.

Ionic ratios computed from ionic concentrations in meq/liter have many applications.

Mg/Ca: For waters flowing through limestone aquifers this ratio is normally in the range 0.5–0.7. Ratios in the range 0.7–0.9 are commonly associated with dolomitic aquifers (Hsu, 1963). Ratios exceeding 0.9 are sometimes found in freshwater from silicate aquifers (Hem, 1970). More often, however, they indicate the admixture of seawater or of a brine. In brackish waters an increase of the Mg/Ca ratio along the flow path may be caused by the precipitation of calcium carbonate or calcium sulfate, if concentrations are sufficiently high.

Na/Cl: Waters related to the normal hydrologic cycle have the ratio characterizing seawater, $0.876 \pm 10\%$. Ratios exceeding 1.0 are attributed to negative ion exchange in which calcium and magnesium are replaced by sodium. Such waters are usually encountered in alkali-rich volcanic, igneous, or metamorphic formations (White, 1957b). Ratios below the seawater range indicate mixing with brines from which sodium has been precipitated, or exchange of sodium from the water against calcium in the aquifer. The latter effect is often encountered when coastal aquifers are affected by seawater intrusion (Hem, 1970; Schmorak and Mercado, 1969).

Na/K: In seawater the ratio is around 47. In rainwater it is low, less than 10, probably because of the rearrangement of ions on bubbles of

TABLE 9.2

Selected Chemical Analyses from Israel[a,b]

		(1)	(2)	(3)	(4)	(5)	(6)	(7)	(8)	(9)	(10)	(11)	(12)
HCO_3	mg/liter	1.58	48.76	255	445	182.9	143.1	286.5	204.2	378	146.3	140	220
	meq/liter	0.026	0.80	4.18	7.30	3.00	2.34	4.7	3.35	6.20	2.40	2.29	3.61
SO_4	mg/liter	0.95	162.15	73	55.1	37.4	1293	12.3	8.6	110.3	819	2650	490
	meq/liter	0.02	3.38	1.52	1.15	0.78	28.92	0.26	0.18	2.30	17.0	53.74	10.20
Cl	mg/liter	2.73	70.91	52	272	92.2	213	61.7	8.5	844	17,747	19,000	210,670
	meq/liter	0.08	2.00	1.46	7.66	2.6	6.01	1.742	0.24	23.90	500.98	535.99	5943
NO_3	mg/liter	0.22	2.3	15.9	22.8	51.4	8.20	18.9	5.0	n.d.	0.0	n.d	0.0
	meq/liter	0.003	0.037	0.29	0.37	0.83	0.13	0.304	0.08		0.0		
Ca^{2+}	mg/liter	0.67	78.09	66	80.1	68.8	312.3	27.6	64.9	122.1	3487.3	400	16,600.
	meq/liter	0.003	3.90	3.30	4.00	3.44	15.58	1.38	3.24	6.10	174.17	19.96	828.34
Mg^{2+}	mg/liter	0.20	8.50	38	44.5	18.9	160.4	25.8	6.0	80.8	616.5	1270	40,570
	meq/liter	0.016	0.70	3.12	3.66	1.56	13.19	2.12	0.49	6.60	50.71	104.47	3337.29
Na^+	mg/liter	1.75	27.61	22	196	47.8	138	79.1	2.7	446	6651.5	10,600	38,470
	meq/liter	0.076	1.20	0.96	8.53	2.08	6.00	3.44	0.118	19.4	289.34	461.1	1673.74
K^+	mg/liter	n.d	n.d	2	2.6	5.7	11.5	2.9	n.d	17.0	339.7	380	7150
	meq/liter			0.06	0.066	0.14	0.29	0.074		0.43	8.69	9.72	182.82
pH	measured	n.d	6.5	7.05	7.05	7.30	n.d	7.6	8.05	n.d	6.5	n.d	n.d
	saturation			7.3	7.08	7.33		7.62	7.49				
EC	micromhos	n.d	n.d	n.d	1956	700	2733	700	384	n.d	47,420	n.d	n.d
TDS	mg/liter	n.d	n.d	544	910	445	2633	n.d	206	n.d	30,010	34,430	304,270
Temperature °C		n.d	n.d	21.8	22.2	24.2	n.d	23.6	14.8	23.8	60.6	26	31.8
S_3O_2	mg/liter	n.d	n.d	15.0	17.4	21.7	n.d	35.6	5.92	n.d	39.1	n.d	n.d
F	mg/liter	n.d	n.d	0.1	0.3	0.2	n.d	0.25	0.15	n.d	2.65	n.d	n.d
	meq/liter			0.006	0.016	0.01		0.014	0.008		0.14		

		(8)	(9)	(10)	(11)	(12)
Br	mg/liter	2.4		197.7	65	5,150
	meq/liter	0.03		2.476	0.813	64.427
H_2S	mg/liter			1.17		
CO_2	mg/liter			12.3		

[a] Data by courtesy of TAHAL, Ltd.

[b] Column headings: (1) Rain, single storm, (2) Dew, (3) Dolomite well 78 m deep, (4) Well, calcareous sandstone 112 m deep, (5) Well, marly sands 97 m deep, (6) Well, gypsiferous sandy strata, 75 m deep, (7) Well, basalt 120 m deep, (8) Jordan spring, (9) Na'aman spring, (10) Kinnereth, thermal spring, (11) Mediterranean Sea, (12) Dead Sea, medium depth.

seawater (Bloch *et al.*, 1966). Close to recharge areas the ratio is, for most types of aquifers, in the range of 15–25 (White *et al.*, 1963). Further downstream the ratio tends to increase to 50–70 because of the adsorption of potassium on clays and on other silicates. Low ratios, less than 15, have been reported from certain brines and attributed to an advanced stage of sodium–calcium exchange (White, 1957a, b).

$(Ca + Mg)/(K + Na)$: Near recharge areas the ratio usually exceeds unity. With the downstream increase in alkali metals resulting from ion exchange, a decrease in this ratio is usually encountered. Brines from which NaCl has been precipitated or in which ion exchange substituted Ca for Na are characterized by high ratios.

HCO_3/Cl; SO_4/Cl: Close to recharge areas the assemblage of anions is usually dominated by bicarbonate, and its concentration usually increases downstream until the solubility product of $CaCO_3$ is attained (Schoeller, 1962). The concentrations of SO_4 and Cl also increase in the downstream direction. In the range of normal salinities the solubility product of $CaSO_4$ is not attained and SO_4 concentrations continue to increase, but chloride concentrations increase more rapidly until chloride becomes the dominant ion.

Cl/Br: In seawater and in waters participating in the normal hydrologic cycle the ratio is close to 300. Lower values are characteristic of formation waters and of brines from which chlorides precipitated. Therefore this ratio is often used to distinguish seawater intrusion from other causes of salination. Values in the range of 500–4000 have been found in waters in direct contact with evaporites (Behne, 1953).

The *trilinear diagram* (Piper, 1944) introduces two separate sets of triangular coordinates for anions and cations, respectively. Concentrations are plotted as percentages of total anion or cation concentrations in milliequivalents. The points in the two triangular grids may then be projected into a rhomboid grid (Fig. 9.1). Circles with diameters at the appropriate scale, or by figures near each point, can be used to indicate absolute concentration values. When three points fall on a straight line, the intermediate point represents a mixture between the two end points.

A triangular diagram reserves equal areas for all possible kinds of water and is convenient for the representation of widely divergent water types. When closely related waters are plotted, the points cluster together obscuring all details, and the rest of the sheet remains blank. Several modifications of the triangular diagram are discussed by Hem (1970), Matthess (1973), and Schneider (1973).

The *logarithmic diagram* (Schoeller, 1962) focuses attention on ion ratios. The ions are identified by vertical equidistant lines, and the respective

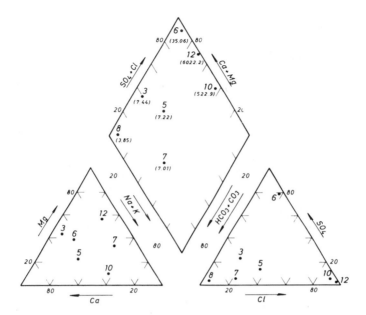

Fig. 9.1 Trilinear diagram. Large figures identify analyses in Table 9.2, small figures in parentheses indicate sum of cations meq/liter.

concentrations are plotted on a logarithmic scale (Fig. 9.2). The zigzag line connecting all points gives a visual impression of the chemical composition. When several analyses are plotted on one sheet, parallel lines indicate equal ion ratios. Appropriately offset logarithmic scales for meq/liter and for mg/liter, respectively, save the bother of converting one unit to the other one. In precomputer days this was a distinct advantage.

The *mixing diagram* is a convenient tool for the investigation of mixing relationships. The example shown in Fig. 9.3 is self-explanatory. The advantage of this representation is that each constituent or characteristic can be plotted on a convenient scale. The points representing a specific characteristic of a mixed water fall on a mixing line between the points representing end members, and all the points representing various character-istics of a mixed water fall on a vertical line that indicates the mixing ratio, in percent, between the end members. Only constituents that are not prone to ion exchange or to reduction–oxidation should be used in this method.

The *natural classification of waters* (Taussig, 1961, 1976) combines equiv-alent concentrations of ion pairs in a fixed sequence. For example, HCO_3 is

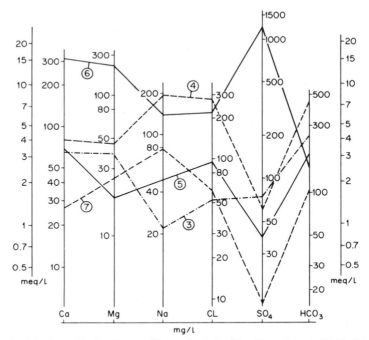

Fig. 9.2   Logarithmic diagram. Figures in circles identify analyses in Table 9.2.

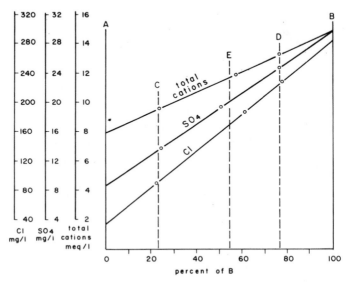

Fig. 9.3   Mixing diagram. The waters represented by C and D are mixtures of the *end members* A and B.

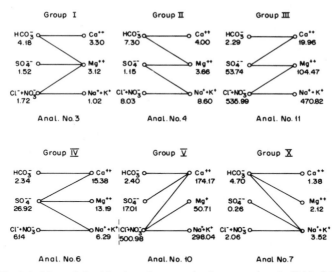

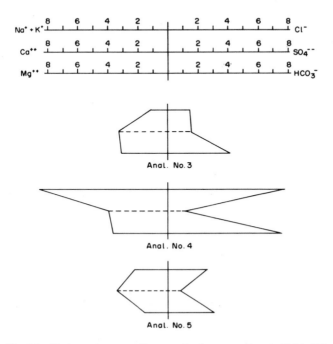

Fig. 9.4   Natural classification of waters. Analyses are given in Table 9.2.

Fig. 9.5   Horizontal pattern diagram. Analyses are given in Table 9.2.

combined first with Ca; the remainder is combined with Mg. The remaining surplus of Mg is combined first with SO_4 and then with Cl. The remaining surplus of Cl is combined with Na + K (Fig. 9.4). Six major groups can be defined in this way. If NO_3 is added to the list of ions, four additional groups are obtained. The ion pairs thus constructed are, of course, only indices, just like ion ratios or points on a diagram. Minerals cannot be reconstituted from ionic solutions in such a simple way.

Taussig's classification combines a simple diagrammatic representation that does not need much space with figures indicating concentrations in meq/liter. The diagram makes it easy to identify significant changes along the flow path of the water.

The *horizontal pattern diagram* (Stiff, 1953) is useful for the representation of hydrogeochemical data on maps and cross section. It is illustrated in Fig. 9.5. Many other symbolic representations have been proposed for this purpose. Schneider (1973) discusses hydrogeochemical legends in some detail. It should, however, be remembered that the purpose of a legend is to simplify map reading. Very elaborate legends are apt to defeat their own purpose and are better replaced by explanatory notes attached to the maps.

9.6   QUALITY CRITERIA FOR GROUNDWATER SUPPLIES

Water quality is judged by five principal criteria: (1) solid mineral particles; (2) dissolved anorganic constituents; (3) dead organic matter; (4) live organisms, especially bacteria; (5) radioactivity. For some purposes the original temperature of the water is also of importance.

Particulate matter such as sand, silt, and suspended clay is objectionable for hygienic and aesthetic reasons, and because it plays havoc with water supply installations. Only primitive irrigation installations are insensitive to dirty water. Sand can be removed by *sand traps*, composed of wide sections of pipe where flow velocities are so small that the sand settles. Clay particles can be removed only by costly flocculation and filtration. Properly constructed and thoroughly developed wells should not draw any particulate matter. Attention to these points during well construction prevents much trouble.

Table 9.3 gives an abbreviated list of standards that seem to be generally accepted. Dead organic matter and heavy bacterial contamination that pose a grave problem are encountered only in polluted groundwater. The major dissolved constituents are acceptable or at least tolerable within a wide margin of concentrations. A large amount of research has been done on minor constituents, especially fluoride.

TABLE 9.3

Standards for the Chemical Composition of Drinking Water

Major constituents	Concentrations (mg/liter)		Trace constituents	Maximum concentration (mg/liter)
	Desirable range	Maximum concentration		
TDS	$\leqslant 500^a$	1500	NH_4^+	0.5
pH	7.0–8.5	6.5–9.2	F^-	1.5^c
Cl^-	$\leqslant 300$	600	Fe	1.0
SO_4^{2-}	$\leqslant 200$	400	Pb	0.05
NO_3^-	-	50	Cu	1.0
Ca^{2+}	75–200		Cd	0.01
Mg^{2+}	$50–150^b$	150^b	Se	0.01
$MgSO_4 + Na_2SO_4$	$\leqslant 500$	1000	Ag	0.05
			Zn	5.0
			Cr^{6+}	0.05
			Cyanide	0.01
			Phenols	0.002

[a] $\leqslant$ means smaller than, or equal to.
[b] If SO_4 exceeds 250 mg/liter, Mg should not exceed 30 mg/liter
[c] Desirable ranges of fluoride were specified by the U.S. Public Health Service (1962; cited also in Hem, 1970, p. 332). *Sources:* U.S. Public Health Service (1962) and World Health Organization (1970, 1971).

Quality criteria for irrigation water depend on the influence of the water on the soil and on the crop, on climatic factors, and on irrigation methods. A rough quality criterion for irrigation water is TDS measured as EC. The relevant ranges are as follows:

excellent waters   less than 250   micromhos/cm at 25°C
good–permissible
    waters   250–2000   micromhos/cm at 25°C
doubtful–unsuitable more than 2000   micromhos/cm at 25°C

Doubtful waters can still be used for the irrigation of some crops, provided that wetting of the leaves is avoided, that the soil is well drained, and that a downward flux of irrigation water is maintained at all times.

A commonly used criterion for the soil–water relationship is *SAR* (sodium adsorption ratio) defined by

$$SAR = \frac{Na}{\sqrt{\dfrac{Ca+Mg}{2}}} \tag{9.8}$$

where Na, Ca, Mg are in meq/liter.

A high SAR value indicates that sodium from the water is likely to replace calcium and magnesium in the soil with a consequent deterioration of soil texture. Low SAR values are smaller than 10, medium values are between 10 and 18, and high values exceed 18. In well-drained soils the danger of sodium exchange is smaller than in heavy, badly drained soils.

A minor constituent that has received much attention is boron. Small concentrations up to 0.5 ppm B are conducive to plant growth; concentrations in excess of 4 ppm B are destructive to all crops. The tolerance of crops to boron concentrations varies between these limits.

The field of water suitability for various purposes is very wide and cannot possibly be encompassed by any one person. The investigator of a groundwater resource should confine his work to the provision of complete analyses, including trace elements that seem to merit attention in the particular setting and to the application of the simple criteria given above. In cases of doubt, specialists in the respective fields should be consulted.

FURTHER READINGS

American Water Works Association (1971). "Water Quality and Treatment," 3rd ed. McGraw-Hill, New York.

Arad, A. (1966). Hydrogeochemistry of groundwater in Central Israel. IASH bull 7, 122–146.

Arad, A., Kafri, U., and E. Fleischer, (1975). The Na'aman spring Northern Israel, salination mechanism of an irregular seawater–freshwater interface. *J. Hydrol.* **25**, 81–104.

Atkinson, T. C. (1977). Carbon dioxide in the unsaturated zone, an important control of groundwater hardness in limestone. *J. Hydrol.* **35**, 111–124.

Batard, F., Billet, C., and Risler, J. J. (1979). Prospection de CO_2 d'origine profonde dans le Massif Central (France). *Hydrogéologie, Géologie de l'ingenieur,* Sect. 111, No. 2, pp. 157–163, B.R.G.M. Orléans, France.

Behne, W. (1953). Untersuchungen zur Geochemie des Chlor und Brom. *Geochim. Cosmochim. Acta* **3**, No. 4, 186–215.

Bentor, Y. K. (1969). On the evolution of subsurface brines in Israel. *Chem. Geol.* **4**, 83–110.

Bloch, M. R., Kaplan, D., Kertes, V., and Schnerb, J. (1966). Ion separation in bursting air bubbles. *Nature (London)* **209**, 802–803.

Castany, G. (1968). "Prospection et Exploitation des Eaux Souterraines," pp. 238–265. Dunod, Paris.

Chetboun, G. (1977). A mathematical model for predicting the concentration of nitrogen compounds in surface and g'water streams. Ph.D. Thesis, Hebrew Univ., Jerusalem.

Daniels, F., and Alberty, R. A. (1966). "Physical Chemistry," 3d ed. Wiley (Interscience), New York.

Garrels, R. M., and Christ, C. C. (1965). "Solutions Minerals and Equilibria." Harper, New York.

Hem, J. D. (1970). Study and interpretation of the chemical characteristics of natural waters. *U.S. Geol. Sur., Water-Supply Pap.* 1473.

Hsu, K. J. (1963). Solubility of dolomite and the composition of Florida groundwaters. *J. Hydrol.* **1**, 288–310.

IHD-WHO (1978). "Water Quality Surveys Studies and Reports in Hydrology," Vol. 23, UNESCO, Paris.

Jacobson, R. L., and Langmuir, D. (1972). An accurate method for calculating saturation levels of groundwater with respect to calcite and dolomite. *Trans. Cave Res. Group. G.B.* **14**, 104–108.

Kitano, Y. (ed.) (1975). "Geochemistry of Water." Dowden, Hutchinson and Ross, Inc. distributed by Academic Press, New York.

Lafuente, J. G. (1969). "Quimica del Aqua." Blume, Madrid.

Matthess G. (1973). "Die Beschaffenheit des Grundwassers." Borntraeger, Berlin.

Mercado, A., and Billings, J. K. (1975). The kinetics of mineral dissolution in carbonate aquifers as a tool for hydrological investigations. *J. Hydrol.* **24**, 303–331; **35**, 365–384.

Miotke, F. D. (1974). Carbon dioxide. *Abh. Karst-Hoehlenk., Reihe A* No. 9. Geographische Zeitschrift, Franz Steiner, Wiesbaden, Federal Republic of Germany.

Piper A. M. (1944). A graphic procedure for the geochemical interpretation of water analyses. *Trans. Am. Geophys. Union.*, **25**, 914–923.

Reardon, E. J., Allison, G. B., and Fritz, P. (1979). Seasonal chemical and isotope variations of soil CO_2 at Trout Creek, Ontario, Canada. *J. Hydrol.* **43**, No. 1/4, 355–371.

Schmorak, S., and Mercado, A. (1969). Upconing of the freshwater–seawater interface below pumping wells. *Water Resour. Res.* **5**, 1290–1311.

Schneider, H. (1973). "Die Wassererschliessung," Chap. 3.7. Vulcan Verlag, Essen.

Schoeller, H. (1956). "Geochemie des Eaux Souterraines." Technip. Paris.

Schoeller, H. (1962). "Les Eaux Souterraines," pp. 257–384. Masson, Paris.

Schoeller, H. (1964). La concentration des eaux souterraines en chlore. *Bull. BRGM* No. 2, pp. 51–90.

Schoeller, H. (1969). L'acide carbonique des eaux souterraines. *Bull. BRGM, Sect. III* No. 1, pp. 1–32.

Shuster, E. T., and White, W. B. (1972). Source areas and climatic effects in carbonate groundwaters as determined by saturation indices and carbon dioxide pressures. *Water Resour. Res.* **8**, 1067–1073.

Sillen, L. G., and Martell, A. E., (1964). Stability constants of metal ion complexes. *Chem. Soc., Spec. Publ.* No. 17.

Stiff, H. A., Jr. (1951). The interpretation of chemical water analyses by means of patterns. *J. Pet. Technol.* **3** (10), 15–17.

Stumm, M., and Morgan, J. J. (1970). "Aquatic Chemistry." Wiley, New York.

Summers, W. K. (1972). Factors affecting the validity of chemical analyses of natural waters. *Groundwater* **10**, 12–17.

Talsma, T., and Philip, J. R. (1971). "Salinity and Water Use. A National Symposium on Hydrology Sponsored by the Australian Academy of Science." Macmillan, London.

Taussig, K. (1961). "Natural Groups of Groundwater and their Origin," PN 205. TAHAL, Water Plann. Isr., Tel Aviv.

Taussig, K. (1976). "Water Chemistry." Mekoroth Water Co., Tel Aviv.

Tebbutt, T. H. Y. (1971). "Principles of Water Quality Control." Pergamon, Oxford.

Todd, D. K., ed. (1970). "The Water Encyclopedia," pp. 319–321. Water Inf. Cent., Port Washington, New York.

UNESCO-WHO (1978). "Water Quality Surveys. A Guide for the Collection and Interpretation of Water Quality Data." Studies and Reports in Hydrology, No. 23. UNESCO, Paris.

U.S. Public Health Service (1962). "Drinking Water Standards." U.S. Dep. Health, Educ., Welfare, Washington, D.C.

Valyashko, M. C. (1958). Some general rules with respect to the formation of the chemical composition of natural brines. *Tr. Lab. Gidrogeol. Probl., Akad. Nauk SSSR* **16**, 127–140.

Water Research Center. (1977). Groundwater Quality, Measurement and Protection. Papers and proceedings of the conference held at the Univ. of Reading in 1976. Water Research Center, Medmenham, U.K.

White, D. E. (1957a). Thermal waters of volcanic origin. *Geol. Soc. Am., Bull.* **68**, 1637–1658.

White, D. E. (1957b). Magmatic, connate and metamorphic waters. *Geol. Soc. Am., Bull.*, **68**, 1659–1682.

White, D. E. (1960). Summary of chemical characteristics of some waters of deep origin. *U.S. Geol. Surv., Prof. Pap.* No. 400-B, pp. B452–B454.

White, D. E., Hem, J. D., and Waring, G. A. (1963). Chemical composition of subsurface waters. *U.S. Geol. Surv., Prof. Pap.* No. 440-F, pp. F1–F67.

World Health Organization (1970). "European Standards for Drinking Water." 2nd ed. UNESCO, Paris.

World Health Organization (1971). "International Standards for Drinking Water." UNESCO, Paris.

Yaalon, D. H. (1961). "On the Origin and Accumulation of Salts in Groundwater and in the Soils of Israel," Dep. Geol., Publ. no. 255., Hebrew Univ., Jerusalem.

CHAPTER
10
Environmental Isotope Techniques

10.1 HYDROLOGICALLY IMPORTANT PROPERTIES OF ISOTOPES

The atoms of a chemical element may be pictured as consisting of a *nucleus* around which there circle a number of electrons. Chemical properties depend on the number of electrons; the mass (*atomic weight*) of the element is concentrated in its nucleus. *Isotopes* of an element differ in their atomic weight but have an equal number of electrons. Many chemical elements are a mixture of several isotopic species. Usually one species constitutes the bulk of the element and the others only a few percent or fractions of a percent.

Several natural processes are accompanied by the partial separation of isotopic species, so that one part of the environment becomes enriched in a particular isotope while another part is simultaneously depleted of it. The use of *stable (nonradioactive) isotopes* in hydrology depends on processes of this kind. The complete separation and quantitative analysis of stable isotopes is carried out in specialized laboratories by *mass spectrometers*. The nuclei of *radioactive isotopes* tend to break up spontaneously, creating one or several *daughter elements* or *daughter isotopes*. The process of nuclear *disintegration (radioactive decay)* is accompanied by the emission of discontinuous bursts of *radiation*, which can be detected and measured by *radiation counters*. There are three kinds of radiation: *Gamma rays* are very short electromagnetic waves, *beta rays* are electrons carrying one negative charge, and *alpha rays* are nuclei of helium atoms carrying four positive charges.

The energy of radiation is measured in millions of electron volts (MeV). Each radioactive element emits one or several rays. Gamma and alpha rays are emitted at discrete energy levels that characterize the specific emitter. Beta rays are emitted at energies that vary continuously up to a maximum, characteristic of the specific beta emitter. The intensity of radiation (number of energy bursts per second) is termed *activity*. The law of radioactive decay states that activity is proportional to the number of atoms present, the proportionality factor being characteristic for the particular radioactive isotope. The very small activity of natural waters can be measured only in specially prepared, concentrated samples with the aid of highly sensitive laboratory instruments.

The mathematical formulation of the law of radioactive decay leads to the equations

$$A = A_0 \exp(-\lambda t) \tag{10.1a}$$

$$t = (1/\lambda) \ln A_0/A \tag{10.1b}$$

where A_0, A are the activity at the beginning and the end of a time interval, respectively; t is the time interval; and λ the decay constant (T^{-1}).

The half-life $T_{1/2}$ is the time interval during which activity decays to one half of its initial value.

$$T_{1/2} = (1/\lambda) \ln 2 \approx (1/\lambda)0.6921 \tag{10.1c}$$

The term *half-life* is widely used because it appeals to intuition. For computations, the decay constant λ is more convenient.

Several radioactive isotopes originate in the atmosphere and are carried into the groundwater system as constituents of natural replenishment. The *radioactive age* of a water sample can be determined by Eq. (10.1b) if the activity of the sample and the initial activity of natural replenishment are known. The measured activity of a sample is, however, influenced not only by radioactive decay but also by mixing processes that occur in the aquifer and during sample taking. Therefore it is necessary to relate radioactive age to a system characteristic, the *residence time*, which is defined as

$$t_r = \frac{V_g}{\overline{R}_g} = \frac{V_a n}{\overline{R}_g} \tag{10.2}$$

where V_a and V_g are volumes of saturated aquifer and of water upstream from the sampling point, respectively (m³), $\overline{R}_g$ is average annual replenishment upstream from the sampling point (m³/yr), n total porosity, and t_r the residence time. The residence time is of great practical interest because of its simple functional relation to other aquifer parameters. It should be noted that the definition of depletion time (Sections 1.1 and 8.1) is formally similar but refers only to the dynamic reserves and to the effective porosity of a phreatic aquifer.

At the present state of the art, mixing effects cannot be determined with accuracy. The range of their influence on the radioactive age of a sample will be evaluated with reference to two extreme models.

The piston flow model assumes that mixing does not occur. Each batch of water that enters the aquifer is shoved onward by the succeeding batch "as if by a piston." It is obvious that under those conditions

$$t_r = t_a \qquad (10.3)$$

where t_a is the radioactive age of the sample. Vertical piston flow is approximated in phreatic aquifers and causes an *age stratification* of the water. Horizontal piston flow is approximated in confined aquifers at a large distance from the replenishment area.

The *complete mixing model* assumes that each incoming batch of water mixes completely and instantaneously with all the water upstream from the sampling point. The mathematical formulation of this model yields

$$t_r = (1/\lambda)\left[\exp(\lambda t_a) - 1\right] \qquad (10.4a)$$

The following indicative results are expressed in terms of the half-life $T_{1/2}$ (Eq. 10.1c):

For	$t_a = T_{1/2}$	$t_r \approx 1.4\,T_{1/2}$ (10.4b)
"	$t_a = 0.1\,T_{1/2}$	$t_r \approx 0.1\,T_{1/2}$ (10.4c)
"	$t_a > T_{1/2}$	$t_r \gg T_{1/2}$ (10.4d)

Instantaneous complete mixing cannot occur in the aquifer, but samples withdrawn from a phreatic aquifer by a fully penetrating pumped well approximate the complete mixing model.

10.2 STABLE ISOTOPES OF HYDROGEN AND OXYGEN

Deuterium (^{2}H or D) occurs in natural waters in the form HDO at concentrations of about 320 ppm. It can be measured by mass spectrometry with an accuracy of $\pm 0.02\%$. Oxygen 18 is more abundant and much easier to analyze. It occurs in the form $^1H_2{}^{18}O$ at concentrations of about 2000 ppm and can be determined with an accuracy of $\pm 0.002\%$.

During changes of phase the heavy isotopes tend to concentrate in the liquid phase (fractionation). Water vapor rising from the ocean is isotopically lighter than the vapor from which it originates. Precipitation is isotopically heavier than the vapor from which it originates. Each "rainout" depletes the remaining atmospheric moisture of heavy isotopes. Succeeding rainouts become, therefore, progressively lighter.

The isotopə composition of a sample is expressed in terms of its deviation from *standard mean ocean water*, (SMOW) (Craig, 1961).

$$\text{Deviation (Del)} = \delta = \left(\frac{R_s}{R_{SMOW}} - 1 \right) 1000 \, (\text{promille}) \qquad (10.5)$$

where $R_s = D/H$ or $^{18}O/^{16}O$ of the sample and $R_{SMOW} = D/H$ or $^{18}O/^{16}O$ of SMOW.

The lightest Del values are found in polar ice, D about -200, ^{18}O about -30. The heaviest Del values occur in terminal lakes, D about $+20$, ^{18}O about $+2$.

Del values of individual rainfalls show a wide scatter, but yearly averages are fairly constant climatic characteristics. The standard ^{18}O deviation in a worldwide network comprising 30 stations with at least three years' records was 6.1 promille. In very arid regions with irregular rainfalls the scatter is probably larger (Gat, 1971). Oxygen 18 has been successfully used in investigations concerning the following groundwater problems:

(1) *Identification of recharge areas.* The fractionation of heavy isotopes depends on the temperature at which a change of phase occurs. In regions with orographic precipitation, the precipitation falling on the mountains is generated at colder temperatures and more strongly depleted in ^{18}O than precipitation falling at lower elevations. In Europe ^{18}O depletion amounts to about Del 0.2 promille per 100 m difference in elevation.

(2) *Identification of waters that were replenished during colder climatic phases.* By this method it has been shown that the water in deep confined aquifers in North Africa and in the Negev desert of Israel stems from a period when the climate was colder than it is today, probably during the Pleistocene.

(3) *Investigations concerning the origin of a saline component in groundwater.* If salination is due to the admixture of a highly concentrated brine, the water is heavier in ^{18}O than it is when seawater is involved.

(4) *Investigations in hydrothermal areas.* At high temperatures ^{18}O exchange occurs between the water and carbonate minerals and the water is enriched in ^{18}O.

Deuterium by itself has found little application in groundwater research. In conjunction with ^{18}O, however, it is used to identify water bodies that were affected by rapid evaporation.

Del values of rainwater show a linear relation between D and ^{18}O:

$$\delta D = 8 \times \delta^{18}O + d \qquad (10.6)$$

The intercept d stems from fractionation at the ocean–atmosphere interface and varies from region to region. It is about 10 in Europe and about 24 in the eastern Mediterranean. The invariant slope 8 reflects fractionation processes in the cloud (Dansgaard, 1964). This linear relation, the so-called *meteoric water line*, is maintained in terrestrial water bodies as long as water evaporates under quasi-equilibrium conditions. If evaporation occurs under dynamic conditions (i.e., if there is a pronounced temperature gradient at the air–water interface), the residual waters fall on an *evaporation line* with a slope smaller than 8.

Figure 10.1 shows the results of a regional investigation by this method (Mandel *et al.*, 1972, Section 2.4). An artificial lake on the Foix River near Barcelona (Spain) had been leaking for many years. The ^{18}O–D relation clearly identified the flow path of an "evaporated" water body from the reservoir into an adjoining limestone aquifer and made it possible to plan recovery of the escaped water by pumping from wells.

The interpretation of stable isotope analyses is not always as straightforward as the above summary may suggest. Fractionation at the cloud level is

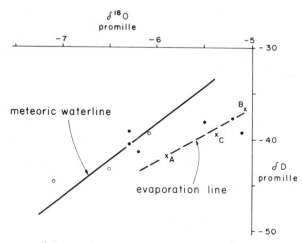

```
  o   well in sandstone aquifer
  •   well in limestone aquifer
A x   sample from river
B x   sample from reservoir (tail)
C x   sample from reservoir (dam)
```

Fig. 10.1   Meteoric water and evaporation lines.

sometimes masked by subsequent processes such as isotope exchange between air moisture and raindrops and partial evaporation of raindrops before they reach the ground. The state of the art of stable isotope methods is discussed by Gat (1971).

10.3   TRITIUM

Tritium (^{3}H or T) is the radioactive isotope of hydrogen. It emits weak beta radiation with a maximum energy of 0.018 MeV and has a half-life of 12.26 years. Concentrations are measured in *tritium units* (TU), one TU being defined as one atom ^{3}H to 10^{18} atoms ^{1}H. The accuracy of analyses is ± 1 TU.

Tritium is generated by the interaction of cosmic rays with nitrogen in the upper layers of the atmosphere. This mechanism generates concentrations of 5–10 TU in precipitation. Much more tritium has been added to the atmosphere by thermonuclear explosions. Tritium concentrations in rainfall increased from the beginning of the 1950s onward. In 1962–1963 they reached a maximum of about 8000 TU (in the Northern Hemisphere) and declined from that time because of restrictions on thermonuclear explosions. Tritium rainout is monitored by a network of stations maintained by the *International Atomic Energy Agency* (IAEA). In most locations the record of T concentrations in precipitation can be reconstructed by reference to IAEA data with fair accuracy. Generally concentrations increase with latitude and show a maximum in late spring and summer. For the purpose of groundwater investigations only yearly averages are of interest. Tritium is widely used for dating in the following contexts:

(1) Very low T concentrations, around the level of detectability, show that the water stems from the prebomb period. Relatively high T concentrations, say 10 TU or more, indicate that the water originates partly or wholly from post-1960 precipitation (the situation slowly changes with the T peak receding into the past). In investigations concerning recharge mechanisms or aquifer delineation such semiquantitative indications are often of considerable value.

(2) For more precise tritium dating the changing activities of rainfall and have to be taken into account and assumptions regarding the mixing model have to be made.

Assume that piston flow occurs and that a record of T concentrations in groundwater is available.

$$\ln A_n = \ln B_{n-t_r} - \lambda t_r \tag{10.7}$$

where A, B are the activities of the sample and of precipitation, respectively, and n is the number of years since the beginning of sample taking.

The residence time t_r is determined by matching records of A with the measured or reconstructed record of B in such a way that Eq. (10.7) is satisfied.

Complete mixing is simulated by the exponential model (Eriksson, 1962):

$$A_n = (1 - 1/t_r)^n A_0 \exp(-\lambda n)$$
$$+ 1/t_r \sum_{i=1}^{n} B_i (1 - 1/t_r)^{n-i} \exp(-\lambda n + \lambda i) \qquad (10.8)$$

The unknown A_0 can be estimated if a prebomb year is taken as starting point. Equation (10.8) enables the estimate of residence time from groundwater activity measured in a single year.

Two assumptions implicit in the preceding dating procedures have to be mentioned: (a) T concentrations in groundwater replenishment are assumed to equal those of rainfall. In reality replenishment is a selective process: weak showers are likely to evaporate; short, intense rainstorms may produce much surface runoff but relatively little replenishment. (b) The radioactive age of the water includes residence time in the nonsaturated zone, whereas the mixing model refers only to flow in the saturated zone. Generally, the errors introduced by these assumptions are insignificant as compared to errors stemming from grossly simplified mixing models.

(3) The vertical age stratification of water in a phreatic aquifer may be used to estimate groundwater replenishment. The T age of a layer of groundwater is determined either by identifying a well-defined marker, such as the T peak of 1963, or by curve matching with T records of rainfall. The thickness of the layer multiplied by the effective porosity of the aquifer equals replenishment during the identified age interval. The reasoning may be expanded to the nonsaturated zone by substituting moisture content for effective porosity. Implementation of the method requires sampling points for successive small-depth intervals. The observation points must be drilled without using water. These experimental difficulties restrict the application of the method to shallow unconsolidated aquifers.

10.4   CARBON 14

The radioactive isotope ^{14}C emits beta radiation at the maximum energy 0.156 MeV, and has a half-life of 5568 years. (A more accurate figure is 5730 years, but according to the decision of an international conference, the smaller figure is still being used in carbon dating.) Carbon 14 is generated in the upper atmosphere by neutron interactions with nitrogen; ^{14}C thus generated oxidizes to $^{14}CO_2$. Until 1950 atmospheric carbon dioxide contained approximately one molecule $^{14}CO_2$ to 10^{12} molecules of $^{12}CO_2$. Nuclear explosions added large amounts of ^{14}C to the atmosphere, and in 1963 atmospheric ^{14}C concentrations were about twice the natural prebomb level.

Concentrations are reported as *percent of modern carbon* (pmc), the ^{14}C concentration in the wood of a tree growing in 1950 being defined as 100 pmc. Because of this choice of standard, actual ^{14}C concentrations in the atmosphere are, paradoxically, larger than 100 pmc. Carbon 14 concentrations in living tissues remain in equilibrium with the atmosphere. When the organism dies, ^{14}C concentrations decrease because of radioactive decay. Carbon dating of organic material is based on this property.

The factors that influence the ^{14}C age of a groundwater sample are complex and incompletely understood. According to Eq. (9.7) (Section 9.4), one-half of the dissolved carbonic species stems from the atmosphere and the other half from carbonate minerals that are presumably "dead" with respect to ^{14}C. Maximum concentrations in groundwater should therefore be around 50 pmc, except in recent postbomb waters. As a matter of fact, much higher pmc values are often found in samples that cannot have been in contact with postbomb ^{14}C. The most plausible explanation for this anomaly assumes that interactions occur at the rock–water interface: In the course of millennia ^{12}C in the minerals may be exchanged against ^{14}C in the water, or when supersaturation temporarily occurs, a film of "young" calcite may be deposited on the rock. Therefore the subsequently dissolved minerals are not really dead with respect to ^{14}C. On the other hand, low pmc values do not necessarily indicate a high age; they may reflect $^{12}CO_2$ derived from fossil organic material or from volcanic exhalations.

A method to determine zero carbon age with the aid of the stable isotope ^{13}C did not prove to be of universal validity (Pearson, 1965). The present practice is to measure ^{14}C concentrations of water samples that are known to be fairly young, on the basis of hydrogeologic reasoning or with reference to tritium data. Alternatively, the value $85 \pm 5\%$ pmc is defined as initial concentration, on the basis of statistical data. However, these procedures do not remove uncertainties regarding the processes that influence ^{14}C concentrations in much older water samples.

Carbon 14 has been used to determine the transit time of groundwater between two points. This method seems to be reliable when applied together with T dating in well-mixed carbonate aquifers (Hufen *et al.*, 1974). It has also been used together with isotope and chemical data for the delineation of large aquifer systems.

10.5   SULFUR 34

Sulfur has four stable isotopes. Sulfur 32 constitutes about 95% of the sulfur on the earth's crust, ^{34}S approximately 4.2%, and the other two isotopes, ^{33}S and ^{36}S, about 0.8%. Concentrations of ^{34}S are measured in delta values with reference to an arbitrary standard sample (Canyon Diablo Troilite):

$$\delta^{34}S = \left(\frac{R_S}{R_{CDT}} - 1 \right) 1000 \tag{10.9}$$

where $R_S = {}^{34}S/{}^{32}S$ in the sample and $R_{CDT} = {}^{34}S/{}^{32}S$ in the standard. Reduction of SO_4^{2-} to H_2S renders the resultant H_2S isotopically lighter; isotope exchange between a liquid and a gaseous phase renders the gaseous phase lighter.

Atmospheric sulfur stems from the decay of organic matter, from airborne salts, and from the combustion of fuel. Sulfur washed down by precipitation may subsequently be augmented by the dissolution of evaporites, by H_2S generated from organic matter and from sulfates contained in rocks, and, in some cases, by seawater intrusion. Approximate ranges of $\delta^{34}S$ are as follows:

Seawater	$+18.9$ to $+20.7$
Marine evaporites	-8 to $+32$
Precipitation	-1.5 to $+19.4$
Biogenic sulfur	-35 to $+4$
H_2S derived from gypsum	-35 to $+32$
Oil from the Persian Gulf	-5.4

Sulfur 34 has been used, in conjunction with other isotopes, for the delineation of aquifer systems (Wakshal, 1979) and for the distinction of volcanic sulfur that has a delta value around zero, from sedimentary sulfur.

10.6   THE URANIUM RATIO $^{234}U/^{238}U$

Uranium 238 has a half-life of 4.51×10^{19} yr. It emits alpha rays at 4.19 MeV and decays through two short-lived beta emitters (^{234}Th and ^{234}Pa) to ^{234}U, which has a half-life of 2.48×10^5 yr and emits alpha rays at 4.77 and 4.72 MeV. In a closed system the activities of both isotopes become equal after about 1 million yr. Almost all rocks are much older than that.

Uranium compounds occur in two stable oxidation states, U^{6+} and U^{4+}, with the lower, U^{4+}, being much more soluble than the higher one.

For reasons that are still incompletely understood, radioactive decay favors the formation of the more soluble lower oxidation state. Therefore circulating groundwater preferentially leaches ^{234}U compounds.

The uranium ratio has been used in the study of a deep groundwater system (Cowart and Osmond, 1974). Its use for the delineation of karstic groundwater systems has been suggested (Wakshal and Yaron, 1974; Wakshal, 1979). In carbonate aquifers uranium occurs in concentrations of about 2 ppm incorporated into the crystal lattice of carbonate minerals. If it is assumed that ^{234}U is quickly leached from the relatively small surface of large solution channels, the water flowing through them should be depleted of ^{234}U in comparison with water flowing through narrow channels or through a porous aquifer. Complete confirmation of this intriguing idea is, however, still outstanding.

10.7   SAMPLING FOR ISOTOPE INVESTIGATIONS

Number of Samples

As a rule, samples should be taken from several points in the investigated aquifers; from adjoining aquifers, if any; from springs and surficial water bodies in the investigated area; and from precipitation. In the case of ^{14}C, S, and U, it may also be necessary to take samples of soils and of rock material. Each point should be sampled repeatedly in order to spot errors. Sample taking requires careful planning. A common mistake in applied isotope work is to expect significant results from only a few haphazardly collected samples.

Interaction of the sample with air, with materials used in pumping installations, and with suspended matter has to be minimized. Water from boreholes should be sampled after 2–3 h of pumping. The best procedure is to take the water through a plastic hose from the faucet that is usually attached to the outlet pipe of the pump, in order to avoid splashing. Two filters, 400 mesh, installed in the hose collect silt and fine sand. Clayey suspended matter may have to be filtrated in the lab, with care being taken to minimize exposure to air.

Surficial waters should be sampled below the surface of the water body. Portable submergible pumps with the previously mentioned filters installed in their outlet pipe are excellent for this purpose. Springs have to be sampled at the original outlet, not in the diversion channel or near a hydrometric installation. Rainfall samples are usually collected daily, from a standard rain gauge, and put into a bottle large enough to hold one month's sample. At the end of the month the cumulative sample is stirred to ensure mixing. It is a good idea to ask the laboratory that carries out the isotope analyses for detailed instructions regarding the size of the samples, bottling, arrangements for storing and transportation, and—in the case of ^{14}C, ^{34}S, and U—procedures for sample preparation. The following guidelines are usually adhered to, but they are no substitute for detailed specifications, which depend to a certain extent on local conditions.

Samples for Oxygen 18, Deuterium, and Tritium

The minimum size of samples for deuterium and ^{18}O analyses is 20 cm^3. Tritium requires a larger sample, about 500 cm^3, and more if low tritium levels are expected. Bottles should be rinsed with distilled water in the lab; transported tightly closed to the sample points; rinsed twice with the water to be sampled, completely filled, leaving only a tiny air bubble below the stopper; labeled; and sent for analysis. During transportation and if storage is required they must be kept at an even cool temperature and not exposed to bright light.

Carbon-14 Samples

Three to four grams of carbon are required for analysis. This quantity can, in most cases, be obtained by precipitating the dissolved carbonic species as $BaCO_3$ from about 120 liters of water. Precipitation is usually carried out in a conical vessel made of fiberglass, standing with its apex downward on a tripod. A transparent container holding 1–2 liters is screwed onto the lower end of the conus. The vessel is filled through an opening in its upper, wider end. A solution of carbonate-free NaOH is added to increase the pH to 8 and to convert bicarbonates into carbonates. Phenolphthalein serves as convenient pH indicator. One liter of concentrated $BaCl_2$ is added and the upper opening is closed to minimize interaction with atmospheric carbon dioxide during precipitation, which takes about 1–2 hr. Then the transparent container is detached, closed tightly, and taken to the lab.

Sulfur-34 Samples

Water samples of 10–30 liters, depending on sulfur concentrations, are collected and further processed in the lab. The water is acidized to about 2 pH in order to prevent precipitation of carbonates and is concentrated by boiling to about one-fourth of its original volume. A 5%-$BaCl_2$ solution is added in sufficient quantity to ensure complete precipitation of all SO_4^{2-} as $BaSO_4$. The precipitate is filtered and is dried in a porcelain crucible. A minimum of 100 mg is sent for spectrometric measurements.

Sampling for Uranium Isotopes

A sample of about 50 liters of water is collected in polyethylene containers that have previously been rinsed in the lab with distilled water and concentrated NHO_3, and in the field with filtered water from the sampling point and about 100 cm³ of concentrated NHO_3. The pH of the sample is lowered to 1–2 by the addition of HNO_3 and the containers are taken to the lab. Further processing includes the addition of a little ^{232}U as *spike*, in order to facilitate measurements, collection of uranium on a resin, elution from the resin, a number of steps for further purification, especially for the removal of iron and thorium, and finally deposition on a stainless steel planchet. These procedures demand a high degree of skill and a well-equipped laboratory.

FURTHER READINGS

Ataken, Y., Roether, W., and Muennich, K. O. (1974). The Sandhausen shallow groundwater tritium experiment. *Proc. IAEA Vienna Symp.* 1, 21–42.

Bochin, N., Dumitrescu, S., *et al.* (1972). Status and reasons for using isotope techniques in hydrology. *Proc. IAEA-UN Peaceful Uses At. Energy* 14, 441–423.

Bosch, B., Guegan, B., *et al.* (1974). Tritium et le bilan hydrogéologique de la nappe alluviale du Rhône entre Donzère et Mondragon (France). *Hydrogeologie, Sect. 3* No. 3, pp. 246–260.

Bradley, E. (1974). Nuclear techniques in groundwater studies. *In* "Groundwater Studies" (Brown, R. H., Konoplyantsev, A. A., Ineson, J., and Kovalevsky,V. S.,eds.), Vol. 10, UNESCO, Paris.

Calf, G. E. (1978). Isotope hydrology of the Mereeni sandstone aquifer, Alice spgs (Australia). *J. Hydrol.* 38, 343–356.

Cowart, J. B., and Osmond, J. K. (1974). ^{234}U and ^{238}U in the Carrizo sandstone aquifer of South Texas (USA). *Proc. IAEA Vienna Symp.* 2, 131–149.

Craig, H. (1961). Standards for reporting concentrations of deuterium and oxygen 18 in natural waters. *Science* 133, 1833–1835.

Dansgaard, W. (1964). Stable isotopes in precipitation. *Tellus* 14, 436–468.

Davis, G. H., Dincer, I., *et al.* (1967). A combined environmental isotope approach for studying waters in developing countries. *Proc. UN Int. Conf. Water Peace* 2,

Eriksson, E. (1962). Radioactivity in hydrology. *In* "Nuclear Radiation in Geophysics" (H. Israel and A. Krebs, eds.), pp. 47–60. Springer-Verlag, Berlin and New York.

Evin, J, and Vuillaume, Y. (1970). Etude par le radiocarbone de la nappe captive de l'Albien du basin de Paris. *Proc. Vienna Cong. Isotope Hydrology*, pp. 315–331. IAEA, Vienna.

Fontes, J. C., and Garnier, J. M. (1977). Determination of the initial ^{14}C activity of the total dissolved carbon age estimation of water of confined aquifers. Univ. Pierre et Marie Curie, Laboratoire de Geologie Dynamique, Paris.

Friend, J. P. (1973). The global sulfur cycle. *In* "Chemistry of the Lower Atmosphere," pp. 177–201. Plenum, New York.

Fritz P., Reardon, E. J, and Barker, J. (1978). The carbon isotope geochemistry of a small groundwater catchment in northwestern Ontario. *Water Resour. Res.* **14** No. 6, 1059–1067.

Gat, J. R. (1971). Comments on stable isotope methods in regional groundwater investigations. *Water Resour. Res.* **7**, 980–986.

Gat, J. R. (1975). Elucidating salination mechanisms by stable istotope tracing of water sources. *Proc. Int. Symp. Brackish Water Factor Dev., Ben Gurion Univ., Beer Sheba, Isr.* pp. 15–23.

Gat, J. R., and Carmi, I. (1970). Evolution of the isotopic composition of atmospheric waters in the Med. Sea area. *J. Geophys. Res.* **75**, 3039–3048.

Gat, J. R., and Dansgaard, W. (1972). Stable isotope survey of freshwater occurrence in Israel and the Northern Jordan Rift Valley. *J. Hydrol.* **16**, 177–211.

Gat, J. R. and Issar, A. (1974). Desert isotope hydrology, water resources of the Sinai desert. *Geochim. Cosmochim. Acta*, **38**, 1117–1138.

Geyh, M. A. (1972). On the determination of the initial ^{14}C content in groundwater. *Proc. Conf. Radiocarbon Dat., 8th, Wellington* pp. D58–D69.

Halevy, E., and Payne, B. R. (1967). Deuterium and oxygen in natural waters, analyses compared. *Science* **156**, 669–670.

Hanshaw, B. B., Back, W., and Rubin, M. (1967). Carbonate equilibria and radio-carbon distribution related to groundwater flow in the Floridan limestone aquifer. IASH–UNESCO, Symposium on Fractured Rocks, Dubrovniki, 1965. **2**, 601–614.

Hoefs, J. (1973). "Stable Isotope Geochemistry." Springer-Verlag. Berlin and New York.

Hufen, T. H., Lau, L. S., and Buddemeier, R. W. (1974). Radio carbon, ^{13}C and tritium water samples from basaltic and carbonate aquifers in the island of Oahu, Hawai (USA). *Proc. IAEA Vienna Symp.* **2**, 316–334.

IAEA (1963). *Proc. Tokyo Symp. Radio Isot. Hydrol.* Publ. No. 71.

IAEA (1964). *Proc. Vienna Symp. Isot. Tech. Groundwater Hydrol.* Publ. No. 373, 3 vols.

IAEA (1966). *Proc. Vienna Symp. Isot. Hydrol.* Publ. No. 141.

IAEA (1970). *Proc. Vienna Symp. Isot. Hydrol.* Publ. No. 225.

IAEA (1975). *Proc. Vienna Advis. Group Meet. Interpretation Environ. Isot. Hydrochem. Data Groundwater Hydrol.* Publ. No. 429.

Kaufman, M. I., Rydell, H. S., and Osmond, J. K. (1969). $^{234}U/^{238}U$ disequilibrium as an aid to the hydrologic study of the Floridan aquifer. *J. Hydrol.* **9**, 374–386.

Kronfeld, J., and Adams, J. A. S. (1974). Hydrologic investigations of the groundwaters of central Texas using $^{234}U/^{238}U$ disequilibrium. *J. Hydrol.* **22**, 77–88.

Mandel, S., Mercado, A., and Gilboa, Y. (1972). Groundwater flow in calcareous rocks in the vicinity of Barcelona, Spain. *Bull. IASH* **17**, No. 1, pp. 77–83.

Nielsen, H. (1974). Isotopic composition of the major contributors to atmospheric sulfur. *Tellus* **26**, 213–221.

Nir, A. (1964). On the interpretation of tritium "age" measurements of groundwater. *J. Geophys. Res.* **69**, 2589–2595.

Nir. A., and Lewis, S. (1975). On tracer theory in geophysical systems in the steady and non steady state, part 1. *Tellus* **27**, 372–387.

Olsson, I. U. (1968). Modern aspects of radiocarbon dating. *Earth-Sci. Rev.* **4**, 203–218.

Pearson, J. F. (1965). Use of $^{13}C/^{12}C$ ratios to correct radiocarbon ages of materials initially diluted by limestone. *Proc. Int. Conf. Radiocarbon Tritium Dat., 6th, Pullman, Wash.* USAEC Conf. No. 650652, pp. 357–366.

Pearson, J. F., and White, D. E. (1967). Carbon 14 ages and flow rates of water in Carrizo sands, Atascona City. Texas (U.S.) *Water Resour. Res.*, **3**, 251–261.

Rabinovitz, D. D., Gross, G. W., and Holmes, C. R. (1977). Environmental tritium as hydrometeorologic tool in the Roswell Basin, New Mexico. *J. Hydrol.* **32**, 3–46.

Tamers, M. A. (1975). Validity of radiocarbon age dates on groundwater. *Geophys. Surv.* **2**, 217–239.

Thatcher, L. L. (1967). Water tracing in the hydrologic cycle. *American Geophysical Union. Proc.* Symp. Isotope Techniques in the Hydrologic Cycle, Illinois, 1965. pp. 97–106.

Vogel, J. C., Lerman, J. C., and Mook, W. G. (1975). Natural isotopes in surface and groundwater from Argentina. *Hydrol. Sci. Bull.*, **20**, 203–221.

Wakshal, E. (1979). Karst evolution of the Cenomanian-Turonian aquifer in Galilee, Northern Israel. Ph.D. Thesis, Hebrew Univ., Jerusalem. (In Heb.; Engl. summ.)

Wakshal, E., and Yaron, F. (1974). ^{234}U/^{238}U disequilibrium in waters of the Judea Group (Cenomanian–Turonian) aquifer in Galilee, N. Israel. *Proc. Vienna Symp. Isot. Tech. Groundwater Hydrol.* IAEA/STI Publ. No. 373, **2**, 151–177.

Wigley, T. M. I. (1975). Carbon 14 dating of groundwater from closed and open systems. *Water Resour. Res.* **11**, 324–328.

Wigley, T. M. C. (1976). Effect of mineral precipitation on isotopic composition and ^{14}C age of groundwater. *Nature* No. 263, pp. 219–221.

CHAPTER
11

Delineation of Groundwater Systems

In surface water studies the river basin is easily defined as the natural unit to which hydrologic studies refer. The identification of a groundwater system—the underground equivalent of a river basin—is more problematic, because it is not necessarily related to topographic or geologic features visible at the surface.

Delineation of groundwater systems aims at the recognition of the boundaries enclosing the system, of areas and mechanisms of recharge and discharge, and of the flow paths of groundwater from the recharge areas to discharge areas. In addition, processes that may eventually constitute constraints on groundwater exploitation should be identified. Thus the delineation of a groundwater system involves essentially the recognition of patterns that form the basis for subsequent quantitative work.

There are three types of boundaries. *Fixed boundaries* are created by impermeable rocks. *Movable boundaries* reflect hydraulic conditions. Examples of this category are the freshwater–seawater interface in coastal aquifers and the groundwater divide that is formed in an aquifer draining toward two different outlets. *Arbitrary boundaries* have to be introduced, sometimes, in order to restrict the research area to a part of a larger natural system. They should correspond as much as possible to flow lines and to equipotential lines (Section 12.2).

Replenishment areas are those in which an addition of water to the regional zone of saturation takes place. The replenishment area of an aquifer may consist of different geologic strata, and it may be covered by rocks and soils with widely differing infiltration capacities (Section 12.3).

Part of the water may infiltrate into local perched horizons and reappear within the recharge area in the form of small springs as rejected recharge (Mifflin, 1968). There are two types of natural replenishment mechanisms: precipitation on a replenishment area and infiltration of surface flows. Unintentional man-made mechanisms, such as return flow from irrigation and seepage from storage reservoirs and from urban water supply and sewage systems, play an increasing role. A rough appraisal of rainfall, surface runoff, and evapotranspiration helps to identify areas where replenishment from rainfall may occur (Sections 12.1 and 12.3).

The areas where a net outflow from the zone of regional saturation takes place are termed *discharge areas*. They are usually much smaller and easier to locate than recharge areas. It is for this reason that the investigation of a groundwater flow system should start from the discharge end. Discharge can take the form of spring flow, evaporation from swamps, desert mud flats and areas covered by phreatophytic vegetation, seepage into rivers, and subsurface drainage into the ocean or into lakes. Springs are easily identified and gauged. Spring discharge constitutes an ascertained minimum of groundwater outflow, but the possibility of additional outflow has to be investigated. Techniques of analyzing spring flow with reference to the groundwater system are detailed in Chapter 8. Seepages into rivers are sometimes visible. Persistent dry weather flow may indicate the existence of an exploitable aquifer. In many rivers groundwater is discharged, at low stages, through the river banks and replenished, at high stages, by infiltration into the river banks. Swamps may be caused either by the seepage of groundwater or by poor surface drainage, or both. Drilling of a few relatively shallow test holes can prove whether all or part of the water originates from groundwater. If the water level rises and artesian flow appears, the swamp is at least in part groundwater fed. Quantitative estimates of evaporation from swamps are subject to a wide margin of error.

Exploitation areas are the parts of a groundwater system in which groundwater can be abstracted through wells. Their limits are determined by the depth, thickness, and permeability of the aquifer, and by the depth of the water level. The term *groundwater basin* has been proposed to designate them (Mifflin, 1968).

In some cases it is possible to delineate groundwater systems, in a rough way, even prior to drilling. Where visible outflows occur in the form of springs or seepages, it is logical to assume that they are fed from potential aquifers that can usually be identified on the basis of geologic data. Rough quantitative arguments should be introduced at this stage by balancing the estimated outflows against the probable replenishment through assumed recharge areas. The results of this chain of reasoning remain, however, highly speculative until the existence of an exploitable aquifer is proved by drilling.

In most research areas groundwater systems are delineated with the aid of data from producing wells by the following criteria:

(1) Wells belonging to one groundwater system should be identifiable by prima facie geological evidence.

(2) Water level gradients should be well defined and relatively small, say less than 1%. Large gradients indicate a poor aquifer, and a local break in the gradient may indicate a hydraulic barrier (Section 7.3). In the immediate vicinity of outlets, however, large gradients may be caused by the convergence of flow lines and by the transition to turbulent flow. In hard rock aquifers water level gradients need not necessarily coincide with flow directions.

(3) The occurrence of dynamic interference among wells constitutes conclusive proof for a hydraulically connected system. Pumping tests (Sections 6.1–6.6) can, however, rarely be used for the purpose of system delineation since their range is limited. Where exploitation is already in a fairly advanced stage, cyclic water level changes in observation holes may help to identify hydraulically connected areas.

(4) Geochemical criteria (Sections 9.3 and 9.5) are valuable mainly for checking the validity of conclusions derived by other methods. Geochemical data by themselves can usually be interpreted in several different ways and do not furnish reliable evidence for the existence or absence of hydraulic connections.

(5) If the system is relatively undisturbed, estimates of natural replenishment derived by hydrometeorological or salt balance methods (Sections 12.3 and 12.4) should be approximately equal to the steady state flow through the aquifer [Eq. (12.4), Section 12.2] and to natural outflows.

(6) Replenishment areas can sometimes be identified by the ^{18}O method (Section 10.2).

(7) Springs that issue at the sea bottom or at the bottom of a lake can sometimes be located by infrared photography or imagery (Sections 3.1 and 4.7).

(8) Conclusive evidence for the connection of an intensively exploited aquifer to a visible outlet may be obtained from changes in the slope of the depletion line (Section 8.1).

(9) River–groundwater relations can be determined, by visual inspection or by flow gaugings, in small rivers where inflow from or losses to groundwater constitute a large part, say 20% or more, of river flow. In large rivers outflowing or inflowing conditions may be indicated by the shape of water level contour lines, provided that the lines are based on a sufficiently

dense network of observation wells, and not mainly on the preconceived notion of the person who drew them.

Constraints on groundwater exploitation are discussed in Section 13.2. During the phase of system delineation, it is important to draw attention to the relevant conditions and mechanisms, so that they can be investigated before damage occurs.

FURTHER READINGS

Domenico, P., and Stephenson, D. (1964). Application of quantitative mapping techniques to aid hydrologic system analysis of alluvial aquifers. *J. Hydrol.* **2**, 164–181.

Ineson, J., and Downing, R. A. (1964). The groundwater component of river discharge and its relationship to hydrogeology. *J. Inst. Water Eng.* **18**, 519–541.

Kiraly, L. (1978). La notion d'unité hydrologique essai de définition. *Bul. Centre d'Hydrogeologie* **2**, 83–221, Neuchatel, Switzerland.

Mandel, S. (1961). Properties and genesis of the Turonian-Cenomanian aquifer of western Israel as example of a large limestone aquifer. Ph.D. Thesis, Isr. Inst. Technol., Haifa. (In Heb.; Eng. summ.)

Maxey, G. B., and Hackett, E. J. (1963). Application of geohydrologic concepts in geology. *J. Hydrol.* **1**, 35–45.

Mifflin, M. D. (1968). "Delineation of Groundwater Flow Systems in Nevada," Tech. Rep. Ser. H. W., Publ. No. 4. Cent. Water Resour. Res., Desert Res. Inst. Univ. of Nevada, Reno.

Mifflin, M. D., and Hess, J. W. (1979). Regional carbonate flow systems in Nevada. *J. Hydrol.* **43**, No.1/4, 217–235.

Monopolis, D. (1973). Holokarst, distinction en bassins hydrogéologiques. *Hydrogéologie, Sect. 3* No. 1, pp. 45–53.

12

Groundwater Balances

12.1 GLOBAL FORMULAS

Global formulas purport to estimate the *water crop* (surface runoff and groundwater replenishment combined) on the basis of a few annual or average annual climatic characteristics. If surface runoff is negligibly small, these estimates may be regarded as referring to groundwater replenishment only. A formula for which universal validity is claimed has been proposed by Turc (Castany, 1967, p. 40):

$$\bar{R} = \bar{P} - \frac{\bar{P}}{\sqrt{0.9 + \bar{P}^2/L^2}} \tag{12.1a}$$

$$L = 300 + 25T + 0.05(T)^2 \tag{12.1b}$$

where $\bar{R}$ is the average annual water crop (mm/yr), $\bar{P}$ the average annual precipitation (mm/yr), and T the temperature (centigrades).

In a Mediterranean climate where the type and density of the natural vegetative cover reflect primarily water availability, the following formula is likely to yield reasonable approximations:

$$\bar{R} = a(\bar{P} - b) \tag{12.2}$$

where a (dimensionless, smaller than 1) and b (mm/yr) are empirical constants.

The parameter b can be considered as threshold value, indicating the minimum yearly water supply that is needed to keep perennial trees and shrubs alive. The parameter a indicates the additional loss of water that occurs when rainfall exceeds the threshold value, through annual vegetation, and through the growth of trees and shrubs.

For an annual rainfall in the range of 450–650 mm/yr Goldschmidt (1959) found the relation

$$\bar{R}=0.9(\bar{P}-360) \qquad (12.3)$$

Where average annual rainfall exceeds 650 mm/yr, dense Mediterranean brush is likely to develop and the threshold value increases. Where average annual rainfall is less than 450 mm/yr, trees and shrubs tend to be replaced by a steppelike annual vegetation and the threshold value decreases.

An important general conclusion derived from Eq. (13.3) concerns the variability of the water crop in a semiarid, Mediterranean climate. For example, in an area with 650 mm/yr average annual rainfall, the average annual water crop is 261 mm/yr. If, in any one year, rainfall increases to 605 mm/yr or decreases to 495 mm/yr, the yearly water crop increases to 220.5 mm/yr or decreases to 121.5 mm/yr. Thus a deviation of annual rainfall by $\pm 10\%$ from the average causes the water crop to deviate by $\pm 28.9\%$ from the average. In semiarid regions groundwater replenishment is an erratic event. Only the large storage capacity of aquifers makes it possible to talk in terms of annual averages.

In the early days of hydrologic research many other global formulas were devised, and some of them are still in local use.

12.2 GEOHYDROLOGIC METHODS

In an area where groundwater abstraction is negligible a quasi-steady state of groundwater flow can be assumed to prevail. Under these conditions groundwater flow across a water level contour line is approximately equal to average annual replenishment upstream from the line

$$\bar{R}_g \approx Q_g = (ITl)365 \qquad (12.4)$$

where I is the water level gradient, T the transmissivity (m^2/day), l the length of the selected water level contour line (m), 365 the number of days in a year, Q_g the groundwater flow across the water level contour line (m^3/yr), and $\bar{R}_g$ the estimated average annual replenishment.

Gradients are computed from the water level contour lines upstream and downstream from the line l. Transmissivity is obtained from pumping tests or estimated from geologic data. In practice, straight line segments are substituted for l and the partial flow is computed for each segment. Finally all partial flows are added up to yield the total throughflow (Mandel, 1974). Unfortunately, water level contour maps and estimates of transmissivity are rarely available in almost unexploited areas.

If groundwater levels have become stabilized after a long period of exploitation, average annual replenishment should be equal to the sum of average annual groundwater abstraction and the remaining outflow from the area (see also Section 14.2). The impression that a quasi-steady state has been attained may, however, be misleading, since a small continuous decline of water level is easily masked by fluctuations resulting from changes of rainfall and of pumping. Therefore the application of a steady-state equation to significantly exploited aquifers cannot be recommended.

The *nonsteady-state balance method* applies the equation of continuity to an area bounded by flow lines and equipotential lines (Fig. 12.1):

$$\Delta t\{(ITl)_{\text{in}} - (ITl)_{\text{out}} - G_{\text{a}} + R_{\text{g}}\} = \overline{\Delta h}\ AS_y \qquad (12.5)$$

where Δt is the number of days, G_{a} the groundwater abstraction (m³/day), A the area (m²), S_y the specific yield (dimensionless), $\overline{\Delta h}$ the weighted average

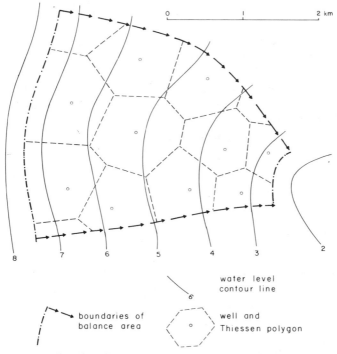

Fig. 12.1 Definition of groundwater balance area.

of water level changes, and in, out are the indices denoting lateral inflow and outflow sides, respectively. Water level changes are weighted by drawing a Thiessen *polygon* (Bruce and Clark, 1966) around each well. The area of each polygon is the weight of water level observations in the respective well. If there are many wells in the balance area, it is more convenient to draw contour lines for equal water level changes and to use the area between these contour lines as weights.

Transmissivities are obtained from pumping tests; gradients from the water level contour map; and groundwater abstraction from pumping records. The specific yields can be determined by solving the equation for a dry period during which no replenishment occurs. Alternatively, S_y has to be estimated by reference to pumping tests and to similar aquifers. The remaining unknown, groundwater replenishment, can then be computed. In actual applications it is convenient to refer to fixed time periods, say six months, and to adjust all input data, including transmissivity, to this period. Values of groundwater replenishment for each one of the selected periods are thus obtained.

Return flows from irrigation and from urban effluents enlarge the apparent values of specific yield and of groundwater replenishment. This source of error can be corrected for by estimating return flows, say, as a certain percentage of the water supplied to the area, and adding them as an additional term to the left-hand side of Eq. (12.5). It must be admitted, however, that the procedure adds another margin of uncertainty to the results.

The nonsteady-state balance method is useful during the phase of increasing exploitation (Section 1.4), when some records of water levels and of groundwater abstraction become available. It should be replaced by a *digital aquifer calibration* technique as soon as sufficient data have been assembled.

12.3 HYDROMETEOROLOGICAL METHODS

The water crop of an area is defined by

$$R = R_s + R_g = P - E_a \qquad (12.6)$$

where R is the water crop, R_s the surface runoff, R_g the groundwater replenishment (dimensions LT^{-1}), P the precipitation, and E_a the evapotranspiration. If adequate methods for the measurement of evapotranspiration were available, it would be easy to compute the water crop and groundwater replenishment with the aid of this simple balance equation. At the present state of the art, evapotranspiration has to be computed with reference to soil moisture, which in its turn depends on rainfall and infiltration. As a consequence, it becomes necessary to simulate the terrestrial part of the hydrologic cycle (Fig. 1.1b) instead of evaluating just one balance equation. The parameters and functional relations that are usually introduced for this purpose stem from a more descriptive phase of hydrologic science. It is doubtful whether precise meaning can be attached to them, but nothing better seems to have appeared on the scene.

(1) *Potential evaporation* denotes the evaporative power of the atmosphere and is defined as the "evapotranspiration that would occur, under given climatic conditions, if an unlimited supply of water was available." Potential evaporation can be measured with the aid of evaporation pans or computed from climatic data with aid of various formulas (Veihmeyer, 1964).

(2) *Field capacity* is the quantity of water that a soil is able to hold by capillary forces against the pull of gravity. It is measured as centimeters of water per meter thickness of soil.

(3) *Evapotranspiration* is defined by the relations

$$\text{for } L_a \geqslant L_m, \quad E_a = E_p$$
$$\text{for } L_a < L_m, \quad E_a = E_p(L_a/L_m) \tag{12.7}$$

where E_a is the evapotranspiration, E_p the potential evapotranspiration, L_a the actual soil moisture content, and L_m the soil moisture content at field capacity.

(4) *Infiltration capacity* or *infiltrability* is the maximum rate (LT^{-1}) at which water can be soaked up by a soil. Generally, it is larger when the soil is dry than when it is wet.

(5) Surface runoff occurs when rain intensity exceeds infiltrability.

(6) Percolation to groundwater occurs when soil moisture content exceeds field capacity.

Various simulation models incorporating the preceding and other simplifying assumptions have been proposed. The bookkeeping procedure (Thornthwaite and Mather, 1955) is designed for manual computation and uses a relatively long time basis, one week to one month, in order to keep the number of computational steps within reasonable bounds. A variant of the Stanford watershed model (Linsley and Crawford, 1960), adapted to regions with significant groundwater replenishment has been proposed by Mero (1978). It is designed for computerized work and uses one day as a time basis. Hydrometeorological simulation techniques are useful in areas that have reasonable records of rainfall and streamflow but almost no data on groundwater. It should be remembered, however, that the simulation of surface runoff with which these techniques are mainly concerned does not automatically produce reliable estimates of groundwater replenishment. Hydrometeorological groundwater balances have to be accepted with reservations until they can be checked against hydrogeologic data.

12.4   THE SALT BALANCE METHOD

Consider an aquifer in a "well-flushed" region where airborne salts are the only source of chloride in groundwater (Section 9.4). The salt balance of the aquifer is given by

$$A\left(\bar{P}\bar{C}_p + \bar{F}_d\right) = Q_g C_g \tag{12.8}$$

where A is the size of the replenishment area (m^2), $\bar{P}$ is the average annual rainfall (m/yr), C_p the average annual chloride content of rainwater (mg/liter, Cl$^-$), C_g the chloride content of groundwater (mg/liter, Cl$^-$), $\bar{F}_d$ the average annual dry fallout of chloride (g/m^2/yr, Cl$^-$), and Q_g the groundwater outflow (m^3/yr).

Under equilibrium conditions (Section 14.2)

$$A\bar{R}_g = Q_g \tag{12.9}$$

where $\bar{R}_g$ is the average annual groundwater replenishment (m/yr).

Average annual replenishment is, therefore, given by

$$\bar{R}_g = \bar{P}\left(\frac{\bar{C}_p}{C_g}\right) + \frac{\bar{F}_d}{C_g} \tag{12.10}$$

Chloride concentrations in rainwater are determined by collecting cumulative yearly samples in rainfall gauges distributed over the area and computing the weighted areal average by Thiessen polygons. Dry fallout can be collected on plastic sheets covered with a sticky material, such as Scotch tape, and similarly averaged over the area. Alternatively, dry fallout may be estimated from the duration of the dry period and prevailing wind directions. The other variables on the right-hand side of Eq. (12.10) are easily obtained.

Strictly speaking, the averages in the equations refer to a period equal to the *residence time* of groundwater [approximately equal to the depletion ratio (Section 1.1)], which is generally of the order of decades. Hence the preceding procedure implies the assumption that conditions of airborne salt transport remained fairly constant during this long antecedent period and are adequately represented by a few years' records.

The method is open to several objections: (1) The assumption that a certain research area is well flushed cannot objectively be proved. (2) It may be doubted whether a few years' samples of airborne chlorides adequately represent the average of a large number of years. (3) Salt adheres to sticky sheets, whereas much of it is probably blown away from natural surfaces. Estimates of the dry fallout component are even less satisfactory.

In spite of these limitations application of the salt balance method is recommended in all areas that are judged to be suitable because it requires relatively little efforts and because it furnishes an independent check on estimates derived by other methods. In Israel it has been applied with reasonable success by Eriksson and Khumakarem (1969), Fink (1963), and Mercado (1970).

12.5   OTHER WATER BALANCE METHODS

The average annual replenishment of an aquifer draining through springs is easily determined by measuring the average annual discharge of the springs. A method for the computation of seasonal replenishment is described in Section 8.1. It makes no sense simply to correlate annual spring discharges with records of annual precipitation, since any reasonably large aquifer "remembers" many previous replenishment events. A *tritium method* has been used in order to determine the replenishment of a phreatic aquifer (Section 10.3). Water samples have to be taken from the undisturbed aquifer at short depth intervals below the water table. This means, in practice, that special research wells are required. *Lysimeters* are installations that collect water below the root zone of vegetation. Large lysimeters may be assumed to be representative of a reasonably large area, but they are costly to build and operate. This method is used mainly for investigations concerning the consumptive water use of agricultural crops. *Energy balance methods* measure the energy needed for evapotranspiration. Until now they have been used mainly on open water surfaces and on areas under irrigated cultivation. It is not unlikely that perfected energy balance methods will make it possible to measure evapotranspiration directly from any surface under any condition and will thus effectively solve the problem of drawing up water balances.

FURTHER READINGS

Bruce, J. P., and Clark, R. H. (1966), "Introduction to Hydrometeorology." Pergamon, Oxford.
Castany, G. (1965). Etablissement du bilan hydrique dans les massifs calcaires de Tunisie. *Chron. Hydrogeol.* **7**, 79–84.

Castany, G. (1967). "Prospection et Exploitation des Eaux Souterraines." Dunod, Paris.

Conrad, G., Marce, A., and Olive, P. (1978). Mise en evidence par le tritium de la recharge actuelle des nappes libres de la zone aride Saharienne. *J. Hydrol.* **27**, 207–224.

Cornet, A., and Roguon, P. (1976). Estimation de la valeur des debits circulants dans la nappe du continental intercalaire en Sahara. *Chron. Hydrogeol.* B.R.G.M, Orléans **11**, 84–96.

Erikson, E., and Khumakarem, V. (1969). Chloride concentration in groundwater, recharge rate, and rate of deposition of chloride in the coastal plain of Israel. *J. Hydrol.* **7**, 178–197.

Fink, M. (1963). "Hydrological Report on the Groundwater Horizon in the Jerusalem Area," PN 2419. TAHAL, Water Plann. Isr. Tel Aviv. (In Heb.)

Goldschmidt, M. (1959). "On the Water Balance of Several Underground Water Catchments in Israel and their Flow Patterns," Hydrol. Pap. No. 4. Hydrol. Serv. Isr., Jerusalem.

Hambert, M. (1976). Bilan hydrochimique d'un bassin versant de moyenne montagne. *Hydrogeologie, Sect. 4* No. 12.

Hillel, D. (1971). "Soil and Water." Academic Press, New York.

Hoffmann, K. (1979). Investigation of groundwater recharge (a regional development project in Madagascar). "Natural Resources and Development, " vol. 9, pp. 51–71. Institute for Scientific Cooperation, Tuebingen Federal Republic of Germany.

Linsley, R. K., Jr., and Crawford, N. H. (1960). Computation of a synthetic stream flow record on a digital computor. *IASH Publ.* **51**, 526–538.

Mandel, S. (1974). The groundwater resources of the Canterbury Plains. Lincoln Papers in Water-Resources No. 12, New Zealand Agric. Engineering Institute, Lincoln, New Zealand.

Mercado, A. (1970). "Hydrological Investigations by Electric Analogue Model in the Southern Coastal Plain of Israel," PN 3217. TAHAL, Water Plann. Isr., Tel Aviv. (In Heb.)

Mero, F. (1978). "The MM08 Hydrometeorological Simulation System, Basic Concepts and Operators Guide," T/78/02. TAHAL Consulting Engineers Ltd., Tel Aviv.

Santing, G. (1957). "Investigation of Groundwater in the Coastal Plain," PN 23. TAHAL, Water Plann. Isr., Tel Aviv.

Thornthwaite, L. W. (1948). An approach toward a rational classification of climate. *Geophys. Rev.* **38**, 55–94.

Thornthwaite, L. W., and Mather, Y. R. (1955). The water balance. *U.S. Geol. Surv., Prof. Pap.* No. 269.

Van der Beken, A. and Bylros, J. (1977). A monthly water balance model including deep infiltration and canal losses. International Assoc. of Hydrological Sciences. *Hydrol. Sci. Bull.* **22**, No. 3. 341–351.

Veihmeyer, F. Y. (1964). Evapotranspiration. *In* "Handbook of Applied Hydrology" (Ven Te Chow, ed.). McGraw Hill, New York.

Vink, F. (1971). Measurement of evaporation in arid regions. *Natur. Resour. Devel.* **10**, pp. 22–34. Institute for Scientific Cooperation, Tuebingen, Federal Republic of Germany.

CHAPTER

13

Criteria for the Regional Exploitation of Groundwater

13.1 GROUNDWATER ABSTRACTION AND GROUNDWATER RESERVES

For the purpose of this discussion it is convenient to distinguish several kinds of groundwater reserves (Fig. 13.1). Reserves held in *live storage* are depleted by natural drainage and can also be recovered by pumping. Generally they are situated above the outlet. In a coastal aquifer the volume of freshwater between the interface and sea level also belongs to this category. Reserves held in *dead storage* can be recovered only by pumping after the live reserves have been exhausted. However, they are not stagnant. As long as flow persists anywhere in the aquifer, the flow lines spread through its entire extent and effect a slow, continuous exchange of water throughout the aquifer. Cones of depression are formed by the abstraction of *local reserves* from the vicinity of pumped boreholes. Eventually all cones of depression spread outward over the aquifer, depleting one or the other of the preceding reserve categories. A fourth kind of reserves, not shown in Fig. 13.1, comprises those that are held in *irreversible storage* in semiconsolidated sediments. When the water level is lowered, the sediments undergo irreversible compaction, squeezing out water from their interstices. The process leads to soil subsidence and frequently also to the deterioration of water quality because of the influx of connate water from fine-grained strata.

229

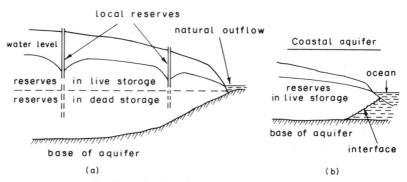

Fig. 13.1   Classification of groundwater reserves.

Abstraction of water from an aquifer sets in motion the following sequence of events: At first local reserves are withdrawn from the vicinity of boreholes. The resultant cones of depression spread outward over the aquifer, depleting the live reserves. The water level near the outlet is lowered, and natural outflow decreases.

The last stages of the sequence, the influence of pumping on the live reserves of the aquifer and on natural drainage from it, are easily analyzed with the aid of a unicell model (Fig. 8.1 and discussion in Chapter 8).

Assuming that pumping and replenishment are constant and that pumping is smaller than replenishment, we obtain the following from continuity:

In the natural steady state
prior to exploitation
$$Q_0 = R \qquad\qquad (13.1a)$$

In the final
quasi-steady state
$$Q_s = R - P_s \qquad\qquad (13.1b)$$

where R is the natural replenishment, P_s the rate of pumping, $P_s < R$, and Q_0, Q_s are the initial and final rates of natural drainage, respectively.

For the period of transition we obtain from continuity and Eq. (8.4)

$$-\frac{dV}{dt} = -t_0 \frac{dQ}{dt} = Q(t) - (R - P_s) \qquad\qquad (13.2a)$$

where V is the volume in live storage and t_0 the depletion time. Integration yields

$$Q(t) = (R - P_s) + P_s \exp(-t/t_0) \qquad\qquad (13.2b)$$

The last term on the right-hand side of Eq. (13.2b) is outflow in excess of the rate, which corresponds to the final equilibrium state. Integration of this asymptotic expression yields

$$P_s \int_0^\infty \exp(-t/t_0)\, dt = t_0 P_s = \Delta V \tag{13.3}$$

where ΔV is the volume of water that is lost through natural drainage until the final equilibrium state is established (*wasting reserves*).

The speed of the process of transition may be judged by calculating the time that elapses until a large part, say 75%, of the wasting reserves is lost.

$$0.75\Delta V = P_s \int_0^{t_{0.75}} \exp(-t/t_0)\, dt = 0.75 P_s t_0 \tag{13.4a}$$

$$-t_{0.75} = t_0 \ln 0.25 \approx -t_0 \times 1.386 \tag{13.4b}$$

were $t_{0.75}$ is the time from the beginning of pumping until 75% of the wasting reserves are lost.

Since t_0 is usually of the order of decades, the final steady state is approached only after many years.

If pumping equals natural replenishment the entire live reserve will be lost, natural drainage will be stopped and the water level will be stabilized at the elevation of the outlet. Continued pumping in excess of replenishment will eventually deplete also the reserves in dead storage until the aquifer practically "dries up." If a recharge boundary is present (Section 6.6), an equilibrium state will be attained when the influx through the boundary equals excess pumping.

The influence of the cones of depression can be computed only if a full description of the actual situation is given. A few qualitative conclusions can, however, be derived intuitively.

Dynamic drawdowns created by wells near the outlet will decrease natural drainage almost immediately. As a consequence, the time of transition will be prolonged and the loss of reserves will be delayed. The obverse will happen if wells are situated at a large distance from the outlet.

In an aquifer with large transmissivity the cones of depression will spread relatively quickly. In an aquifer with small transmissivity, deep localized cones of depression will be formed and the regional influence of pumping will be delayed.

13.2   EXPLOITATION ON A SUSTAINED BASIS

The maximum *sustained yield* (or *safe yield*) of a groundwater basin may be defined as "maximum rate of groundwater abstraction that can be maintained for an indefinite time without causing unacceptable consequences." A discussion of the concept in hydrologic terms follows.

(1) The safe yield refers to the supply capacity of the entire groundwater system, not to limitations caused by inappropriate location of wells or by the excessive concentration of many wells in a small part of the aquifer.

(2) The first undesired but unavoidable effect of groundwater abstraction is a lowered water level that may, in its turn, induce other unwanted effects. The most common effects to be reckoned with are diminished well discharges in thin phreatic aquifers, intrusion of saline water from the sea or from other sources, soil subsidence, reduction of the dry weather flow in rivers and springs, and deterioration of water quality because of the access of air to oxidizable compounds in the stratigraphic column.

(3) Whether an effect is "unacceptable" or merely a nuisance has to be decided on the basis of water use and economic criteria, in short by human judgment; it is futile to look to physical sciences for guidance in this respect.

(4) Almost all the adverse effects are brought about by slow processes. From the water users' point of view, sustained yield exploitation usually means that their water supply is being frozen at a certain level because of the seemingly unfounded apprehensions of a hydrologist. Great difficulties are often encountered on this score.

(5) For sustained yield exploitation two hydrologic conditions must be met: A quasi-steady state as defined in the preceding section must be reached, and all the other unwanted effects, including those that take a very long time to materialize, must be kept within "acceptable" limits. The maximum rate of exploitation commensurate with the first condition equals average annual replenishment. The actual sustained yield is usually smaller because of unacceptable effects that occur already at a lesser rate of exploitation.

(6) It is assumed that the climate and soil cover of the area remain unchanged and that man-made pollution does not occur. In such ideal circumstances one should be able to exploit the aquifer at the sustained yield "forever". In a realistic sense the expression *indefinite period* means simply a time span in excess of any normal planning horizon, say 100 years and more.

(7) Under the above conditions the aquifer may be regarded as a simple *system* with only three major *system variables*: annual groundwater abstraction, areal distribution of groundwater abstraction, and water levels. Minor system variables, such as the depths of boreholes, and monthly pumping schedules are neglected. The task is to maximize the yearly *output* of the system (the recovery of groundwater through boreholes) while observing certain *constraints* (avoiding unacceptable consequences). For sustained yield operation only equilibrium states of the system have to be considered, and this simplifies analysis.

The procedure for estimating the sustained yield of an aquifer can be summarized in the following six steps: (1) Determine average annual replenishment. (2) Identify the *most stringent constraint*, i.e., the first unacceptable effect that will occur when water levels are lowered. (3) Find the quantitative relation between water level elevations and the occurrence of this unacceptable effect. In many cases it is possible to confine attention to certain key locations that are especially sensitive to water level changes. (4) Define minimal water levels for the whole aquifer or for the above-mentioned key positions. (5) Compute the rate of natural outflow that will occur when a quasi-steady state of flow commensurate with minimal water levels is established. (6) The sustained yield is the difference between (1) and (5).

The coastal aquifer shown in Fig. 13.2 will serve as example for this procedure.

(1) Average annual replenishment may be estimated by one of the methods presented in Chapter 12.

(2) Seawater intrusion into the aquifer may contaminate exploited wells and constitutes, therefore, the most stringent constraint.

(3) The laws governing seawater intrusion are presented in Section 2.7.

(4) Intensive groundwater abstraction on a sustained basis is possible only at the landward side of the toe of the interface. In order to stabilize the

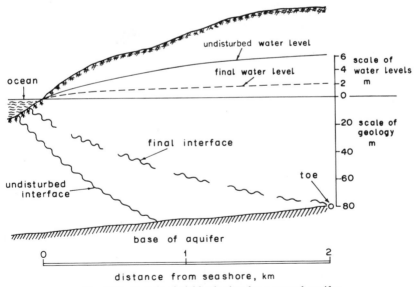

Fig. 13.2   Sustained yield criterion for a coastal aquifer.

toe at some predetermined position, it is necessary to maintain the water level in this key location at a minimal elevation. This minimal elevation is easily computed by Eq. (2.2) if the depth of the aquifer base is known.

(5) Outflow into the ocean is a function of the distance of the toe from the shore [Eq. (2.5)]. From a hydrological point of view, the optimal distance is the one that minimizes outflow into the ocean [Eq. (2.6)]. Water supply engineers and administrators will, however, prefer to keep the extent of seawater intrusion as small as possible, and the area that remains exploitable by wells as large as possible. The final position of the toe has to be decided on the basis of hydrologic, administrative, and engineering criteria.

(6) The sustained yield is the difference between natural replenishment and the outflow that occurs when the toe is stabilized at the selected final position [Eq. (2.5)]. Alternatively, one may compute the steady state flow above the final position of the toe [Eq. (2.4)], and substract it from the estimated steady state flow in the undisturbed aquifer at this location.

Coastal aquifers are relatively easy to deal with since seawater intrusion is governed by the simple Ghyben–Hertzberg rule. A major difficulty, inherent in all quantitative groundwater work, stems from the discrepancy between the real situation and the idealized model on which computations have to be based. In many cases all that can be achieved is a "rough approximation" or an "informed guess."

In other aquifers difficulties are compounded by the fact that the most stringent constraint and its relation to water levels are far from self evident. However, no effort should be spared to evaluate sustained yield criteria, even in a rough way, during the initial phases of groundwater development. At this stage hydrological considerations have a chance to prevail against the interests of potential water users. Facts that have been created in the field are unlikely to be changed by the results of even the most meticulous hydrological investigation.

13.3   EXPLOITATION OF GROUNDWATER RESERVES

Overexploitation, in excess of the safe yield, enables the provision of increased water supplies for a limited time. Overexploiting an aquifer means that groundwater reserves are being recovered that, under safe yield conditions, would either be lost through outflow or remain in storage. Two principal kinds of overexploitation can be distinguished according to the degree of reserve depletion they entail.

(1) The aquifer is overexploited until water levels commensurate with the safe yield are reached. From then onward groundwater exploitation is reduced to the sustained yield. Thus a part of the "wasting reserves" [Eq. (13.3)] is recovered and the period of transition [Eq. (13.4)] is shortened without adverse effects on the aquifer.

(2) Overexploitation is continued beyond this point and the remaining reserves are progressively depleted. In this case damage to the groundwater resources is unavoidable, but because of slowness of hydrologic processes, it usually takes many years before one or the other of the undesired effects cited in Section 14.2 enforces the gradual cessation of groundwater abstraction. If overexploitation is discontinued before large-scale damage has occurred, it is possible to restore safe yield conditions by severely restricting groundwater supplies for some time and/or by replenishing the aquifer artificially.

Several alternative strategies for reserve exploitation will be illustrated with reference to a coastal aquifer. From a hydrologic point of view the most efficient procedure would be to remove the required volume of water as quickly as possible, "as if" by a surgical operation, before losses and deterioration affect the volumes to be exploited. In practice, however, exploitation of reserves must be spread over a certain period of time.

In order to minimize losses by natural drainage, it is desirable to start overexploitation in the seaward portion of the aquifer and to locate boreholes farther inland, as soon as the interface has reached a predetermined position. The procedure is risky inasmuch as the excessive mixing of freshwater and seawater resulting from upconing may easily destroy the very reserves one wishes to preserve. Close hydrologic supervision by observation wells is necessary. The economic feasibility of such a scheme has to be judged by comparing the value of the amounts of water that can be saved with the cost of relocating boreholes.

Another alternative is to locate boreholes inland, as far away from the interface as possible. The cone of depression thus formed will only slowly extend toward the seashore, so that outflow into the sea will continue unabated for a long time. On the other hand, this procedure requires less hydrologic supervision and no relocation of boreholes.

The extreme alternatives illustrated above are of a quite general nature. One can either maximize the exploitable volume of reserves by quick abstraction, minimize losses by shifting the centers of groundwater abstraction over the area, or opt for a simple and relatively trouble-free scheme at the price of reducing the exploitable volume of reserves. In practice, some compromise solution dictated by the hydrogeology of the area, by its legal and administrative infrastructure, and by economic considerations has to be adopted.

Overexploitation can be an important tool for the development of an area if its extent and time schedule are planned in advance and if close control over groundwater abstraction is exercised.

A scheme of planned reserve exploitation was implemented in Israel, in the area between Tel Aviv and Beer Sheva, where the bulk of Israel's agricultural lands are situated (Fig. 2.7). The area has two major water resources, a sandstone aquifer draining into the Mediterranean Sea with an estimated safe yield of 160 MCM/yr, and a limestone aquifer draining through the Yarkon spring (Section 2.4) with a sustained yield of about 200 MCM/yr.

During the years 1955–1964 the coastal aquifer was exploited at the average yearly rate of 330 MCM/yr, and the limestone aquifer was exploited at the rate of 260 MCM/yr. The overdraft, amounting to a total 230 MCM/yr, made it possible to expand irrigated agriculture and to supply water to rapidly growing towns without waiting for additional, imported water supplies.

The Jordan conduit, which diverts water from Lake Kinnereth in the north to the central and southern parts of the country, started to operate in 1964. By this time seawater intrusion had occurred in the heavily overexploited area of Tel Aviv, and Jordan water was injected in order to repair the damage quickly. In the whole area groundwater exploitation was gradually reduced to sustained rates and a switch to the conjunctive use of Jordan water and groundwater was effected (Mandel, 1977).

FURTHER READINGS

Aguado, I., and Remson, I. (1974). Groundwater hydraulics in aquifer management. *J. Hydraul. Div. Am. Soc. Civ. Eng.* **100**, 103–118.

Albinet, M., and Castany, G. (1972). Evaluation rapide et cartographique des resources en eaux souterraines (Appliqué en Venezuela). *Bull. BRGM* No. 2, Sect. 3, pp. 3–26.

Anonymous (1970). International survey on existing water-recharge facilities. *I A S H*, *Publ.* No. 87.

Castany, G., Kunin, V., Mandel, S., *et al.* (1975). "Groundwater Storage and Artificial Replenishment," Natural Resources/Water Series, No. 2. United Nations, New York.

Combe, M., *et al.* (1974). Etude hydrogeologique et économique d'un plan de suréxploitation de la nappe de Souss (Maroc) afin d'accroitre la disponibilité des eaux pour l'éxtension des irrigations. *Hydrogeologie*, Sect. 3 No. 1, pp. 137–144.

Cunningham, A. B., and Sinclair, P. J. (1979). Application and analysis of a coupled surface and groundwater model. *J. Hydrol.* **43**, 129–147.

Domenico, P. A., Anderson, D. V., and Case, C. M. (1968). Optimal groundwater mining. *W. Resour. Res.* **4**(2), 247–255.

Erdelyi, J., *et al.* (1968). "Estimation of Groundwater Resources." Res. Inst. Water Resour. Dev., Budapest.

Mandel, S., ed. (1975). "The Mining of Groundwater Resources as a Tool for Regional Development," Publ. 04/75/28. TAHAL Consulting Engineers Ltd., Tel Aviv.

Mandel, S. (1977). The overexploitation of groundwater resources in dry regions. *In* "Arid Zone Development, Potentialities and Problems," pp. 31–51. Ballinger, Cambridge, Massachusetts.

Mandel, S. (1979). Problems of large scale groundwater development. *J. Hydrol.* **43**, 121–127.

Moore, J. E. (1979). Contribution of groundwater modelling to planning. *J. Hydrol.* **43**, 121–127.

Peck, H. M. (1969). Effects of large scale mining withdrawals of groundwater. *Groundwater* **7**(4), 12–20.

Toth, G. (1973). Hydrogeology and yield evaluation of a municipal well field, Alberta, Can. *Bull. IASH* **18**(26), 165–189.

U.S. Agency for International Development (1973). Techniques for assessing hydrological potentials of developing countries (state of the art and research priorities). U.S. Gov. Printing Off., Washington, D.C.

Widstrand, C. (1978). "The Social and Ecological Effects of Water Development in Developing Countries." Pergamon Press, Oxford.

Willis, R. (1976). Optimal management of the subsurface environment. *Hydrol. Sci. Bull.* **21** (2), 324–333.

CHAPTER

14

Groundwater Observation Networks

One of the results of a groundwater project should be recommendations for the systematic, continuous monitoring of the resource.

In the course of the investigations, water levels should be measured at monthly intervals in all wells (Section 6.12). Exploration boreholes drilled for the purpose of hydrogeologic prospection should be equipped with a small-diameter casing and screen, so that they can be used for routine water level observations. This point is of particular importance, since exploration holes are usually located where exploited wells are scarce. On the basis of about one year's records the observation network can be thinned out by eliminating redundant observation points as well as boreholes that are, for some reason, unsuitable or uncharacteristic. The density of the final, permanent network depends on aquifer characteristics and on the purpose of the observations.

Quantitative work, such as aquifer calibration, requires reliable water level contour maps. Water level gradients are commonly in the range 0.1%–1%. Observation points spaced at 2 km distance from each other will enable the drawing of contour lines at 2–10 m intervals, and this is approximately the minimum required for quantitative work. Much closer spacing is often desirable, at least in certain parts of the area.

For administrative purposes wider spacing is acceptable. It can often be shown by statistical correlations that water levels in a certain area are represented, fairly well, by observations in one borehole. However, this conclusion remains valid only as long as the pattern of groundwater abstraction does not appreciably change. Periodic checks of such networks are therefore indicated. An upper limit of allowable spacing may be defined

238

by the stipulation that the maximum distance between observation points must be smaller than the distance over which geologic aquifer characteristics can be reliably interpolated.

Records obtained by monthly water level measurements are sufficiently detailed for most purposes. Recording instruments are indispensable for specialized researches that require the continuous monitoring of water levels, but their installation for the purpose of routine observations does not always prove to be advantageous. The processing of unnecessarily detailed records takes up the time of office staff, and maintenance of the instruments requires a good workshop. It is unwise to leave recording equipment for a long time unattended in the field. Therefore savings in travel time and transportation are also likely to be marginal.

Monitoring of water quality is almost always carried out by water samples taken from exploited wells. Yearly or twice yearly measurements of electrical conductivity are required for the purpose of general supervision. Closely spaced observations and more detailed analyses are necessary when and where electrical conductivity changes significantly or where, for some reason, significant changes of water quality are anticipated.

The position of the interface in coastal aquifers is best monitored by conductivity measurements in specially constructed observation wells. In the open hole diffusion is more rapid than in the aquifer and results in the apparent widening of the zone of transition. In order to minimize this effect it is recommended to construct multiple screen wells of the type illustrated in Fig. 5.1 and to keep each screened section relatively short, say about 3 m.

Water level and water quality data can be interpreted only if reliable information on groundwater abstraction is available. Methods available are metering devices, the conversion of power consumption into pumped quantities, and estimates based on the size of irrigated areas or standards of domestic consumption. Legal and administrative problems and the lack of cooperation by well owners often render this intrinsically simple task extremely difficult.

The motivation of personnel operating the network is an important factor in the reliability of the data that are obtained. Experience shows that field observers do their tedious and often difficult job conscientiously, as long as they feel that their data are being used. Data sent to a distant filing system, without evidence of being used, stand a poor chance of being reliable.

FURTHER READINGS

Auriol, J., and Canceill, M. (1974). Constitution de fichiers de mésures de niveaux piézometriques périodiques. *Bull. BRGM, Sect.* 3 No. 1.

Garber, M. S., and Koopman, F. C. (1968). Methods of measuring water levels in deep wells. *In* "Techniques of Water Resources Investigations," Book 8, Chap. A. U.S. Geol. Surv., U.S. Gov. Print. Off., Washington, D.C.

Heath, R. C. (1976). Design of groundwater level observation well programs. *Groundwater* **14**(2), 71–77.

Mandel, S. (1965). Design and instrumentation of hydrogeological observation networks. *IASH Publ.* No. 68, pp. 413–424.

U.S. Geological Survey (1976). "Design of Groundwater Level Observation Networks." Open file report prepared in cooperation with hydrological service of Israel, No. 84, E-7, pp. 76–165. U.S. Gov. Print. Off., Washington, D.C.

The Methodology of Groundwater Investigations

15.1 ORGANIZATIONAL ASPECTS

The Division of Labor

The participants in a project of groundwater investigations are easily grouped according to the specific functions they fulfill, although, unfortunately, functional relationships are not always expressed in clear-cut lines of authority.

The Client. The client is the juridical personality who ordered the investigations. The client may be a government department, sometimes in cooperation with an international organization such as an agency of the United Nations or a private corporation or individual. The client defines the aims of the project and its administrative framework in the form of *terms of reference* that are handed down to the investigator. This formal step should, however, be preceded by informal consultations between the two parties in order to ensure mutual understanding. Then the client approves the work program drawn up by the investigator, and for the duration of the project, he receives progress reports at regular intervals, reserving the right to approve or veto major changes in the work program. When the project is completed, the client usually reserves exclusive rights on its results.

The investigator. This group of workers comprises the investigator in charge and his staff. When international financing is involved there may be two persons in charge, an expatriate expert and his local counterpart. It is only natural that the local team leader takes over the major part of administrative duties and that the foreign expert is more involved in technical work, including education of personnel. However, mutual trust between the two team leaders is more important than any formalized division of authority.

The size of the investigator's team should be governed by three considerations: (1) the part of the job that has the most direct bearing on the expected results, such as selection of drilling sites, must be carried out by the team itself; (2) other items, such as drilling and extensive geophysical work, are usually carried out by contractors but have to be supervised by team members, and (3) the team should not be so large that the task of administering it places an excessive burden on the team leader.

Only a small permanent nucleus has to be kept on the job throughout the project. Additional personnel may join the team for limited periods. For example, a geophysicist may be hired to direct and evaluate the work of a geophysical contracting firm if the complexity of the job exceeds the capacity of the permanent staff, or well sitters—preferably junior geologist —may be hired for as long as drilling is in progress.

Where training constitutes an important part of the project, special consideration must be given to this aspect. The recommended procedure is to put each trainee under the guidance of an expert staff member. It should be realized, however, that training requires time and may slow down the progress of the work.

Contractors and suppliers. Costly items of work requiring specialized machinery and expertise, such as drilling, are often entrusted to contracting firms on the basis of a public tender. The contract usually stipulates that the contractor has to pay a fine if he fails to carry out the work according to specifications, but the investigator derives little satisfaction from a fine he or his client may belatedly collect. Therefore only well-established, reputable firms should be entrusted with important work. The lowest bid is not necessarily the best buy.

Less costly items of work, such as chemical analyses, car hire, or other logistic support, may be obtained from suppliers without public tender. Written agreements are advisable also in this case, especially if the work amounts to more than just occasional orders or if there is only one supplier around who practically holds a monopoly.

Cooperative agencies. Cooperative agencies are nonprofit organizations, usually government departments, that carry out some part of the work. Thus a meteorological service may cooperate by installing special observation stations, or a geological survey department may map an area on special request. Sometimes even exploratory drilling and geophysical measurements are carried out by cooperative agencies rather than by commercial firms.

The trouble is that formal arrangements made at the highest level do not necessarily ensure fruitful cooperation. Government departments in particular find it difficult to carry out work in excess of their routine duties according to a strict timetable, or to hire the additional personnel that may be required. When such arrangements are made, the investigator should try to establish personal contact with the workers who have to do the job, and to judge for himself what they can really accomplish within the limitations imposed on them.

The Work Program

The following points should be taken into account when drawing up the work program:

(1) Time should be allowed for an adequate study of the existing situation in the research area. The first item should be the study of all available information on the area and reconnaissance trips; the second one, a campaign of pumping tests in existing wells (drawdown and recovery), water level measurements, and sample collection for chemical analyses. (The last three items can be accomplished by a well-organized team at one time.) The result of this work will be an updated map of well locations, data on existing wells that are not available anywhere else, information on specific discharges, some indication of transmissivity values that should be correlated with the available information on the subsurface geology of the area, indications regarding the natural flow regime and distinct aquiferous units, and sometimes indication of danger spots, where an eventual deterioration of water quality is to be feared.

(2) From the administrative point of view it is preferable to carry out the work in a simple sequence—for example, geologic mapping, geophysical work, drilling, and pumping tests in the new boreholes. Such a program facilitates supervision and accounting but leaves no room for the incorporation of new information in subsequent stages of the work. It is much preferable to proceed in an *iterative sequence*, such as geologic mapping followed by several geophysical measurements, well drilling, subsurface correlation of the new data, verification and calibration of previous geophysical work with the aid of the new data, more extensive geophysical work, and a final phase of well drilling and pumping tests.

(3) The terms of reference frequently specify, in addition to the general investigative effort, the provision of *water supplies* in certain locations.

These locations may be of little scientific interest, but nevertheless the investigator is well advised to allot them high priority and to show tangible positive results early in his work.

(4) The *duration* of the project should allow for the collection of at least one yearly cycle of hydrologic data, as well as for "running-in" and "winding-up" periods. For this reason a regional groundwater investigation rarely takes less than 24 months.

(5) The time schedules of all items must be specified so that they can be adhered to within reasonable limits. Nothing is more galling in a project than having to wait for delayed results. In this context it is of special importance to take into account foreseeable climatic obstacles, such as, for example, the inaccessibility of certain areas during the rainy season.

The simplest form of the *work program* is a bar chart, (Fig. 15.1). PERT procedures may be helpful in a very complex project but, usually, the critical path depends on well drilling and is self-evident. It is desirable to submit the work program to the client for formal ratification and to make sure, at this occasion, that the requisite financial and administrative arrangements are put on a firm basis.

Communications and Decision Making

The work program delineates only the major stages of the investigation. Details have to be worked out by a sequential process of decision making in which each new data becomes an input for the subsequent step. Committee work appears to be the most efficient instrument for this purpose. The following committees are suggested:

The *Research Committee* is composed of the investigator in charge (chairman) and of the senior personnel on his staff. Other workers, junior staff, contractor personnel, personnel from cooperating agencies, and, sometimes, invited experts should take part in the meetings of the committee whenever required by the topic under discussion. The committee should meet about once a month. At each meeting, progress in selected items of the work should be presented by the persons who actually carried it out, irrespective of their rank or the organization to which they belong. Then the chairman should invite comments, criticism, and suggestions on how to proceed further. Formal voting procedures are out of place in this kind of meeting. When a general consensus cannot be arrived at, the chairman is the final arbiter. Finally the chairman summarizes the conclusions in a short written record. Dissenting opinions should be recorded only on explicit request by their proponents.

The *Drilling Committee* supervises all drilling work and decides on new drilling sites. When drilling is in progress the committee should meet once

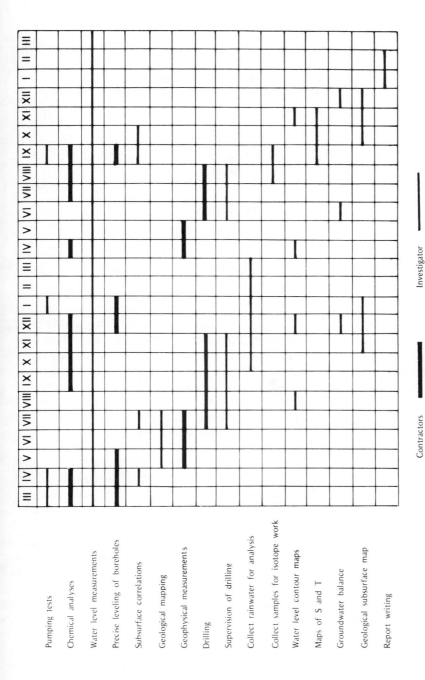

Fig. 15.1 Bar chart for work program.

Contractors ▬▬ Investigator ▬▬

weekly or, at least, once in a fortnight. Its composition and working procedures are described in Section 5.6.

The *Steering Committee* effects communication between the client and the investigator. It should not number more than five members. Representatives of contractors or other specialists may be invited in an advisory capacity. The committee should meet at three- to six-month intervals, review the progress of the project, and authorize major changes in the work program. Its conclusions have to be put to a formal vote and a protocol must be drawn up and ratified after each meeting.

The Data Bank

The investigator needs a data bank containing all the material on his research area, old material as well as data collected in the course of the project. (This ad hoc data bank should not be confused with a permanent nationwide system of data keeping that requires a different approach.) It is convenient to classify the material into five categories.

(1) *The card index and the base location maps* are the heart of the data bank. A simple card index without cross references will usually suffice. The selection of an obligatory set of base maps requires meticulous attention, since available maps often show considerable discrepancies. As a rule, each location should be identifiable by one name and by two grid coordinates.

(2) *Data and information* comprise borehole sections, the results of pumping tests, complete chemical analyses, etc., in short items that are collected only once or at rare intervals. This material is conveniently kept in folders.

(3) *Records*, comprise the results of observations carried out on a routine basis. This material that continually accumulates and is frequently taken out for updating and copying is best kept on sturdy, space-saving filing cards. For example, monthly observations for a period of one year in a borehole, including water levels, groundwater abstraction, and water quality (total dissolved solids, not complete chemical analyses), are represented by 36 figures that can easily be accommodated on a card 20 by 10 cm large. The figures should be written in black ink so that they are easy to copy and difficult to erase. The graphic representation of records is a waste of time and of storage space. The user who requires them should draw them for himself on the scale he thinks most appropriate.

It should be noted that the distinction between data and records is a matter of convenience, not of principle. Water level records are better kept separate from borehole sections, because otherwise very bulky files result that eventually disintegrate by frequent use. On the other hand, the few constant characteristics of river gauging stations and climatic stations may easily be accommodated on the same cards on which the records are kept.

(4) *Reports* comprise old reports, reprints of published papers, internal reports, geologic maps and sections together with their explanatory notes, various yearbooks, field notes, and typewritten, or even handwritten, material from archives. However, books of a general character and administrative documents are excluded. The former find their place in a hand library; the latter belong to the files of the investigator in charge.

(5) *Borehole samples* consist of the boxed collection of samples described in Section 5.4.

The data bank needs the full-time attention of a meticulous, patient person. Elderly or physically handicapped workers are the best candidates for this important but not very rewarding job. With some effort it should be easy to keep the relatively small amount of data in perfect order. Computerized data-keeping systems that interpose machinery and skilled workers between the data and their users are likely to cause more complications, errors, and delays than is tolerable in ongoing work.

A problem that frequently crops up concerns the recompilation of old data and the double filing of new ones. Two examples will illustrate this point. Is it worthwhile to copy all ancient water level data onto the standard cards, or can this work be dispensed with? Is it necessary to file separately each chemical analysis, or is it preferable to leave this material on the desk of a staff member until a geochemical report is eventually issued? The answer to the first question is qualified: Old material has to be copied when it is in danger of being lost, or for the purpose of interpretation, but there is no need to copy it just for the sake of file keeping. The answer to the second question is unqualified: The result of all work should be filed in the data bank as soon as possible. No harm is done if the analyses are double filed, once as separate items and a second time in the geochemical report, but much inconvenience results when they are eventually mislaid by an untidy worker.

Report Writing

A few rules will help to minimize the labor of report writing without prejudice to the quality of the final report.

All team members should be required to prepare their work in a standard format. Graphic and tabulary presentation is preferable; verbal texts should be reduced to indispensable "explanatory notes." After discussion by the research committee and approval by the team leader, these documents should be filed in the data bank. Periodic reports should not be required. Contractors and cooperating agencies should be encouraged to conform to the same standards. The progress reports to the steering committee should consist of the above material supplemented by the research committee conclusions. A short explanatory note may be added.

The final report should be divided into two parts, a volume containing the substantive part and one or several volumes of appendixes containing all the data that were collected by the project. The material for the appendixes can be lifted straight from the data bank, and the research leader should be free to devote his undivided attention to the formulation of the important substantive part. The layout of this volume will depend on the nature of the investigations, but a few general guidelines may nevertheless be suggested.

For the benefit of decision makers who lack the time for a detailed study, the original terms of reference and a summary of findings and conclusions should be put at the head of the volume. Positive conclusions and operative recommendations must be emphasized. Nothing is more maddening to the client than having the need for further investigations presented to him as the first and principal result of the work.

The technical text should be self-contained. The reader should be able to find all the relevant tables and drawings at hand, and as a rule he should not be referred to the appendixes. The scientific principles of the interpretative techniques should be mentioned and literature references should be given, but lengthy theoretical digressions are out of place. If the client specifically requires this material or if it cannot be found in literature, it should be relegated to an appendix. The text should refer to the following points:

(1) exposition of the hydrologic and engineering aspects of the problems that were investigated;

(2) description of the investigated area;

(3) summary of the scope of the work (i.e., the number of man-months, boreholes geophysical measurements, pumping tests, etc., that the project involved);

(4) succinct and lucid presentation of the technical reasoning leading up to the conclusions;

(5) convincing reasons for any suggested further work.

15.2   REMARKS CONCERNING THE LOGICAL STRUCTURE OF GROUNDWATER INVESTIGATIONS

It is necessary to define several widely used words, although this may entail the risk of restating the obvious.

Hydrologic investigations are based on *data* observed or measured in the field. A *technique* is a set of instructions on how to obtain *information* from data, specifying the data needed and prescribing the procedure for interpreting them. For example, a technique of pumping tests produces information (transmissivity and storativity) from data (measurements of water level, time, discharge, and distance between boreholes). A field geologist who describes a certain rock stratum as limestone produces a datum; when he deduces the position of the rock layer in the stratigraphic column, he produces an item of information. Data may contain random errors, information unavoidably reflects these errors as well as the assumptions that underlie the method of interpretation. An indispensable technique that is often applied without even being noticed is the construction of a continuum, such as a smooth line or a "continuous" aquifer, from a set of point data. Errors made right here falsify all subsequent deductions. Practical work rarely starts from scratch on a "bedrock" of data. Some input information usually has to be accepted without very detailed scrutiny. However, the investigator should resist the common tendency to accept as proven fact everything that has been printed.

The ultimate purpose of the investigation is to serve the *practical aims* of a *client*. In this context the investigator is called on to solve *hydrologic problems* that are simply requests for information. The *solution* of the problem (i.e., the required item of information) must conform to certain *standards of accuracy* that depend on the nature of the practical aims and on local circumstances. For example, if the client wishes to exploit a coastal aquifer by wells near the shore, precise information on the seawater–freshwater interface is required, but if the wells are situated at some distance from the shore and if conditions are favorable, a rough estimate of the final position of the interface may suffice. The *formulation of the problem* should specify the information that has to be found and also indicate the required degree of accuracy.

There are two classes of problems, those that call for the *determination of a quantity* and those that call for the *delineation of a pattern*. Pattern delineation requires, in essence, the distinction of relevant "signals" from irrelevant "noises." The greater the noise and the fainter the signal, the more difficult the problem becomes. For example, the identification of sources of salination is a trivial matter in a well-flushed coastal aquifer; it may become very difficult in a dry area where important sources of salination are masked by many minor, slightly saline patches of water. There are no standard techniques to solve such problems and it is rather naive to expect that a mass of accumulated data will fall into a pattern all by itself.

A more fruitful approach involves *heuristic reasoning*. The idea is imaginatively to discern a pattern behind scant items of information and to formulate a working hypothesis that is then supported, modified, or disproved by subsequent work. A useful working hypothesis should bind together several seemingly disparate items of information, and it should be amenable to verification—or otherwise—without undue effort. The best working hypotheses are those that must be either true or false. Unfortunately, such "white" or "black" hypotheses can rarely be formulated in hydrology. Here the investigator has a chance to show his mettle as a scientist.

Quantitative problems require the measurement of certain pattern characteristics, such as the depths of brines below ground. Arrangement of these quantities on a map or a graph will again indicate patterns (e.g., patches of highly saline water in an aquifer) that in their turn may form the input for subsequent quantitative work. Any actual campaign of investigations goes only through a small part of the sequence. It starts on the basis of some previous work (maps, data from existing boreholes, etc.) and it is stopped as soon as the results are deemed to be accurate and reliable enough for the purpose at hand.

15.3   A FLOW CHART FOR GROUNDWATER INVESTIGATIONS

The explanations below refer to Fig. 15.2. Indentification numbers are put into brackets in order to distinguish them from the numbering system of chapters and sections. It should be remembered that the purpose of flow charts is not to present new findings but to draw attention to hidden pitfalls and that the utility of charts becomes apparent only when they are applied to projects of sufficient magnitude and complexity.

(1)   Preliminary Work

(1.1)   Define practical aims.   The client explains his practical aim to the investigator who has to acquire a thorough grasp of the client's needs and expectations before he can decide what to do about them. It is not always easy to establish clear communication since the client and the investigator may attach different meanings to the same quasi-professional terms. Plain speaking, a distrust of professional jargon, and a great deal of patience are called for at this initial stage of the work.

(1.2)   Draw up terms of reference.   Although, formally, the terms of reference are handed down from the client to the investigator, they should be drawn up only after the above thorough discussion.

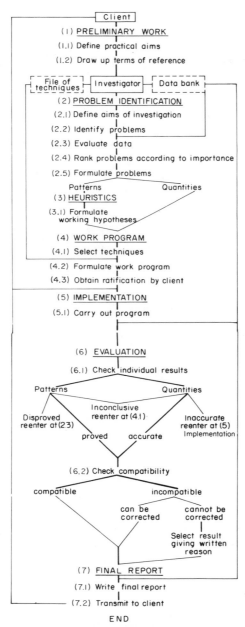

Fig. 15.2   Flow chart for groundwater investigations.

(2)   Problem Identification

(2.1)   Define aims of the investigation.   The investigator defines in a few words, unencumbered by details, what his finished product should be; for example, "drill wells with a certain hourly capacity, observing given standards of water quality" or "determine the maximum sustained yield of an aquifer under a given set of constraints in regard of well locations, pumping lifts and water quality." This involves essentially a process of translation from the client's language into the technical language of groundwater research.

(2.2)   Identify problems.   The problems that have to be solved in order to achieve the aims of the investigation can now be identified. A complete list of problems is drawn up.

(2.3)   Evaluate available data and information.   The investigator evaluates all the available information that has any bearing on the project, such as data on wells and water levels, geologic and topographic maps, and sometimes even seemingly extraneous data, such as road conditions in wet weather or the availability of semiskilled manpower. The idea is to assimilate what is already known, to spot lacunae in the existing data, and to foresee the difficulties that lie ahead. The flow chart assumes that the data can be taken from a data bank. Under actual conditions it is more often the case that the data bank has to be assembled from various sources and that a great deal of effort has to be expended on this task.

(2.4)   Rank problems according to importance.   The major part of the work effort should be expended on the more relevant problems and only a small part on the less important ones. For example, if the project aims at supplying drinking water to widely dispersed cattle stations, water levels and the required depth of drilling will merit detailed attention, but the maximum sustained yield will be far less relevant.

(2.5)   Formulate problems.   The formulation of each problem has to indicate the required degree of accuracy, which in turn depends on the relative importance of the problem. For example, the formulations "estimate groundwater replenishment," "determine average annual replenishment" and "determine yearly replenishment as a function of rainfall" refer to the same problem but at different levels of accuracy.

The end product of problem identification is a list of properly formulated problems divided into two types, quantitative problems and pattern delineation, respectively.

(3)   Heuristics

This step refers only to pattern delineation problems. It has been discussed in Section 15.2.

(4) The Work Program

(4.1) Select techniques. The "file of techniques" mentioned in the flow chart represents the accumulated knowledge of the investigators' team and technical literature. Important problems should be solved by the application of several independent techniques, since results supported by several independent lines of evidence are more reliable, if not more accurate. For example, if the water balance is important, at least two of the techniques given in Chapter 12 should be applied. The investigators' choice is limited by considerations of cost, by the local availability of knowhow and instruments, and by a crowded time schedule. Under these circumstances the task of selecting the most appropriate techniques involves weighty decisions.

(4.2) Formulate work program. See discussion in Section 15.1 and bar charts in Figure: 15.1.

(4.3) Obtain ratification by the client. See discussion in Section 15.1.

(5) Implementation

(5.1) Carry out program. Field work is now carried out and data are interpreted. The data and the results derived from them are filed in the data bank.

(6) Evaluation

(6.1) Check the individual results. The purpose of this action is to find out whether each result satisfactorily solves a particular problem or not. Sufficiently accurate quantitative results and sufficiently proven patterns are passed on to the next step. Results that do not pass this test can be examined again by reentering the flow chart at the appropriate places (see Fig. 15.2). In actual practice, however, the project will near its contractual termination when the results become available. There will be little room for additional field work, and the possibility of reentering the flow chart will probably be restricted to a theoretical reevaluation.

(6.2) Check compatibility of the results. Results that look acceptable, each one by itself, may still contradict each other. Thus a groundwater balance derived by a hydrometeorological method may be incompatible with the known gradients and transmissivities, or conclusions regarding mechanisms of salination may be at variance with the known hydraulic gradients.

Compatible results are accepted and passed on to the next step. Incompatible results may be due to methodological errors that can be spotted and

corrected. If the source of the error cannot be identified, the investigator has
to select the results that, according to his personal judgment, are more likely
to be correct and to reject the other ones. A reasoned statement to this effect
should be written and incorporated in the final report.

(7)   Final Report

This step consists of the writing of the final report and of its transmission to the client.

FURTHER READINGS

Bishop, E. E., Eckel, E. B. *et al*. (J. H. Eric, coordinator) (1978). "Suggestions to Authors of
the Reports of the U. S. Geol. Survey." *U. S. Geol. Surv.*, Govt. Printing Office,
Washington D. C.
Brown, R. H., Konoplyantsey, A. A., Ineson, J., and Kovalevskv, V. S., eds. (1972). "Ground-
water Studies, an International Guide for Research and Practice," UNESCO, Paris.
Cochran, W., Fenner, P., and Hill, M. (1974). "Geowriting, a Guide to Writing, Editing, and
Printing in Earth Science." Amer. Geol. Inst., Falls Church, Virginia.
Kabbaj, A. (1974). Organisation des recherches relatives aux ressources en eaux du Maroc.
Hydrogeologie, B.R.G.M, Orléans *Sect. 3* No. 1, pp. 9–13.
Mitchell, J. H. (1960). "Writing for Professional and Technical Journals." Wiley, New York.
Wagner, H. M. (1975). "Principles of Operation Research," pp. 535–540. Prentice-Hall,
Englewood Cliffs, New Jersey.

Units of Measurement and Conversion Factors

Metric units[a]		American units[b]		1*	2*
Length					
millimeter, mm		inch		0.0394	25.4
centimeter, cm	10 mm	inch		0.394	2.54
meter, m	100 cm	foot	12 in.	3.279	0.305
kilometer, km	1000 m	mile	5280 ft	0.621	1.609
Area, A					
cm^2		$in.^2$		0.155	6.452
m^2	$10^4\ cm^2$	ft^2	$124\ in.^2$	10.764	0.093
hectar	$10^4\ m^2$	acre	$43{,}560\ ft^2$	2.469	0.405
km^2	$10^6\ m^2$	$mile^2$	640 acres	0.368	2.589
Volume, V					
cm^3		$in.^3$		0.061	16.387
liter	$1000\ cm^3$	gallon	$231\ in.^3$	0.264	3.785
m^3	1000 l	ft^3	7.48 gal.	35.714	0.028
million m^3, MCM	$10^6\ m^3$	acre ft	$43{,}560\ ft^3$	809.716	1.23×10^{-3}
Discharge, Q					
l/sec		$in.^3/sec$		16.387	0.061
m^3/hr		gal/min		4.4	0.227
m^3/sec		ft^3/sec		35.714	0.028
million m^3/yr	MCM/yr	million ft^3/yr		35.714×10^6	0.028×10^{-5}
million m^3/yr	MCM/yr	acre ft/yr		809.716	1.235×10^{-3}
Hydraulic conductivity, K					
m/day		$gal/day/ft^2$		24.546	4.074×10^{-2}

Continued

255

Metric units[a]	American units[b]	1*	2*
	Transmissivity, T		
m²/day	gal/day/ft	80.58	1.24×10^{-2}
	Temperature, T		
centigrades °C °C = 5/9 (°F − 32)	Fahrenheit °F °F = 9/5 °C + 32		

[a]Multiply metric units by 1* to obtain American units.
[b]Multiply American units by 2* to obtain metric units.

Index